The
Rosetta Stone
of
God

James Davis

ECKANKAR
Minneapolis

The Rosetta Stone of God

Copyright © 2000 James Davis

The terms ECKANKAR, ECK, EK, MAHANTA, SOUL TRAVEL, and VAIRAGI, among others, are trademarks of ECKANKAR, P.O. Box 27300, Minneapolis, MN 55427 U.S.A.

Printed in U.S.A.

Edited by Joan Klemp, Anthony Moore, and Mary Carroll Moore
Author photo by Ann Stokes

Library of Congress Control Number: 00-132244

Publisher's Cataloging-in-Publication
(Provided by Quality Books, Inc.)

Davis, James Paul.
    The Rosetta stone of God / James Davis. — 1st ed.
    p. cm.
    ISBN: 1-57043-150-7

    1. Spiritual life—Eckankar (Organization) 2. Eck masters. 3. Eckankar (Organization) I. Title.

BP605.E3D38 2000   299'.93
                                    QBI00-281

∞ The paper used in this publication meets the minimum requirements of the American National Standard for Information Sciences—Permanence of Paper for Printed Library Materials, ANSI Z39.48-1984.

Contents

Acknowledgements

My sincere thanks to Judith Irwin for reviewing the manuscript and offering many valuable suggestions. She volunteered to give this task high priority despite other concerns in her life at the time.

Cherie Fontaine gave me support and encouragement during the yearlong writing process. She also read the manuscript and provided excellent proposals on behalf of future readers.

I give a grateful nod to Millie Moore. In a personal letter she shared a long-range vision of where my writing could go. This was like a bottle of champagne broken upon the bow of my ship—it helped launch this book upon its voyage.

Finally, my deep appreciation to Peddar Zaskq and Wah Z. They gave much inner guidance and inspiration on this manuscript, and have served as mentors in both my writing and my spiritual journey.

Dedication

I dedicate this book to the serious seekers of the world.

Introduction

*I*magine that a treasure of sacred wisdom is in your hands, but it has no value to you because it's written in an unknown language. If you only knew the key to decipher the writing, you could access the wisdom. I believe this book reveals the key that will place a great spiritual treasure in your hands. This is the story of how it was revealed to me, its potential value to you, and how you can begin to apply it in your everyday life.

The title of this book originates from the historic discovery of an ancient stone tablet in Egypt. In 1799, an officer in Napoleon's engineering corps found the tablet near the City of Rosetta (Rashid) on the Nile. The stone is a heavy slab of black basalt almost a foot thick, close to four feet high and two feet wide.

Carved upon the stone in three languages is the decree of a long-dead king of Egypt. The stone provided the key that enabled scholars to decipher the riddle of the perplexing Egyptian hieroglyphics. This unsealed the door to the great library of ancient Egyptian literature. The phrase *Rosetta stone* is applied to tools, ideas, or processes which give people a clue to understanding or help them gain access to things of great worth.

The Egyptian Rosetta stone unlocked the writings of a lost civilization. The Rosetta stone of God is the key to something even more valuable: a seeker's treasure from

xi

the vaults of heaven. What could be so valuable and yet be unknown? Wouldn't it have been discovered by now? Come read my story, then judge for yourself.

I have written this book for the serious seeker. If you are such a one, you have already been on the foothills and slopes of the mountain of God for some time. Perhaps your clothes are threadbare from the journey, but you are spiritually lean and fit.

Your travelog surely contains some of the truths to be found in these regions: the importance of love and gratitude, the Law of Economy which teaches you to make the best use of every effort expended, the importance of a skilled guide who can steer you toward the safe passes, and a number of discoveries which are special just to you.

You probably no longer listen to fast-talking guides who promise easy shortcuts. Your map is worn from use, and you have come now to the place where you must venture beyond its borders.

We meet somewhere on the mountain and greet each other, sitting down to swap stories. Condensed from my travelog, this book contains my notes as a gift to you. I have winnowed out the fluff. We both know the steep terrain that lies ahead. It forces us to pack just the essentials.

However, our most valuable assets add no extra weight, for they lie within us—determination, persistence, self-reliance, discipline, patience, and above all, a burning love for God.

At this writing, it has been 200 years since that officer in Napoleon's army chanced upon that strange stone tablet in the mud of the Nile Delta. May this book open to you a timeless treasure—one recovered from the gem fields of the immortals.

Part One

A Seeker in the Foothills

1

Sparks in the Tinder

Once you taste the sweet nectar of divine love, you will move steadily ahead toward God—never happy with the old ways again.

—Harold Klemp
The Living Word, Book 2[1]

G od is often kind to the tenderfoot. Our first steps along the spiritual path can be an easy walk. The ground is smooth, the sky is clear, the birds are singing, and the steep mountain ahead is mercifully shielded from our sight.

This is not to say we haven't been through a dark night of Soul in our search for the trailhead. But once we find it, we are sometimes blessed with a number of wondrous miracles that seem to drop from heaven. Further up the trail the terrain gets rocky and the sky turns gray, and we may think we're in another dark night of Soul. But meanwhile we rejoice in having found our heart's desire. This is the honeymoon phase of the spiritual path.

These initial miracles are sparks in the tinder for the holy fire which God is lighting in our hearts. Quickly the tinder is consumed, and the flames die down. But

These initial miracles are sparks in the tinder for the holy fire which God is lighting in our hearts.

the fire at least is started. If we feed it with contemplation and love, it will surely grow.

The sparks in my tinder The sparks in my tinder were six simple miracles which came my way between the ages of eighteen and twenty-one. Though I didn't see it at the time, each was a gift, intended to open a different window to heaven. One or more of them may remind you of your own gifts from heaven.

The sparks in my tinder were six simple miracles which came my way between the ages of eighteen and twenty-one.

These miracles provided an important understanding I would later need to receive the insights which form this book. A natural progression of insights which led me to the Rosetta stone of God.

The first miracle occurred the summer after I finished high school. I was working for a forest protection agency on a fire-fighting crew. When there were no fires, we went into the mountains and practiced. One afternoon we were in heavy brush. It was nearly impossible to push through it. I spotted a fallen tree. Its long, straight trunk would make an easy path through the tangled bushes.

After walking its length, I found a wall of branches. Leaning heavily against the branches, I pushed hard to break through. Suddenly the wall gave way, and I staggered forward two steps, only to find myself teetering on the end of the log as it jutted out over the edge of a cliff. I looked down some thirty feet to a bed of jagged boulders.

My momentum had carried me past the point of regaining my balance. I flailed my arms wildly, as if I could save myself by flapping them. But it was too late—I pitched forward to my doom.

At that moment a firm hand appeared out of thin air and pushed against my chest to stop my fall. It gave me just the extra moment I needed to look around and find a branch to grab. I pulled myself back from the brink and quickly sat down to calm myself.

A loving presence rested like a cloak upon my shoulders. I wondered if this was a guardian angel. As the pounding of my heart subsided, I struggled to come up with a logical explanation. But I had none. Looking back I can see that this first gift from God opened a small window to heaven that had been closed before. A little notetaker somewhere in the back of my mind wrote down a first entry:

A loving presence rested like a cloak upon my shoulders. I wondered if this was a guardian angel.

1. I am protected (but by whom?).

Later that summer I joined the United States Navy, volunteering for submarine duty. My specialty was to be a sonarman. It would be my pleasure to travel around the world beneath the waves, listening to the sounds of the ocean deep and all that swam and dove and crept therein.

Every day I spent long hours just listening intently. This heightened my sensitivity to sound. An unexpected benefit emerged in my dreams. Though I had always been a strong visual dreamer, I became a better aural one as well. I would awaken in the morning with vivid memories of music, voices, and other sounds.

One night I dreamed a voice was speaking to me. It spoke of many new spiritual ideas which I had not thought of before. The instruction began with basics, then progressed as the nights passed.

The teachings covered a wide range of concepts and wove them all together with compelling clarity. After each nightly instruction the voice ended with the same refrain, "All the universe." I had no clue what this meant, but it sounded impressive, and it served as a cue for me to wake up and write down what had been given.

After several weeks I had a notebook full of inspiring knowledge. Some of the topics included things I had never pondered before, like the nature of Soul, karma and reincarnation, out-of-body travel, and God's plan for the world. Yet each was taught to me in a way that seemed so natural and obvious that I found myself changing my beliefs.

After about a month the instruction stopped. My dreams returned to normal. The notetaker in the back of my mind got out his little notebook and added entry number two:

1. I am protected (but by whom?).
2. I can be taught in my dreams (but by whom?).

One winter when I was twenty, the submarine I served on was in port in Groton, Connecticut. It was the year 1972, and meditation was becoming popular. I wasn't much interested in it, but one of my buddies was. When he asked me to join him in town for a lecture about meditation, I went along.

I popped out of my body and found myself hovering above the circle of people, looking down from the ceiling.

We joined an audience of about fifteen people. A young, articulate man spoke eloquently about the benefits of meditation to our physical and spiritual health. He invited us to put our chairs in a circle, close our eyes, and chant a word together. He wanted us to feel the immediate benefits.

I had hardly chanted the word two or three times when suddenly I popped out of my body and found myself hovering above the circle of people, looking down from the ceiling.

Hey, this really works! I thought. I caught a glimpse of someone else hovering nearby. He looked familiar, but I couldn't place him. He was not anyone from the group below us. He just smiled, then disappeared. "Hmmm," I said to myself, "this is all very curious."

When we finished chanting, I bounced back into my physical body. The speaker asked if anyone wanted to share their experiences. I waited to see what others had to say. Most of the people mentioned feeling inner peace or calm. Some had no special experience. When it was my turn, I leaned forward and delivered an enthusiastic report of my out-of-body adventure.

The look on the speaker's face betrayed a touch of confusion and bewilderment. Apparently he hadn't encountered this kind of response before. Everyone else in the circle, including my buddy, looked at me strangely. The speaker found his voice and muttered, "I'm not sure what you are talking about."

That out-of-body experience was the third miracle. Another window to heaven opened for me that day.

I leaned back in my chair and let the discussion pass to the next person. This was still the early seventies, and the study of near-death experiences had yet to make out-of-body experiences familiar to the public. I wondered if I had outgrown this man's meditation path before I even got started.

That out-of-body experience was the third miracle. Another window to heaven opened for me that day. The diligent little notetaker in the back of my mind added item number three to the growing list:

1. I am protected (but by whom?).
2. I can be taught in my dreams (but by whom?).
3. I can leave my physical body (but who was that other person nearby?).

This third item on the list, I soon learned, was truly God's gift to a tenderfoot. By this I mean it was beginner's luck. Try as I might over the next few months, I could not repeat the trick of getting out of my body. In fact, it would be years before I succeeded in doing it at all, except in the dream state.

Later that year the Navy sent me to San Diego, California, for more sonar training. I rented a studio apartment in the suburb of Ocean Beach, to better enjoy the beach lifestyle. I also made frequent trips to the library and various bookstores, seeing what I could learn about the unusual experiences I had been having.

Flitting from book to book like a butterfly in search of the best nectar, I only succeeded in whetting my appetite. Whatever I was searching for eluded me.

One afternoon the heartfelt yearning for this elusive mystery took hold of me. I put down the book I'd been reading. Then I knelt on the floor of my little studio apartment and closed my eyes. "Dear God," I prayed, "if there is a teacher for me on this weary old earth, please lead me to him."

"Dear God," I prayed, "if there is a teacher for me on this weary old earth, please lead me to him."

Something went thump on the floor. I cracked open one eye to peek at what had made the noise. A direct look might scare away whatever it was. The book I had just placed on the table had somehow managed to scoot over to the edge and fall to the floor! That was a little spooky. Were there ghosts afoot in broad daylight?

When the book bounced, two bookmarks had popped out of it. One was the bookmark I'd put there. The other I hadn't noticed before.

I reached over and picked up the unfamiliar bookmark. Someone had handwritten a note on one side which said, "Look not to the pond to see the moon, for that is only a reflection. The real moon is in the sky above."

Turning the bookmark over, I saw the silhouette of a man and a quote which said, "I am eternal, therefore, I am free. All who come unto Me shall experience the freedom of eternity."

The quote was attributed to someone named Paul Twitchell. Beneath the quote was the local address of something called ECKANKAR (rhymes with check-in-car). I stared at the silhouette. It seemed vaguely familiar.

Was this the answer to my prayer already? If so, it had arrived in record time. I couldn't wait to find out. So I got into my car and drove to the address given on the bookmark. It was a small office along a city street in San Diego. A sign in the window said Open, so I went in. I was greeted by a man in his late twenties and an attractive young woman.

After introductions, we sat down to chat. I showed them the bookmark and asked what Eckankar was all about. They explained that the word meant the path of ECK, another name for Divine Spirit. They said the teachings provided a way for anyone to have their own spiritual experiences. With my growing list of miracles, this caught my attention and prompted me to ask more.

I showed them the bookmark and asked what Eckankar was all about.

As they answered my questions, I recognized these were the same teachings I had gotten from the voice in my dreams while at sea on the submarine.

Then I noticed several portrait photos upon the wall. One looked familiar. For a few moments I searched my memory for a match. Then the amnesia lifted. This was the man who had hovered nearby during my out-of-body experience at the meditation meeting! "Who is that?" I asked.

"Paul Twitchell," they replied. "He was the spiritual leader of Eckankar until his translation (death) in 1971."

"I'm surprised he passed on," I said, "because I feel he has been guiding me."

The couple smiled, exchanging knowing glances. "Paul Twitchell and other ECK Masters often work with students on the spiritual path," the woman explained.

After an hour or so, I'd heard all I needed to hear— I wanted to find out more about this man and his ideas about life. I bought one each of the dozen or so books available and talked the couple into giving me a membership brochure as well. They had encouraged me to go more slowly and digest what I was reading. But I was starved for this spiritual food and not at all interested in polite table manners.

As I prepared to leave, the man asked where I was living. "I'm renting an apartment in Ocean Beach," I said.

"Well that's interesting. Paul Twitchell used to live in Ocean Beach when he first presented Eckankar here back in the early sixties. I guess that's a good sign you're in the right place!"

As I drove home on the freeway, whistling a happy tune, I watched the notetaker add a fourth little miracle to the list in the back of my mind. He also erased the parenthetic "whom?" questions that had suffixed the first three items. I knew now the mystery man was Paul Twitchell:

1. I am protected.
2. I can be taught in my dreams.
3. I can leave my physical body.

"Paul Twitchell and other ECK Masters often work with students on the spiritual path," the woman explained.

4. I am being guided.

That evening I read through the biography of Paul Twitchell, *In My Soul I Am Free,* by Brad Steiger. Twitchell was a fascinating man. He had developed the ability to move out of his physical body even as a child (he called it Soul Travel). This and his deep interest in all things spiritual led him on a quest and mission to learn everything the world claimed to know about God.

He traveled widely, read voraciously, and investigated firsthand the religious practices and metaphysical techniques of the world. As he worked at his task, Twitchell patiently sifted the gold from the sand.

Eventually his quest led him to the grand goal of his life—what he called God-Realization. This was his term for someone who had traveled upward through the many levels of heaven until he finally reached the Secret Place of the Most High, the abode of God. He called this high heaven the Ocean of Love and Mercy.

Of great interest to me was Paul's claim that he could meet inwardly with any sincere student and begin teaching him what he needed to know, so that he too might reach the heights of God.

Paul offered to meet the seeker in contemplation, through Soul Travel or in his dreams. It was at this point that the value of my earlier experiences smoothed the path.

Paul offered to meet the seeker in contemplation, through Soul Travel or in his dreams.

"Oh yes," I said to myself, "that's using miracle number two from that checklist, I can be taught through my dreams, and number three, I can move out of my body."

As I prepared for bed that evening, I felt a strong presence in the apartment. So strong it was unsettling. I'd never felt anything like it. I kept opening the closet door and looking in the bathroom to assure myself that nobody was hiding there.

I finally went to bed and fell into a fitful sleep. But the usual transition into deep sleep was interrupted. Instead of falling soundly asleep, I found myself slipping gracefully out of my physical body in full awareness. The room had a glow to it coming from the walls and furniture.

Instead of falling soundly asleep, I found myself slipping gracefully out of my physical body in full awareness.

I felt light and happy. The feeling was similar to the one I'd felt some months before when I was hovering above the circle of people at the meditation meeting. Then I felt that presence again. It was coming from behind me.

Turning around I saw a man standing near the head of the bed. I recognized him from the photograph on the cover of his biography. It was definitely Paul Twitchell, though a younger-looking and more radiant version than the picture of him.

"All right," he began matter-of-factly, "you know why I'm here. You want to learn how to Soul Travel in the dream state. Right now you're in the Astral body, not the Soul body. But I like to start people out this way. Soul is hardly more than a viewpoint in these lower worlds of space and time.

"Soul Travel can be so subtle it doesn't even register on the human consciousness. It takes practice to recognize the experience. The Astral form, though subtler than the Physical, is close enough to it that you should be able to more easily relate this experience to your waking life."

"Well this is really something!" I exclaimed. "I feel as free as a bird!"

He smiled with understanding. "Tonight we'll keep

it simple. I'd like you to practice just circling the room a few times, like an airplane in a holding pattern."

I could propel myself by just thinking of where I wanted to go. I circled the room slowly. After a few circles I got more confident, moving faster each time. Then, just for fun and variation, I went under a chair on my way around. This maneuver brought a chuckle from Paul.

I could propel myself by just thinking of where I wanted to go.

"That's it for now," he said abruptly. Then he turned and walked right through a wall.

I felt the tug of my physical body. In a moment I was awake in bed with a vivid recall of the experience and an awe of Paul Twitchell. Here was a man who made extraordinary claims about his ability to teach and guide his students through the inner realms and actually made good on his promises. He had my full attention and interest. I was eager to read more about this man and his teachings called Eckankar.

As I lay in bed, my thoughts passed over the miracles I'd experienced to date. I began to piece things together: the hand that kept me from falling over the cliff, the voice of the spiritual dream instructions while I was serving aboard the submarine, the man who was present during my out-of-body experience with the mediation group, and the being who answered my prayers for a teacher by putting an Eckankar bookmark under my nose. I felt certain that all of these were orchestrated by Paul himself. My list had grown to five miracles:

1. I am protected.
2. I can be taught in my dreams.
3. I can leave my physical body.
4. I am being guided.
5. I have a teacher who can meet me at will via Soul Travel.

Over the next few weeks I read through the pile of books I had bought at the Eckankar center. Once I read through them all, I went back and read them again. I began diligently to practice the spiritual exercises Paul described in these books.

But all this pushing didn't help me break through to any new miracles. My tinder was just about burned up. My beginner's luck was running out. The flashy experiences which I had been given by Paul to catch my interest were dying down.

I sensed it was time to begin the slow and patient work of spiritual unfoldment. This I was willing to do, for I knew that eventually I would be able to feed the flames and build a good spiritual fire within myself.

But one more gift for the tenderfoot remained—the most precious gift of all. It came in a dream and changed forever the chief aspiration of my life, for it showed me what the core teachings of Eckankar were really about.

The dream came to me about three months after my initial nighttime rendezvous with Paul. In the dream I was standing on a mountaintop looking up at the stars when he made a sudden appearance at my side.

In the dream I was standing on a mountaintop looking up at the stars when he made a sudden appearance at my side.

He put a comforting hand on my shoulder and followed my skyward gaze. "You seek the Star of God," he said softly. "The sky is thick with stars which God has cast carelessly across the heavens like diamonds upon a black velvet cloth. How shall you find the one you seek?"

I looked into Paul's eyes, which shimmered with a beautiful inner light. "Something out there is pulling at my heart," I said. "If I just follow my heart, I will find it."

"Then let's go," he said. Taking my hand, we sailed

up and away from the earth. We began to accelerate out into space. Soon the stars were flashing past us at great speed. After traveling silently for a time, we began to slow down, and Paul said, "In a few moments I am going to point to a certain star. I want you to look at it for just a moment, then turn away."

We entered an empty region of space suffused with a deep silence and peace and coasted gently to a stop. Pointing, Paul said, "You may look now."

I turned and looked, gazing into the light of a brilliant blue-white star. It was at once a million miles away and just beyond my reach. There was a moment of suspense, then suddenly I was engulfed in a blaze of love.

Whatever inner body I was wearing went completely limp as I felt my entire being surrender helplessly into an all-embracing rapture. Wave upon wave of divine love washed over me, through me. I felt like a moth whose one desire was to sacrifice all and perish in ecstasy in this cosmic flame.

How could a mortal like me follow the instructions of my guide to look for just a moment upon this sight, then turn away? I had no such powers. Divine love held me close in its most tender embrace.

Somewhere in the distance I heard Paul's voice say, "This is enough," as he pulled me away from the vision. In silence, hand in hand, we flew back through the universe of stars, all the way back to earth atop the mountain. As soon as we landed I slumped to the ground.

"You have been given a tiny glimpse of God's love," said Paul. "You are not yet ready to go closer. That star you saw is not God Itself but only a symbol of Its love for you.

Wave upon wave of divine love washed over me, through me. I felt like a moth whose one desire was to sacrifice all and perish in ecstasy in this cosmic flame.

"One day you shall gaze upon the face of God. For now, let this be your constant reminder that you exist because God loves you. May the blessings be."

I awoke from the dream. In that little notebook in the back of my mind, the notetaker jotted down my sixth and final miracle, the one that got me started on my twenty-year search for the Rosetta stone of God:

"One day you shall gaze upon the face of God. For now, let this be your constant reminder that you exist because God loves you."

1. I am protected.
2. I can be taught in my dreams.
3. I can leave my physical body.
4. I am being guided.
5. I have a teacher who can meet me at will via Soul Travel.
6. I am being led home to God.

So who was this man Paul Twitchell, and how could he work these miracles for me? Where did he acquire these abilities? Did he come from some spiritual tradition or was he working alone? Were these six miracles the extent of his abilities to help me, or were they just a sampling of things to come?

Later I would discover that these were the kind of questions Paul Twitchell liked people to ask. Little did I know that it would take me decades to answer these questions to my satisfaction. They would eventually lead to my search for the Rosetta stone of God.

The stories in this chapter tell how I found the trailhead to the spiritual mountain. Before going further, I need to pause and talk a little about the teachings of Paul Twitchell. He had climbed the spiritual mountain and left valuable notes for those who would follow in his footsteps.

2

The Mystery Man

He had figured out the key—how to teach others to become Co-workers with God. This was the major difference between Paul and many of the other teachers.

—Harold Klemp
The Secret Teachings[1]

*P*aul Twitchell had my full attention. His writings answered many of my questions and provided inspiration to continue the journey. His ability to help me in my spiritual unfoldment answered my desire for a capable teacher.

Paul Twitchell had my full attention.

It's beyond the scope of this book to examine even the outline of this man's complex and fascinating life. I wish to write just enough to move ahead with the story I am telling.

Very briefly, after years of research, study, effort, and exploration, Paul succeeded in his goal of attaining spiritual Mastership. He felt it was his mission to reestablish the ECK teachings in society after they had been hidden and taught in secret for many centuries.

He began to do this in the early sixties. By the time he left this world in 1971, Eckankar was well on its way to becoming known worldwide.

One thing struck me immediately about his writings. And frankly, it took a little getting used to. This was the unusual way he wrote about the immortal part of each of us. He had a habit of referring to the soul in a personal way. Instead of writing "the soul" or "your soul" or "many souls," he would write simply "Soul."

"Soul can leave the body at will and travel to higher planes."

For example, he might write, "Soul can leave the body at will and travel to higher planes." When I'd read a sentence like that, I wanted to edit it, and stick an article in front of "Soul." I wanted it to read "a soul" or "the soul." He seemed to have a personal acquaintance and familiarity with the spiritual nature within us. He would no more say "The Soul is immortal" than we would say "The God is love."

At first this seemed a contrivance to me. But once I caught the point of view this man was trying to share with his readers, my impression changed. After reading several of his books it became hard to think and talk about "the soul" anymore. And as this shift occurred, there came with it a fresh point of view. Bringing about this shift was, I surmised, Paul Twitchell's motive. And I later found my conjecture was correct.

One day I came across a letter Paul wrote on the semantics of spiritual language. "The terminology is wrong in most cases," he wrote. "Take, for example, that which is constantly used in the religious field, 'My soul,' or 'Your soul.' Where is the position from which these people are speaking? Why, it is from the state of the lower consciousness. It is putting a proprietorship upon the most important part of being of man, that of Soul. It is standing back in the physical senses and looking at Soul as a lower object; this of course is a false premise, for we should dwell in the higher self (Soul) and look down upon all the lower senses and physical flesh. We must be in the position as Jesus when he said, 'Destroy this temple, and in three days I will raise it up.' He was speaking from the higher realm of God."[2]

The shift of viewpoint which Paul's writings instilled in me was moving from "I have a soul" to "I am Soul, and I have a body." This may seem an innocuous transition. But it can introduce just the paradigm shift into our thoughts which enables us to take the first step toward a new spiritual identity.

The other term Paul often used differently was the pronoun referring to God. He preferred to use the word "It" rather than "He" or "Him" when referring to God. These pronouns help perpetuate the notion of God as an old man with a long beard sitting on a throne in the sky. Paul used them sometimes too, for poetic effect, or perhaps in deference to tradition. But he usually used the word "It."

Again, his motive was to remind the reader that the supreme being could not be contained by such human attributes as male and female. The word *It* may seem impersonal at first. Yet Paul Twitchell's deep and profound love for God shines through all his writings.

THE LIGHT AND SOUND

The second thing which struck me about Paul Twitchell's writings was their emphasis upon the Light and Sound of God. I was quite familiar with the idea of the Light of God. It has been praised by mystics of all religious traditions.

In modern times the experience of this Light of God has spread well beyond the inner circle of mystics. For example many people who have gone through a

Paul Twitchell's deep and profound love for God shines through all his writings.

near-death experience speak ecstatically of this light. Here is a fairly typical description from author Betty Eadie's near-death account in her book *Embraced by the Light:*

"As I got closer the light became brilliant—brilliant beyond any description, far more brilliant than the sun—and I knew that no earthly eyes in their natural state could look upon this light without being destroyed. Only spiritual eyes could endure it—and appreciate it."[3]

The Sound of God is perhaps less well known. Pythagoras spoke of the music of the spheres. We all know the mysterious power of music to move us, inspire us, and soothe us. Many scriptures attribute the power of the Sound or Word as being of primary importance in the story of creation. "In the beginning was the Word," begins the Gospel according to Saint John, "and the Word was with God, and the Word was God."

Though millions of people have read such passages in scripture, few seem to have connected it with something real and tangible in their own lives. The line of spiritual teachers Paul Twitchell became a member of emphasize the divine Sound Current. In fact they say It is the keystone of the arch of God and the basis of all secret teachings. It is the most important factor in Soul's journey home to God, even more so than the Light.

The line of spiritual teachers Paul Twitchell became a member of emphasize the divine Sound Current.

"The current of Sound from the Godhead contains the total sum of all teaching emanating from God," writes Paul Twitchell in his book *The Tiger's Fang.* "It is God's language to all, and includes all that God has said or done. It is God in expression, and It is the method by which God is made known to all the worlds. It is the Word and the language of God."[4]

This music of God cannot be heard by the outer ears—only by the faculties of Soul. The ability to hear it is developed through certain spiritual exercises, and the assistance of a spiritual Master who knows the importance of the Sound. These teachers are generally the ECK Masters. The word ECK signifies the Light and Sound of God. More about these Masters in a moment.

Paul's writings are filled with beautiful and inspiring descriptions of this music from the Great Composer. Many who practice the techniques he taught have learned to hear this uplifting Word from heaven and see the radiance of the divine Light.

The Sound can come in almost any form, timbre, pitch, and volume imaginable. It can be a sound of nature such as the wind, the songs of birds, or the rumble of thunder. Or it can be a single, pure tone, like a single note from a flute. It can even burst forth in symphonic majesty.

Whatever form It takes, It is God serenading Soul, telling of God's love for us, calling to us to rise and come home. The closer we get to God on our journey home, the more delectable and enchanting the Sound becomes.

As a child, I would hear a soft background sound when all was still at night. It reminded me of the barely audible whisper made when a breeze whisks particles of dry sand along a beach. This sound has comforted me over the years. I never thought of it as unusual.

When I began doing the spiritual exercises taught by Paul Twitchell, I found a change in this background sound. During contemplation it would increase in volume until it was in the foreground. This same increase in volume would come at other special moments, such

This music of God cannot be heard by the outer ears— only by the faculties of Soul.

as when sitting in the audience at an Eckankar seminar.

Over time the background sound made other transformations. I would be doing something ordinary, like sitting at my desk at work, when the whisper would suddenly increase in volume, then turn into a clear, bright tone. This tone would last from fifteen or twenty seconds to a minute, then as quickly quiet down again.

It became clear to me that this background whisper I'd heard all my life was the same Sound of God which Paul had spoken of. The Sound is always pleasant, even joyful, and does not interfere with one's normal consciousness. For me, Its arrival brings happy feelings, and when It departs, It leaves a feeling of lightness and love.

The Sound is always pleasant, even joyful, and does not interfere with one's normal consciousness.

Together these two great attributes of Spirit, the Light and Sound, are God's greatest gifts to Soul. In the higher stages of unfoldment they bring rapture and fill one with the bliss of divine love.

THE ECK MASTERS

Of great interest to the world, and also of great controversy, was Paul Twitchell's assertion of the existence of a group of God-Realized beings, the ECK Masters. He had met and been taught by a number of these Masters and eventually became one of them.

What intrigued some and riled others was his claim that this order of Masters had existed on earth for thousands of years, an unbroken line, teaching and initiating followers largely in secret, and that many of them were of an incredible age and still alive today.

Where was the proof? Paul said the proof would come when one of these Masters made an appearance to the seeker. This was usually in the dream state and on occasion, in the flesh.

Some critics insist that dreams are unreliable proof. They claim our unconscious minds can conjure up just about anything, and therefore, the dream experiences people have with the ECK Masters hardly validate Twitchell's claims.

In seeming response to this point, reports came in from many people (some who had never heard of Paul Twitchell or Eckankar at the time) who had met one or more of these Masters in their dreams years before Paul ever wrote about them.

Reports came in from many people who had met one or more of these Masters in their dreams years before Paul ever wrote about them.

Even stronger validation has come from people who have met one or more of these Masters in the flesh. Some of these encounters occurred years before Paul Twitchell began writing about the ECK Masters. The most resolute critics dismiss these testimonies as fabrications. In other words, if a skeptic is convinced that something cannot be true, no amount of evidence makes any difference. Perhaps this is a case of "You will see it when you believe it."

Though I had met and been taught by a number of ECK Masters in the dream state during my first decade in Eckankar, I had never actually met one of them physically. I wondered at times whether I was fooling myself.

But this doubt was dispelled one evening in 1981. I was living alone in an apartment in Wichita, Kansas. I had been planning to give a series of introductory talks about Eckankar to local communities. When I went to bed that Friday evening I had these thoughts in mind and invited helpful ideas from the ECK Masters in the dream state. This was a habit of mine which usually brought results in the form of new ideas in the morning.

About 2:00 a.m. someone shook me awake. This should have caused me to awaken in alarm. Instead I felt strangely calm. I sat up to find the famous ECK Master Rebazar Tarzs sitting on the edge of my bed.

I sat up to find the famous ECK Master Rebazar Tarzs sitting on the edge of my bed.

This notable man was Paul's main teacher, and Paul painted a striking portrait of him. Rebazar is a leader among spiritual leaders. He's about five-feet-ten-inches tall, of swarthy complexion, robust physique, deep voice, and animated gestures. He wears a short black beard and has dark flashing eyes.

Paul claimed that Rebazar Tarzs, like a number of ECK Masters, is of an extraordinary age. Though he looks to be in his thirties, he is supposed to be some five centuries old. He lives in a remote mountain area in Asia, but appears to followers of Eckankar around the world.

This great ECK Master had made frequent appearances in my dreams and contemplations over the years. I felt a special closeness to him. But I had never met him physically.

"Let's go over your plans," he said that night, matter-of-factly. "I have some suggestions." We talked for a few minutes; then he got up to leave.

"Never mind the professional critics and debunkers of the ECK Masters," he said. "These people are just parasites who live off the labor and efforts of others. They find it a vain pleasure to attack any worthy cause set up for the benefit of mankind. If Paul Twitchell and Eckankar didn't exist, they would seek out another host to feed upon. It is the nature of this world, and there will always be such people." He raised his hand in blessing, then dissolved his form into the darkness of the night.

I mention this incident because it can be a stretch for some seekers to believe that such beings as the ECK Masters really exist. I will, on many occasions in this book, refer to various ECK Masters. They do exist, and their existence is one of the great fortunes of the serious seeker.

THE MAHANTA

Of the many fascinating subjects Paul Twitchell wrote about, the most arresting to me was a being he called the Mahanta. (Not to be confused with the title Mahatma which is used sometimes in India.)

Paul variously defined the Mahanta as: the highest state of consciousness on earth; a spiritual mantle passed from one Living ECK Master to the next; an ancient being who is ever present to help the seeker find his way home to God. And these were but a few of the definitions he gave of who or what the Mahanta was.

No matter what spiritual topic he touched upon, Paul almost always showed how it was linked to the Mahanta. Such a diversity of viewpoints initially served only to confuse the subject in my mind.

Among all the ECK Masters there is only one who holds the title of the Mahanta, the Living ECK Master. For his term of office he is directly responsible for assisting any seeker who wishes to follow the path of ECK. The other ECK Masters work in the background and support his mission.

Among all the ECK Masters there is only one who holds the title of the Mahanta, the Living ECK Master.

Paul Twitchell held this position from 1965 to 1971. As the full title of the position implies, there is a sort of union of two principles involved. The Mahanta part, and the Living ECK Master part. These are the two faces of the Master: the inner face and the outer face.

It would be many years before I began to sense the importance of who or what the Mahanta is in the larger scheme of things. It gradually dawned on me that here was a vital key to the spiritual history and destiny of the human race. I felt that a fact of utmost importance had been revealed to humanity, especially to the serious seekers. Yet hardly anyone outside of Eckankar had even heard of it.

It gradually dawned on me that here was a vital key to the spiritual history and destiny of the human race.

I began a thorough research effort on the subject of the Mahanta. After reading all that was available in the writings of the ECK Masters, I went to the inner planes to see what more could be discovered. I did this through contemplations and by looking for insights in my dreams.

For over twenty years I pursued this elusive subject until exhausting all my known sources of research. I was near the end of the trail but not there yet. Feeling a breakthrough discovery lay hidden just beyond my grasp, I didn't suspect my reward was near at hand. The many threads of my research had begun to weave together into a discernible pattern. I only needed someone to help me see it.

Like a two-dimensional image that becomes three-dimensional when looked at in just the right way, my pattern needed only the right focus and viewing angle. It was about to come to me from a totally unexpected source. I stood at the threshold of discovery.

3

A Call to Adventure

How strong must be our urge to reach God? Very strong. But at first we don't care much about lofty spiritual goals because they are immaterial to us. So the ECK Masters lead us slowly toward the higher visions.

—Harold Klemp
Soul Travelers of the Far Country[1]

*L*ife has a mischievous way of sweeping us off our feet and tossing us into adventures when we least expect it. Many of us imagine we like adventures—but when they come knocking at the door, we quickly contrive excuses about being too busy at the moment.

In his book *The Hero with a Thousand Faces,* mythologist Joseph Campbell traced the steps of the adventurer's journey as found in myths throughout the world. The journey begins with a call to adventure, often some chance encounter, some ordinary day gone awry.

It seems innocuous—some curious coincidence becomes the bait that lures us into the unknown. Before we recognize what's happening, we get swept out into white water and find ourselves plunging recklessly ahead. At that point we can kick and scream and try

Life has a mischievous way of sweeping us off our feet and tossing us into adventures when we least expect it.

to refuse the call. Or we can grab an oar and start paddling!

My call to adventure began with naive innocence on a most humdrum Monday morning. I arrived at work and drove to my favorite parking space closest to the office. As I opened the door and began to get out of the car, I noticed an old brass key lying on the pavement. With an idle flick of my foot I sent it skidding a few feet away and went into the office.

Later in the day I went out to eat lunch in a restaurant. When I returned, the parking lot was nearly full. I had to circle around until I found an empty spot way in back. As I got out of the car a glint of sunlight drew my attention to something on the ground. It was an old brass key. Or was it the same key? I doubted it was, for this parking space was several hundred feet away from the one I'd used in the morning.

There was a time when I wouldn't have given this coincidence a moment of thought. But experience had since taught me to look for meaning in such events. They are often life's way of getting our attention, of alerting us to some impending message of importance.

These synchronicities often appear to us at important turning points in our lives.

These synchronicities often appear to us at important turning points in our lives. So as I looked at the key, I wondered, *Was this little coincidence of sufficient moment to contemplate its meaning, or was it too minor to matter?*

At the time a late project at work seemed a lot more important. So I gave the old brass key a good hard kick. It spun out of sight under another car. I was too busy for an adventure.

That evening, as I got ready for bed, the incidents with the keys began to distract me. *Maybe there is a message in this somewhere,* I thought. *Keys . . . hmmm . . . keys to what? I don't get it.* The bothersome brass keys needled my thoughts as I drifted off to sleep.

Dreams often join forces with synchronicities in a devious conspiracy to jolt us out of our ordinary consciousness. They will take us in hand as soon as we enter their enchanted land and do their part to undermine our complacency.

Dreams often join forces with synchronicities in a devious conspiracy to jolt us out of our ordinary consciousness.

Sometime in the middle of the night I found myself having a lucid Soul Travel dream. I was floating in a void, peering into its featureless dimensions with a feeling of nervous expectancy. In the distance I spotted a pair of tiny moving lights. One was a beautiful sparkling blue, the other a radiant gold.

They began to grow in size, and I realized they were rapidly approaching. As they came closer, I could hear a deep humming sound. The sound carried an intense yet loving vibration.

Soon the two spheres were hovering in front of me, just beyond arm's reach. They emitted such a radiant light and pure humming sound that I felt out of place with my sluggish vibrations.

The golden one began to shimmer, its outer surface slowly opening to reveal an inner sphere. There was something inside, an object of the purest gold I had ever seen. But what was it? I looked more closely. It was a golden key! I knew it was mine if I simply had the courage to reach in and take it.

Instead, I hesitated and moved back. The golden sphere snapped shut. For a moment these two spiritual beings—for I was sure that's what they were—communicated with each other. Then they sped away, quickly disappearing into the darkness. This was the third time in twenty-four hours I had been offered a key, and I had refused it every time.

I awoke from the dream, cursing at myself for passing up this opportunity. How could I have been so clueless as to miss the significance of the two keys in the parking lot? I was being offered a key to spiritual wisdom but had recklessly kicked it aside. *Well, I failed this test,* I thought. *It may be a very long time before such an opportunity comes again.*

In my experience, Divine Spirit always tests us to see if we are worthy of a gift. It sets up a series of hurdles, learning experiences to teach us what we need to know for the next step. If we don't learn the lessons—whether in relationships, business, health, or keys in a parking lot—we will be sent back through the course until we master the lesson.

I decided not to give up without a struggle. Why wait around for the next opportunity to take this test? As I lay in bed I hatched a plan that I probably would have discarded instantly in the saner hours of daylight: I would get up early, drive to work before anyone else arrived, and search the parking lot until I found that key!

Divine Spirit rarely responds to such plans. And it was a weak assumption that if I did find the key in the parking lot, I would be given a fresh opportunity with the dream key.

The next morning, as I drove to work early, I felt a little foolish. I won't repeat the more colorful word my wife had for such behavior. But having set this plot in motion, stubbornness became the momentum that kept me moving forward.

When I arrived at work I parked my car near the

Divine Spirit always tests us to see if we are worthy of a gift. It sets up a series of hurdles, learning experiences to teach us what we need to know for the next step.

back of the empty lot. Trying to look as casual as possible, I started a systematic search for the brass key. I spent a half hour checking out the entire lot. The key was nowhere to be found. With deep disappointment I gave up the search.

At midday, just before lunchtime, a coworker poked his head inside my cubicle. "Hey, Jim. Here's a present for you. I found it in the parking lot." He pitched an old brass key to me! "It's a key to some new wheels for you," he joked, hinting that he thought my humble older car was due for a replacement.

As he left, I said, "You have no idea what a priceless gift this is. Thanks!" He looked at me strangely and shrugged.

I slipped the key into my pocket and gazed out the window with a big grin. "So, the Beings of Light are giving me another chance!" Little did my coworker know he was serving as a messenger.

Besides synchronicities, another way Spirit talks to us is through the speech of others. Someone may be saying something which is quite ordinary to them, but it has another, more special meaning for the hearer of the message.

For example, someone may be trying to decide whether to move to Colorado. They may be walking along a street absorbed in this question when they overhear a passerby say, "I'd rather be in Colorado." This could be Spirit's way of answering their question. Harold Klemp, the spiritual leader of Eckankar today, has coined the phrase "Golden-tongued Wisdom" to describe these kinds of messages.

My coworker's words were surely Golden-tongued Wisdom. He said the key was to some "new wheels."

My coworker's words were surely Golden-tongued Wisdom. He said the key was to some "new wheels." I felt there was a hidden meaning in his words. Spirit was handing me a golden key, opening a new door to divine wisdom. And the first hint as to the nature of that wisdom was contained in the image of new wheels.

To me, wheels symbolize the movement of life, the cycle of time, and the way our inner potential unfolds through the sequence of the events in our lives. The spokes mark the different stages between birth and death. The hub of the wheel signifies the center or still point of life around which all revolves. The zodiac is a traditional example of such a wheel image writ large upon the celestial canvas. I suspected Divine Spirit was leading me toward some vital new insight on the process of spiritual unfoldment.

I leaned back in my chair and looked out the window. A sunbeam broke through the soggy spring sky and bathed me in its warmth as it poured in through the window. Looking at my watch I saw it was lunchtime and decided to head outdoors for a noontime stroll.

As I walked along a neighborhood street, enjoying the play of sunlight upon the flowers that bordered the yards, the spark of a vision floated quietly into my thoughts. A brightly colored seed from the fields of heaven. My attention was drawn gently within. Elements of a landscape began to unfold there, spun from the ethereal pattern hidden in the seed.

I felt a keen sense of anticipation. When this had happened to me before, it often presaged a new insight of some kind.

A few moments later I was strolling through two parallel worlds. Outwardly the walk continued along the street. But inwardly, the vision had solidified, and I was walking along an ancient road paved with heavy stones. The heat of the stones warmed my bare feet as I padded along. The carefully laid masonry led straight across a grassy plain toward an ancient step pyramid. Each stepped level was about ten-feet thick. A wide row of stairs led from the base up to the top.

I wondered if this was a vivid fantasy or a form of bilocation—a state of consciousness where one becomes aware of another level of reality at the same time he continues to be aware of his physical surroundings.

At the base of the pyramid, I gazed upward. The stairs beckoned, so I began the steady, methodical climb. Nearing the top, I was taken aback by the presence of a man on the flat landing. I hadn't seen him from the bottom.

The wind whipped at his white toga as he welcomed me with a trace of a smile and a friendly yet piercing gaze from pale blue eyes. His bald head and weathered face, coupled with a lean, athletic physique made him look both old and youthful at the same time. His features were hard to define, perhaps a mixture of Caucasian and Chinese.

The wind puzzled me, for I hadn't felt even a breeze up to that moment. I looked out over the plain. The green sea of grass was undisturbed by even a ripple. *Hmmm,* I thought. *There must be a wind just at the top.* But as I ascended the final few steps, I found no wind, except in a close circle around the man himself! The wind calmed as I approached him.

I thought I heard a subtle humming sound in the atmosphere atop the pyramid. It seemed to surround the man in the white toga. I recognized it as the same sound I'd heard in my dream. It was the sound which had come from the golden sphere of light—the one that had held that mysterious key. As this recognition touched

The wind whipped at his white toga as he welcomed me with a trace of a smile and a friendly yet piercing gaze from pale blue eyes.

me, I became aware of a golden aura spreading radiantly outward from the man.

"You have been asking many questions of the higher ones," he began. "You wish to know more about the Mahanta, that mysterious being sometimes called the Ancient One: He who is the secret force in world history; he who stokes the Holy Fire; he who fans the flames of divine love in the hearts of all seekers!"

So! The picture was becoming more clear. It was my incessant spiritual curiosity that pulled me into this new adventure!

I tend to be an inquisitive person and have a fault of asking unnecessary questions. At the same time, I know that spiritual teachers prefer to let the student answer his own questions. So I felt a little cautious, unsure of whether this was a mild reprimand or an invitation to instruction. "Maybe I'm being a little too impatient," I responded.

The first half of any revelation begins with an insightful question, whether consciously voiced or not.

"Not at all," he replied immediately. "The first half of any revelation begins with an insightful question, whether consciously voiced or not. The right question is the key that will open the door. It shows you are ready for a deeper understanding and draws forth from the higher planes an answer of equal measure and worth.

"Examine the history of knowledge. Amazing progress is made by the human race whenever someone asks a simple but profound question no one has thought of before."

My attention was pulled away from the inner reverie for a moment by an outer incident—a dog came trotting over to say hello. I stopped to pat him on the head and scratch his ears; then continuing my walk, I shifted my focus back into the reverie.

"Aren't questions often just an attachment of the mind?" I asked.

"Listen," the man continued. "This is often true. Some questions are born of impatience, idle curiosity, laziness, doubts, or vanity. The true teacher will not waste his time answering them, for nothing fruitful comes of it. The questioner hardly realizes what he is really looking for. He believes it is answers to his questions, but this is not true. Examine your own hidden motives when you ask these kinds of questions, and you will discover there is no genuine thirst for the wellspring of wisdom.

"Now contrast those questions with the ones about the Mahanta which have brought you here today. First you did a thorough study of all you could find about the subject. Next you took it into contemplation many times, looking at it from many points of view. Then you shared what you had learned with others. Through sincere effort and self-discipline you went as far as you could on your own. Only now do you ask for the eye of revelation. See the difference?"

"I do, thank you." Back in the physical world I had reached the end of a dead-end street. I paused to admire some roses then began walking back the way I'd come. I shifted my attention back to the inner. "May I ask your name, sir?"

"You can call me Zan. I will be your mentor for a while. Together you and I will explore more about the Mahanta. You have been given a key. But a key is of little value if you do not know which lock to apply it to. Do you know what this key gives access to?"

I thought a moment. "The Golden-tongued Wisdom tells me it is a key to some new wheels. But I don't yet

You can call me Zan. I will be your mentor for a while. Together you and I will explore more about the Mahanta.

understand what that means. Perhaps there is more to learn about the wheel of karma and rebirth and Soul's long journey through the lower worlds."

Zan said, "Your intuition about new wheels is on track. As events unfold, the meaning of that phrase will reveal itself. Meanwhile, over the next few weeks, be alert to the insights you receive through inner impressions. They may seem to be ordinary thoughts and images, but they will help you organize and solidify your revelations. Do you have a final question?"

Your intuition about new wheels is on track. As events unfold, the meaning of that phrase will reveal itself.

Zan seemed familiar. I was at ease with him, though I also sensed he possessed a rare wisdom. Perhaps even more than this quality though, I sensed a being who carried a very high responsibility with ease and confidence. What that responsibility was I could only guess.

"Zan," I said, "I am eager to proceed in my research with you. But a part of me holds back, suspecting you and this whole scene are nothing but a creation of my imagination—even if a vivid and lively creation! When I have these kinds of inner connections, I am rarely satisfied they are real unless I can find a way to validate them outwardly."

Zan replied, "Nor should you be. It is wise to check their validity. Especially if you plan to apply what you have received on the inner planes to your outer life. Soul lives a dual life. In fact a multiple life, on many planes at once.

"Some of the inner experiences have no relevance to your physical life. So there is little reward in trying to make sense of them using the measures of earth. These are truly parallel worlds. Like the hypothetical parallel lines of Euclidean geometry, they never meet. At other times some of these multiple worlds intersect.

Bridges of consciousness unite them, and across these bridges flow the communications from one world to the other.

"God dwells ever at the center, in sweet repose, contemplating Its vast creations. When It wishes to communicate Its visions to Soul, It does so through the Mahanta!

"So I leave you with this thought: if you pay attention, before the day is over you will receive a confirmation of this inner drama we have created together."

A strong gust of wind suddenly swirled around Zan, whisking his form away like mist and leaving me alone atop the pyramid. I turned and descended slowly. With each step the inner vision gradually faded until, by the time I got to the bottom, the only world I was aware of was the physical one. I finished my walk and went back to the office.

Later that day I took my family to a restaurant for dinner. As we waited for a traffic signal to change, I was wondering how the confirmation would come, if at all. I glanced at the personalized license plate on a sports car in front of us. Written on the plate were just three letters: ZAN!

These were likely the initials of the car's owner. Estimating there must be a million or so automobiles in the state, the odds that I'd pull up behind the one with these particular letters on its plate just at that moment were like the odds of winning the lottery. And how appropriate, considering the wheels symbolism of my adventure, that the name *Zan* had appeared on the license plate of an automobile.

I decided my experience with Zan was real. Now what? He had said he would serve as a mentor for me,

God dwells ever at the center, in sweet repose, contemplating Its vast creations. When It wishes to communicate Its visions to Soul, It does so through the Mahanta!

helping me gain deeper insight into the Mahanta.
Meanwhile, until his next appearance, I would contemplate on where this revelation was leading.

Such contemplations always cleared the way for
further insights. In the past I had tried to simply wait
for the next revelation to come. But that didn't work.

The effort must always be made to probe deeper.

The effort must always be made to probe deeper. The
process is like two people who start digging a tunnel
from opposite ends with a goal of meeting in the middle.
Both must continue digging. And so I kept digging,
knowing I would eventually break through.

4

The Caves of Ajanta

*Many of us have searched for centuries, following
one path or another, and looking—without success—for
the source of the call of Soul.*

— Harold Klemp
Journey of Soul[1]

O ne Saturday I felt a nudge to go to the library
and do some research on the history of wheels
and their religious symbolism. I came across an
interesting account of some old cave art that pertained
to the subject and read it in bed before falling asleep.
I didn't suspect it would open another window of discovery.

The reading induced a dream. In the dream I was
standing on a cliff at the entrance to an ancient, abandoned monastery and series of temples. A number of
caves were also carved into the face of the cliff.

The cliff formed one wall of a deep valley that ended
in a high waterfall. Heat waves from the noontime sun
radiated from the cliff walls. The site was picturesque,
but even the continuous echo of the falling water and
the buzz of insects failed to dispel the sense of isolation
that pervaded the place.

Just then Zan emerged from a cave, carrying a

*In the dream
I was
standing on a
cliff at the
entrance to an
ancient,
abandoned
monastery and
series of
temples.*

39

torch. I joined him, and we surveyed the valley below. Some swallows were diving and playing in the air currents that rose up along the waterfall. They would swoop, disappear a moment behind the falls, then come shooting out and upward. I wondered whether they were chasing insects or just enjoying the pleasure of their winged freedom.

"I see you followed the prompting to go to the library and do some research. Good start!" Zan said. "This is the valley of Ajanta in western India. We are in the past—the time is the mid-nineteenth century. The oldest caves here were excavated by Buddhist monks. I thought this would be a good place to start our journey of discovery, in our search for the answers to your questions.

"This is the valley of Ajanta in western India. We are in the past—the time is the mid-nineteenth century.

"Here we will pick up a trail that winds backward into time, to the early dawn of human history. Hidden in these caves is a clue to the mystery!" Zan turned and quickly disappeared into a cave. I followed him inside, welcoming the cool relief from the hot afternoon sun.

He led me through several cavernous rooms, then paused and held the torch high, near one of the walls. It was covered with beautiful frescoes set in mountain scenery. There were scenes of people preparing food, carrying water, hunting, riding elephants, singing, dancing, and playing musical instruments.

We left the first cave, made our way along a difficult trail, and entered a second. Zan led the way to another series of wall paintings. "This series represents the life of the Buddha—his birth and legends of his life."

"These are amazing," I said.

Zan replied, "Indeed. These works were inspired by the Buddhist scriptures. Come. Let's go to the next cave, which is the object of our journey."

The torch cast animated shadows along the walls as we moved ahead. In a few moments we stepped out into a wider cavern. Zan held up the torch. There on the wall was a painting of a large wheel divided into sections. Each section of the wheel depicted a unique scene.

"Here it is," said Zan. "This painting is an esoteric diagram of human life in the form of a wheel. It represents the long path of Soul in the lower worlds. Each division signifies one of the causes, called nidanas, of Soul's bondage to the earth world. Taken all together they represent the great chain of cause and effect which drives Soul around the wheel through thousands of lifetimes, until It finally masters the lessons of life.

"It takes a keen insight into life and much deep study before one can unravel the intricate laws of karma and reincarnation. Without access to the Soul records on the higher planes and a vision that spans eons, the student cannot gain the needed perspective. Part of my work is to elucidate these laws of karma and reincarnation for the benefit of the human race. Despite the many books which have been written on this subject, only the most rudimentary basics of the subject have yet been revealed."

I examined the wheel painting more closely. "It reminds me of the zodiac of astrology, only with different symbols for the divisions."

Zan replied, "The underlying idea is roughly similar, but there are important differences. The wheels of the various forms of astrology and this Buddhist work of art are all offshoots of a master circular diagram called the Bhavachakra, the wheel of life.

"In its complete and detailed form it is a concise

I examined the wheel painting more closely. "It reminds me of the zodiac of astrology, only with different symbols for the divisions."

formulation of the spiritual laws controlling Soul's destiny in the lower universes. As you know from your studies in Eckankar, the wheel is central to an esoteric system used by the ECK Masters. This system is called the ECK-Vidya, the ancient science of prophecy.

"There's an age-old debate about when astrology split off from the ECK-Vidya system. But I won't add to that debate at this time."

The sweep of history began to open up before me as Zan talked on these matters. "How does all this relate to the golden key to new wheels which you have put in my hands?" I asked. "Clearly we are talking about wheels here. But they are old ones. I understood my quest was leading to something new."

Zan laughed at my impatience. "First we must pick up the trail that will lead us to the treasure. We are following tracks which meander through the dust of history. I shall help you follow the trail of clues back through time."

Zan walked up to the wall. "This particular wheel, and other Buddhist works like it, are fragments of a more complete system which predates it by thousands of years. It appears to have its roots far back in primitive folklore. If the scholars knew just how far back, they would be astonished.

"The ECK Masters have preserved an unbroken record of the spiritual mysteries. These secret teachings have been placed in secure temples where they are under constant guard. These temples are called the Temples of Golden Wisdom, and the records therein include the Shariyat-Ki-Sugmad. This phrase can be translated into English as the Way of the Eternal. When we meet again we shall visit one of these temples. It will be the next

The ECK Masters have preserved an unbroken record of the spiritual mysteries. These secret teachings have been placed in secure temples where they are under constant guard.

stopping point for our research into the past."

Zan reached up to the wheel painting and, with his index finger, slowly traced its circumference on the smooth rock. He seemed to be deeply absorbed in his thoughts.

"The artist who painted this felt the perennial dilemma of humanity," explained Zan. "He saw the broad panorama of history and the long labor of his own past lives. He was an old man who had devoted his life to the Buddhist path. Yet a longing was born in his heart from this work, and he wondered whether he was any closer to spiritual liberation than when he joined this monastery in his youth.

"He knew the four noble truths, and he followed the eightfold way of his religion. Yet he had not attained nirvana, the freedom he longed for. This is the story of so many in the earth world. They follow the religion of their native culture—sometimes by habit; sometimes with a sincere heart. But in the end the goal of God still eludes them."

Zan gave me a long look. "You don't remember, do you?" he said.

"Remember what?" I asked. Zan just kept looking at me. His gaze swallowed me into a stream of images which swept back in time. Suddenly I remembered being an old Buddhist monk, painting the very fresco we were standing before. The recall was vivid and recaptured the poignant feelings of that distant lifetime.

Suddenly I remembered being an old Buddhist monk, painting the very fresco we were standing before.

"Now I remember," I said softly.

Zan nodded. "You left that life with a yearning to find the deeper secret which eluded you. Your final gesture was this painting of the wheel of life. You had dearly hoped this last effort would be your breakthrough to God's love. It was not in vain. Even though centuries have slipped through the hourglass, God has brought you back to this place today, that you may find the secret."

With that, Zan turned and led the way back to the bright sunlight. We startled a hawk that was perched on a rock near the cave entrance. It swooped out over the valley, caught an updraft, then circled back to eye us from a loftier perspective. Zan smiled. Turning to me he said, "We will meet again soon."

5

Lost in Time

While we, the actors, polish away the flaws in our spiritual roles, the ages roll on like a slow, deep river—purifying Soul.

—Harold Klemp
Soul Travelers of the Far Country[1]

*F*or the next several days I was busy with work and family matters and unable to put much attention on Zan and his instruction. Finally a quiet evening came when my wife and daughters were out shopping. I decided to try a Soul Travel technique.

Lying on the bed, I closed my eyes and thought about where I would like to go. I felt drawn to have an experience high in the mountains. So I took a few deep breaths and began to gently focus my attention on the inner screen of my mind.

As I relaxed and began to flow with the imagery, I saw a rugged mountain landscape softly lit by a full moon. I vividly imagined myself being transported into this landscape. As I held to the feeling of being there, the environment in my bedroom gradually began to fade while the mountain scenery became more solid. After three or four minutes the transition was complete. This delighted me. I was rarely so successful with this technique.

I decided to try a Soul Travel technique.

I stood at a wide spot in a trail that wound up the side of a steep ridge. The location was near the peaks of a high mountain range. A cold, biting wind whipped up from the gorge below. Just ahead were some rough stone steps leading up and around a bend.

I started to climb, hugging the rock wall to avoid the force of the wind. After several switchbacks, the trail ended at a heavy wooden gate. I was about to knock when the gate opened. A smiling Tibetan monk welcomed me into a courtyard.

"Using Soul Travel, you could have as easily landed right in the courtyard," he chuckled. "No need to come in through the back door! Let's go inside."

Across the courtyard was a large castlelike structure. I recognized it as the famous Katsupari Monastery, a Temple of Golden Wisdom in northern Tibet.

Across the courtyard was a large castlelike structure. I recognized it as the famous Katsupari Monastery, a Temple of Golden Wisdom in northern Tibet. I had visited it before in the dream state after reading about these temples in a book by Paul Twitchell. He said they held the archives of the true wisdom and that Souls could visit them during sleep to gather esoteric wisdom.

Paul also mentioned that monasteries like Katsupari are so carefully guarded that no one can enter them unless they are first screened by the monks, who can read the seeker's aura like we scan a daily newspaper. I figured this explained why the monk who met me at the gate knew I was coming.

As soon as we were inside, the monk said, "You know your way to the dining room. Why don't you go in and help yourself to a cup of hot tea?" Then he disappeared down a hallway.

I continued straight ahead to the dining room. It must have been very late at night for the room was deserted. I poured some tea, then took a seat by a panel of windows along one side of the room.

On a clear day this spot would offer a spectacular view of the mountains. But tonight there was little to see but my own reflection. I cupped my hands against the glass and peered out into the night. The effect of the moonlight on the snowy peaks created an eerie landscape of vague, ghostly shapes.

"It's a very well-situated monastery, wouldn't you agree?" I turned to find Zan standing behind me, sipping from a cup. "The founding of this place is a story in itself, and a study in the spiritual history of the human race."

At the beginning of each great civilization, or root race, an ECK Master helps establish its spiritual foundation.

He pulled out a chair and sat down next to me. "At the beginning of each great civilization, or root race, an ECK Master helps establish its spiritual foundation. These root-race epochs are not to be confused with the comparatively brief subcivilizations written about in history books, such as your western civilization. The few fragments of knowledge about the root races are preserved in scattered myths and legends.

"Four of them passed into history long ago. These have been called the Polarian, the Hyperborean, the Lemurian, and the Atlantean races. Perhaps the most remembered and discussed is the Atlantean race, which dwelled on the lost continent of Atlantis.

"We are currently living in the era of the fifth root race, called the Aryan. The ECK Master to help lay the spiritual foundation for the fifth race was Rama. He founded this monastery. His life story is one of the most remarkable in spiritual history."

Zan sipped his tea. "Beneath the sands of the Gobi Desert lie the ruins of the original capital of the fifth race. It was called the Uighur Empire and its capital was Khara Khota. Rama received his spiritual training in the high valleys of these mountains. Part of his learning took place via Soul Travel to the secret spiritual city of Agam Des, much in the manner you are gathering spiritual instruction here tonight via Soul Travel.

Agam Des is the headquarters for the ECK Masters and the site of another Temple of Golden Wisdom.

"Agam Des is the headquarters for the ECK Masters and the site of another Temple of Golden Wisdom."

"Could you tell me something about the Uighur Empire?" I asked.

"That historic empire began as the largest and most important subempire of the Lemurian civilization. Lemuria, also known as the lost continent of Mu, once stretched across a large part of the Pacific Ocean. Known as the 'Empire of the Sun,' it was the greatest civilization of the ancient world. The people of Mu were highly civilized and enlightened.

"They sailed around the globe, establishing colonies and building great temples and gigantic carved monuments. Mu was destroyed by a series of earthquakes and cataclysms.

"The Uighur Empire—prize offspring of Lemuria— extended across most of Asia. It also had a chain of settlements across the central parts of Europe. When the empire was at its peak the Gobi Desert was a rich, fertile plain. The Uighurs had well-built cities, huge temples and public institutions, and palaces for the rulers. A highly spiritual group of people from Lemuria, called the Naacals, settled in the Uighur Empire. They brought with them a library of tablets upon which were inscribed the purest of the sacred writings of their motherland.

"In time the Uighur Empire suffered the same fate as Lemuria, being destroyed by a vast cataclysm and floods which buried its capital city, Khara Khota. Some of the Naacals survived in the west. Many years later they journeyed to the ruins of the ancient capital, dug the tablets out, and carried them to their temple to the west. The descendants of the these Naacals eventually settled in Tibet.

"So, was Rama part of that history?" I asked. "Ever since I first read of him, I've been fascinated by the story of his life, what little we know of it. Maybe some day I can meet him."

Zan smiled and said, "He should be arriving, just about now." The words were hardly out of his mouth when a robust man came striding into the room. Rama made quite an impression on me. He reminded me of the actor Charlton Heston in his role as Moses in the movie *The Ten Commandments.*

Rama had a thick, flowing beard, longish wavy hair combed back, and a large, husky frame. He wore boots to his knees, loose-fitting pants, a coarse shirt, and a wide belt.

Zan and Rama nodded to each other, then Rama introduced himself warmly with a crushing handshake. "We have met before," he said, "but I see you do not remember." These Masters never seemed to tire of telling me how poor my memory was. "He you call Zan has filled me in on your research project. He asked me to meet you here and give you a further clue to lead you to the lost treasure you seek."

"Thank you so much for coming, Rama! I've always wanted to meet you, so your gift of time is much appreciated. Zan has just been telling me about the Naacal

In time the Uighur Empire suffered the same fate as Lemuria, being destroyed by a vast cataclysm and floods which buried its capital city, Khara Khota.

tablets—how they were retrieved from the ruins of Khara Khota."

Rama sat down and leaned back, folding his hands behind his head. "That was long after my mission there. Let me give you a little background. My mission occurred in the last decades before the cataclysm wiped out most of the Uighur Empire.

"In my youth I was a seeker. I went in search of anyone who claimed knowledge of the spiritual mysteries. I also learned the art of Soul Travel—the ability to move out of my physical body and explore the inner worlds. My inner journeys led me to the great city of Agam Des, headquarters of the ECK Masters. They began to train me in the ways of the Ancient One, the Mahanta. I became aware I was being prepared for a mission to help renew the religious consciousness of the day.

"The time came for me to start my mission, which was daunting—I was charged with reestablishing the teachings of the ECK Masters throughout the empire and its colonies. It seemed to me that the obvious place to start would be in Khara Khota, the center and capital of the empire. You must realize that in those days the regions outside the main empire were just frontier settlements. Such were the lands of Europe, the Mediterranean, the Middle East, and India.

"I had envisioned a fairly simple plan: establish a center in the capital, train some reliable students, and let the teachings spread out from the center to the periphery.

"Full of confidence I made my way to Khara Khota and set to work. But I quickly ran into resistance from the established religious groups. At first this was just

> "I also learned the art of Soul Travel—the ability to move out of my physical body and explore the inner worlds."

criticism. But many of the people were tired of the old order and were hungry for truth. They began to drift away from the temples of the Uighur priests and come to my group.

"As the number of seekers coming to hear me grew, the threats from the priests grew proportionately. I was too naive at the time to understand this was the age-old obstacle of every ECK Master who comes forth. Our simple message of direct experience with the Light and Sound of God is too much for those with only rituals and faith to offer their followers.

"It wasn't long before the priests used their influence to drum up a list of charges and have me expelled from the city. With some of my trustworthy followers, I went back into the mountains to rethink how I was going to accomplish my mission.

"It was during this time that the inspiration for establishing the Katsupari Monastery came to me. The inner direction of Spirit began to show me I needed to establish a place that would be an anchor for the teachings. I was also being given prophecies that clearly showed the coming collapse of the Uighur Empire, and the political and social upheavals that would roll over Asia. So I had to locate a site that would be remote and secure. After some careful searching we finally found this spot.

"The inner direction of Spirit began to show me I needed to establish a place that would be an anchor for the teachings."

"Stone by stone and plank by plank, we had to haul materials great distances. The original building was very modest. Over the centuries it has been updated and expanded many times until it has become the castle-sized structure you see today.

"I had copies made of all the important sacred writings of the empire, including the Naacal tablets, and brought them here for safekeeping. Having established the monastery, I was ready to go back down from the mountains and start my travels to the frontiers.

"First I went to Europe and got as far as what is today Germany. Then I circled back and went down to Persia where I established a line of teachers who later evolved into the Magi. Then on to India where I planted the seeds for the religious traditions which would later evolve there. You see, the outlying regions were not controlled by the priestly organizations of Khara Khota and were much more open to the new ideas.

Rama paused and seemed to reflect on that distant past. "I could write volumes about the adventures of my wide travels. The greatest satisfaction was always the eager response of those seekers who were hungry for the Light and Sound of God."

This story enthralled me. I found myself trying to sketch the details of the sweeping drama. "I struggle to imagine how one man could do so much," I said. "Your story reminds me of Saint Paul who traveled far and wide, and endured so many hardships in his tireless efforts to establish Christianity."

Rama replied, "I assure you, anyone who dedicates their life to spreading the Word of God will have a life full of adventures."

Rama replied, "I assure you, anyone who dedicates their life to spreading the Word of God will have a life full of adventures."

Zan had been listening quietly. He finished the last sip of his tea and said, "To this day, a good student can trace the teachings of Rama throughout the world. Though the pure ECK teachings were largely lost, hardly a single major religion today is without some debt owned to those initial seeds that were planted."

"Now," said Rama as he stood up, "come with me. It is time to tie this discussion in with your own quest for understanding." Zan waved a hand to the two of us and said to me, "Go with Rama. We shall meet again in several days."

I followed Rama out of the dining area and down a hall which terminated in a large, high-domed room. He pointed to the ceiling. Looking up, I saw a large painting on the ceiling of the Bhavachakra, the Wheel of Life.

"Zan showed me a similar painting in some caves in India," I said.

"A few Tibetan students have been allowed to study here at Katsupari over the centuries," explained Rama. "From here they carried some of the teachings to other parts of Tibet and some down into India. But even this painting was inspired from a previous model. Come with me."

I followed Rama down another hallway. He stopped at a door and knocked. In a few moments it was opened by a rather tall, dark man with white hair and a pointed white beard. "Wait here," Rama said, disappearing into the room. I heard the two men talking in low voices for a few minutes; then the door opened again, and I was invited in.

When I got a closer look at the other man I saw he was the great ECK Master Fubbi Quantz, abbot of the Katsupari Monastery.

When I got a closer look at the other man I saw he was the great ECK Master Fubbi Quantz, abbot of the Katsupari Monastery. I had sat in the audience a number of times in the dream state, listening with rapt attention while he taught students from the Shariyat-Ki-Sugmad, the scriptures of the ECK Masters.

Fubbi Quantz looked at me with kind eyes and said, "I am giving you permission to go into the archives. Rama will show you the way. There is a lot of material down there. Trust your intuition to guide you to what you need."

I thanked the ECK Master sincerely and followed Rama into the hallway. We went down several flights of stairs and along a corridor cut in solid rock, before coming to a heavy, locked door. Rama had a key he'd apparently gotten from Fubbi Quantz. He unlocked the door and let me in. "I'll be back shortly," he said, as he closed the door and locked it from the outside.

My eyes swept the room which was softly lit from an unknown source. The room measured perhaps fifty by fifty feet, with passages leading to other rooms. There were several tables, apparently for laying out manuscripts. The archival records appeared to include books, scrolls, stone and clay tablets, metallic sheets, artifacts, and even some canvases.

It was a large collection. I understood why the abbot had advised me to follow my intuition. There was no reference librarian standing by. It would have taken a long time to find anything, assuming one knew what he was looking for. And I didn't even know what I was looking for!

Taking a deep breath, I closed my eyes a moment to see if I felt drawn in any particular direction. I felt a pull toward a doorway off to the left. I entered this smaller room.

Stone tablets were stacked against three walls. Against the fourth was a stone wheel, about three feet (one meter) in diameter. I knew immediately that this was what I was looking for.

I walked over and knelt to examine it closely. The now-familiar patterns of the Bhavachakra were engraved upon it. There were a number of concentric circles representing various cycles of time, each divided into twelve segments. Various glyphs and engravings

Stone tablets were stacked against three walls. Against the fourth was a stone wheel, about three feet (one meter) in diameter.

in an unknown language adorned the outer edges. I knew instinctively it was tens of thousands of years old, maybe more. When Rama said the ceiling painting upstairs was itself from a prior model, I was sure that this was it. Perhaps this stone artifact was the original prototype of the many wheels of life and zodiacs which can be found in the records of early civilizations.

My thoughts turned back to the beginning of this journey. The Golden-tongued Wisdom had said I had the key to "new wheels." But this was a very old wheel. Why had my quest led me here? There had to be a clue somewhere in this ancient artifact from the Uighur Empire. Or was it even older—maybe from Lemuria?

I carefully examined the wheel for clues, but nothing illuminating came of it. I felt like I was at the door of a great secret but couldn't see how to open it. My attention was interrupted by the return of Rama. "It's time to go now. You can come again later," he said.

Rama locked the door behind us. "Good. You found the wheel of the ancients," he said over his shoulder as we climbed the stairs. "And what did you discover about it?"

"Frankly, I don't know what I'm supposed to be looking for. Whatever it is, I didn't recognize it. Any idea what it might be?"

Rama laughed. "Oh, yes. But this is *your* quest. I believe you have the answer deep inside—buried in your unconscious! Watch your dreams closely for the next few nights and further light may come."

As we climbed the last few steps, I suddenly remembered that this whole episode at the Katsupari Monastery was a Soul Travel experience. Or was it all in my imagination? Or was it both? This puzzle caused me

I suddenly remembered that this whole episode at the Katsupari Monastery was a Soul Travel experience. Or was it all in my imagination? Or was it both?

to lose my focus. In a moment I was back on my bed, rubbing my eyes and stretching. I looked at the clock. About forty-five minutes had passed—much longer than I usually go with this kind of exercise.

I looked up to see a little spider crawling along the ceiling, indifferent to the Law of Gravity. I wondered what would happen if he stopped to think about whether walking upside down on a ceiling was really possible. I imagined he would lose his grip and fall to the floor.

In any case, I felt I was getting closer to the object of my search. The ancient artifact held an important clue. How could I find it?

The ancient artifact held an important clue. How could I find it?

6

The Rosetta Stone of God

The Mahanta, the Living ECK Master, is the em-
bodiment and expression of the SUGMAD [God], which
is the perfection and completion of the number 12.

—Paul Twitchell
The ECK-Vidya,
Ancient Science of Prophecy[1]

S everal days passed during which I ruminated on the meaning of the old stone wheel of life. One evening while thinking about it I toyed absent-mindedly with a small ECK pendant about the size of a dime.

On one side of it is ᗤ and on the other the word *HU.* These are two ancient spiritual words of significance to the world. HU is an ancient name for God which can be traced in many cultures the world over. ᗤ signifies the ECK, the Light and Sound of God.

Of the word *HU,* Harold Klemp, the current leader of Eckankar, writes, "Perhaps least known among the many names is HU, the universal name for God. The brotherhood of ECK Adepts has known of it for centuries. The spiritual hierarchy picked the present age to bring knowledge of it to the modern world."[2]

And of the EK symbol he writes, "The EK symbol is one that has appeared many places in centuries past,

HU is an ancient name for God which can be traced in many cultures the world over. ᗤ signifies the ECK, the Light and Sound of God.

from Greece to the Himalayas. Perhaps in the years to come more will be revealed about its role. The EK symbol is merely a symbol of Spirit, the Voice of God."[3]

I kept idly flipping the pendant, reading the word on each side: HU-EK, HU-EK, HU-EK. Something in this little ritual began to affect the working of my thoughts, prying open a new crack of insight. Suddenly I got the inspiration to grab a piece of paper and draw a circle. I wrote the twenty-six letters of the Latin alphabet around the periphery of the circle in clockwise order, equally spaced. Then I circled the letters H and U. They were exactly opposite each other, bisecting the circle.

I rotated the circle so H was on top and U on the bottom. Then I circled the letters E and K and noticed they were symmetrically placed on either side of the HU axis. (See illustration 1.) I then drew a rectangle with one side passing through each of the four letter points on the circle.

"What a delightful little discovery," I said. These two special words from ancient times formed a remarkable pattern of symmetry in the Latin alphabet—as if by design. What is more, the dimensions of the rectangle look very close to the classical golden section.

The golden section is venerated historically for its many special properties. I explored this in my book *The Dream Weaver Chronicles* where I show the spiritual significance of this "divine proportion" as it is often called. The ratio of the sides of the golden section are about 1 to 1.6. One interpretation of this ratio is that it expresses the relationship of the part to the whole, or the microcosm to the macrocosm. In this view it can signify the bridging connection between Soul and God.

I performed some quick trigonometry on the HU-

The ratio of the sides of the golden section are about 1 to 1.6. One interpretation of this ratio is that it expresses the relationship of the part to the whole, or the microcosm to the macrocosm.

EK rectangle and found its proportions to be about 1 to 1.5, which is quite close to the divine proportion. In fact, it's as close as is possible for a rectangle drawn within the constraints of the twenty-six-point circle of the Latin alphabet.

Though interesting as a quaint mystical tidbit, I asked myself what value it held in my quest for deeper insight on the ancient Wheel of Life. There seemed to be some relevant clues. First of all the alphabet circle was wheel-shaped. Second, it hinted at a divine and ancient connection through the words *HU* and *EK*. Maybe I was getting close to a breakthrough. It was time to turn once more to the trusty Spiritual Exercises of ECK for more light.

I retired to my favorite quiet spot in the house and settled into a state of relaxation in a comfortable chair. Then I slowly sang the words *HU-EK* for several minutes, all the while watching to see what might form on the inner screen of my mind.

Before long I saw the ancient Bhavachakra, or Wheel of Life, take shape before my inner eye.

Before long I saw the ancient Bhavachakra, or Wheel of Life, take shape before my inner eye. It seemed to float lightly in space despite its granite solidity. Then a second wheel, glowing and transparent, appeared just in front of the Wheel of Life. This one was the alphabet circle with the HU-EK and the golden section. Slowly the shining alphabet wheel merged with the old Wheel of Life making the ancient stone glow with a golden tint.

The four letters H-U-E-K began to shine brightly, and a humming sound emanated from the wheel. It was as if the HU-EK rectangle were a golden door holding back a great pressure of light and sound on the other side which might burst through at any moment.

The door began to glow until it was radiant. It slowly opened as brilliant golden beams of light shot out through the opening crack. At that moment I ceased to be an observer. I rose in the Soul body and moved forward toward the opening door. I felt the intensity of the Light and Sound pouring through. Taking a deep breath I girded myself, closed my eyes, and made a rush for the opening, passing through the portal into a higher dimension.

On the other side I opened my eyes to find Zan standing before me smiling. Behind him was nothing but a void of Light and Sound. "Where am I?" I asked him.

He said "You've arrived at your sought-after destination. But you are looking in the wrong direction. Turn around!"

I turned around to behold a breathtaking sight. Zan continued, "The little pendant held the secret—HU on one side and EK on the other. The Wheel of Life has two sides to it also, but you never thought to look on the second side."

Before me shone the other side of the Wheel of Life, an iridescent wheel of the most intricate and beautiful design made out of pure Light and Sound. It reminded me of a huge rose or lotus, and I counted twelve petals. Upon each petal was a holographic image and text. I knew instinctively that this was an inner and higher correspondence to the outer Wheel of Life.

"You have found the Rosetta stone of God," Zan said simply. "This living wheel contains the hidden code needed by Soul to find Its way back home to God!"

I stared in wonder as ripples of rainbow light danced upon the wheel's surface. It was the most beautiful work of art I'd ever seen. Yet it was more than artwork.

I rose in the Soul body and moved forward toward the opening door. I felt the intensity of the Light and Sound pouring through.

It was a living expression of Divine Spirit. I stood silently, savoring the epiphany of the moment.

"This other side of the wheel might well be called the Wheel of the Mahanta," Zan explained. "It is to the Wheel of Life what Soul is to the body. This inner wheel has always been there, hiding behind the outer Wheel of Life for those who sought to discover it."

"When the lower worlds were created for the education of Soul, God organized the lessons to be learned into an orderly sequence. Though each individual spark of God would follow Its own path through life, it was necessary that all go through certain common experiences to get them started.

When the lower worlds were created for the education of Soul, God organized the lessons to be learned into an orderly sequence.

"Collectively these primary lessons of life are called primal karma, which means the first or primary causes in the school of life. Many life experiences are similar to elective courses in a college or university—Soul can pick and choose what is of interest. But primal karma consists of the required curriculum established by the Lords of Karma to get all Souls who pass through the lower worlds started.

"The driving force of the Wheel of Life is the great Law of Cause and Effect which governs the processes of movement and growth. This law is an aspect of the Law of Economy, which governs all the lower creation and assures that the lower worlds run with efficiency in the administration of God's plan.

"The Wheel of Life in full detail is a concise expression of the Law of Economy, of primal karma and the cycles of cause and effect which govern Soul's long journey through space and time.

"Once Soul is nearing the completion of Its lessons on this Wheel of Life under the Law of Economy, It begins to resonate to the higher influences of the Wheel of the Mahanta. This wheel expresses the Law of Love.

"To balance the twelve labors, or major experiences of Soul on the Wheel of Life, God created twelve gifts of love which Soul could draw upon for spiritual liberation. These gifts of God are embodied in the Mahanta, the Living ECK Master. You see? Thus the higher wheel is an expression of the divine Law of Love. The lower wheel is an expression of the Law of Economy, manifesting in the twelve signs of the ECK-Vidya and the zodiac.

"In the subtle body of man are the various energy centers, or chakras. The center near the heart, called the heart center, is a flower-shaped form of twelve petals. When the twelve petals of the heart center in man are fully opened to the twelve gifts of God which flow through the Mahanta, the seeker acquires a golden heart. A golden thread, or cord of Light and Sound, then links the heart of man with the heart of God, through the heart of the Mahanta."

I asked, "What then draws Soul to the Mahanta? If these gifts are readily available, why don't more people discover them?"

"It's a matter of spiritual maturity," Zan explained. "The inexperienced Soul will seek out teachers and guides who demonstrate one or a few of the gifts. And even then, such teachers usually only possess the gifts to a small degree.

"But this is no fault of the teachers, for they too are learning as they go along. In the early stages Soul is simply not aware of all the gifts, because It has not yet discovered the need. But I tell you this, God's efforts are not superfluous. Each of the twelve aspects of the Mahanta are essential to Soul's ultimate liberation."

God created twelve gifts of love which Soul could draw upon for spiritual liberation. These gifts of God are embodied in the Mahanta, the Living ECK Master.

Zan pointed to the wheel. "Tell me what you see," he said.

I looked closely at the holographic image on the first division of the wheel. "I see a man standing on a path which leads up into some hills. He seems to be gesturing toward the path, inviting someone to come with him. He is holding a staff."

"And what does this image evoke in you?" asked Zan.

"It gives me the impression of someone who is showing the way, inviting me to follow him on the path up into the hills. Spiritually, this must be the Mahanta in his role as a spiritual guide."

Zan said, "And that's actually a fairly good modern description. The glyph of light under that picture signifies the Wayshower. This is the first stage in Soul's movement toward spiritual freedom. Each of these aspects of the Mahanta has applications on many levels. The Wayshower, for example, seems simple on the surface. He is everyone's idea of a spiritual guide. But as Soul progresses on the path up into the hills, which signifies the journey upward into the heavenly worlds, the meaning and beauty of who the Wayshower is changes.

The glyph of light under that picture signifies the Wayshower. This is the first stage in Soul's movement toward spiritual freedom.

"Its highest meaning is completely beyond anything the human mind can understand. This is the face of the Wayshower who escorts Soul into the secret place of the Most High. None but those taking the initiations of ECK Mastership can understand the Wayshower's mission in those high heavens.

"And so it is with all twelve gifts of God. They actually constitute a great unity, extending from the highest heavens to the lowest planes of creation. But the cosmic vision of the totality of the Mahanta is simply too much for Soul to grasp until the final stages. So I caution you not to accept the first facile concept that comes to mind as you study these gifts of God expressed on the Wheel of the Mahanta.

"Whatever your understanding of them now, it will become broader and deeper as you progress. Take each one into contemplation. Look at it from as many levels as you are capable of at this time.

The radiant wave of God's love pours forth into the universes from the immortal fountain of the Ocean of Love and Mercy on the twelfth plane.

"The radiant wave of God's love pours forth into the universes from the immortal fountain of the Ocean of Love and Mercy on the twelfth plane. The Mahanta, the Living ECK Master is the embodiment of God's love. According to the sacred numbers of the ECK-Vidya, he is the perfection and completion of the number twelve. He brings to the world a new cycle of manifested truth. The sacred word HU, which represents the Sugmad, expresses all that can be said about this great cycle of twelve.

"This is how the HU-EK combination unlocked for you the secret golden door into this sacred place where we now stand. It is no coincidence that the Latin alphabet evolved in a way that this combination was encoded into the order of the letters. The letters, words, and alphabets of the physical world express the divine Word. Their evolution is given careful attention by those who watch over the unfoldment of the human race.

"Let's finish for now by getting an overview of this Rosetta stone of God. I will give you a modern translation for each of the texts that accompany the engravings."

The second image was of a man with a staff, standing next to a person sleeping under a crescent moon. Zan said, "The man with the staff appears in most of the pictures. This is always the Mahanta. The staff indicates his spiritual authority. I will explain more about this later. This text translates to dream teacher or Dream Master."

The third division showed a man standing at the ready with a silver shield. "This is the Mahanta in his role as the Guardian," said Zan.

The fourth sector showed a man with his usual staff in one hand and a scroll in the other. Zan said, "This is the Vi-Guru, the high teacher of spiritual wisdom."

In the fifth picture the staff was replaced by a torch which was held high. "This signifies the Light Giver," Zan explained.

The sixth showed a tree bent low by a strong wind. "Literally, the text calls this the Purifier, or the Wind from Heaven. Perhaps a good phrase would be the Wind of Change."

Seventh came a picture of the Mahanta figure with his hand raised in a blessing. Zan pondered a few moments. "The Healer," he said.

The eighth image showed the Mahanta setting a bird free from its cage. "The Redeemer," said Zan.

Image nine was the Mahanta figure standing atop a mountain. "This shows the Mahanta as the Godman," Zan continued.

The tenth hologram had the figure with a hawk upon his shoulder. "The hawk represents the high and keen vision of the Mahanta as Prophet," Zan explained.

The eleventh showed two figures. One man was handing his staff to another. "This one symbolizes the Ancient One," said Zan. "The meaning of the glyph will become clear when we discuss this aspect."

The last hologram was simply a brilliant six-pointed

The third division showed a man standing at the ready with a silver shield. "This is the Mahanta in his role as the Guardian," said Zan.

star. Zan said, "This is the Living Word. There is more to say about this wondrous gift of God, as well as the eleven other aspects of the Mahanta. Starting with the first one, we will take each in turn. But for now, you have much to ponder on."

Zan's form turned into light before fading from the screen of my mind. A moment later the Rosetta stone of God also faded, ending my contemplation.

Zan had laid out my task for me. It was time to explore each of these twelve gifts of God that are embodied in the Mahanta, the Living ECK Master— to see what treasures they held in store for the sincere seeker.

It was time to explore each of these twelve gifts of God that are embodied in the Mahanta, the Living ECK Master—to see what treasures they held in store for the sincere seeker.

Part Two

The Ascent of
the Mountain

7

The Wayshower

I always come back to the definition of the Mahanta, the Living ECK Master as a Wayshower. He is not a way-pusher or a way-dragger who kicks and shoves you through the inner worlds. The Wayshower is, quite simply, someone who shows the way.
He can show each of you your own way home to God.

—Harold Klemp
The Dream Master[1]

I thought for several days about the best way to pursue my study of the Rosetta stone of God. My plan was to invite Zan to offer his perspective on each aspect of the Mahanta. Then I would do further research, plus draw on my own experiences. Finally, I would formulate everything on each aspect into a chapter.

One evening I felt ready to try this plan. I closed my eyes and began singing HU-EK to attune myself spiritually as I put my attention on the Wheel of the Mahanta. While doing this I invited Zan into my inner sanctum. After a few minutes he appeared on the screen of my mind.

"It's time to begin a close study of the Wayshower," he said directly. "As said before, the subject of the

I closed my eyes and began singing HU-EK to attune myself spiritually as I put my attention on the Wheel of the Mahanta.

Mahanta is too broad for the mind to grasp as a whole. From the highest view there are no divisions. This is ever true of the God viewpoint. But how many people dwelling on earth can see from the mountaintop?

"So the ECK Masters, in ancient times, organized the teachings to be assimilated in stages, much as a pupil in your school system goes through a sequence of lessons until he has mastered the whole curriculum.

"In Its journey of many lives, Soul will meet the Mahanta in one of his aspects. Later It will discover another aspect, then another. Eventually Soul begins to recognize the same divine being behind each aspect It has come to know.

"Therefore let's study the twelve aspects of the Mahanta by going around the wheel and pausing to elaborate on each, one by one. When the time is right, every person discovers the Mahanta in his own way. There is no set approach.

"The first tentative steps toward God occur when Soul stops Its mad rushing about in the world and asks Itself, 'Where am I going?' It senses the need for direction and instinctively begins to seek a guide. At first It comes upon lesser guides to show the beginning steps."

"The path to God is indeed well-beaten close to the departure point. There are guides aplenty lined up for hire. Think of an early American settler who wanted to leave the civilized eastern seaboard for the frontier.

"If his goal was only to get as far as the Appalachian Mountains, almost any guide would do.

"Were his aim to reach the great Rocky Mountains, he would have to search out a more experienced guide. There would be fewer available with the qualifications.

In Its journey of many lives, Soul will meet the Mahanta in one of his aspects.

"And for the hardy pioneer who sought to journey beyond the Rockies, all the way west, there were very few guides. It is fitting that a spiritual guide is assigned to each person according to individual needs. And when the greater guides have taken him or her as far as they can, they turn the person over to the Mahanta.

"The spiritual journey leads far beyond places that have ground to walk upon; beyond places where Soul needs a body that has legs to walk with," Zan smiled. "When Soul begins to yearn for such climes and has passed the tests, It will be led to the Mahanta forthwith."

I thought back to that day when I kneeled upon the floor of my apartment, pleading to God for a guide who could show me the way home to God. The answer to my prayers had been so swift I counted it a miracle.

Zan continued, "I mentioned before that each of the aspects of the Mahanta has application on many levels and in many contexts. The Mahanta as Wayshower is a vital figure in every stage of the spiritual journey. From something as down to earth as direction for a new job, to the most subtle lessons on the threshold of God-Realization, the Wayshower is ever at work in the seeker's life. He continuously shows the alert Soul the best direction to take."

After a few moments of silence, Zan concluded his comments. "Take some time now to look back over your life and see where the Wayshower has been at work, guiding you with sure direction along the trail."

From something as down to earth as direction for a new job, to the most subtle lessons on the threshold of God-Realization, the Wayshower is ever at work in the seeker's life.

PRACTICAL GUIDANCE

Zan faded from my inner screen. Opening my eyes, I picked up my journal and began writing down what

I had learned in contemplation. Looking out the window I saw a moving van had parked in front of a house across the street. It brought back a memory from years ago when the Wayshower had helped me find a new direction during a major turning point in my life.

The year was 1989. I had just finished two years of college, retraining for a new profession. After sending out resumés to five or six companies and doing a number of interviews, I received several offers.

My wife and I discussed the possibilities. Each offer was quite good. We weighed the pros and cons of each, but it was difficult to decide which one to accept. One night before going to bed I asked the Mahanta if he could give me some guidance.

That night I had the following dream.

I was driving along a major interstate highway in Oregon, and it was getting late. I found a motel and checked in for the night. Just as I got settled, someone knocked at the door. I opened it to find Harold Klemp, the Mahanta, the Living ECK Master.

"Harold, come in! So good to see you." The Master entered the room and took a seat on the edge of the bed. After chatting a few minutes he asked, "Do you have a map?"

I dug through my suitcase, found a map, and handed it to Harold. He spread it out on the bed and took a felt-tipped marker out of his coat pocket. "We're here," he said, circling our current location on the map. "Let's trace a good route for you to follow tomorrow when you get back on the road."

He moved the marker over the map, tracing a bright yellow path all the way to Portland. "That should do it," he said as he popped the cover onto the marker and put

Each offer was quite good. We weighed the pros and cons of each, but it was difficult to decide which one to accept. One night before going to bed I asked the Mahanta if he could give me some guidance.

it back in his pocket. "I need to go now. Good traveling—
and let me know how things work out."

I thanked him as he stepped out the door into the
night. A moment later I awoke from the dream.

As I lay in bed pondering on the dream, I thought
about the one offer I had from a company in Portland.
It paid somewhat less than the others, which would
mean a few lean years for the family. But it was a solid
company with good opportunities for growth and ad-
vancement. The Wayshower was clearly showing the
best route to the next step in my life. I accepted the job
in Portland. Over the ensuing years it proved to be a
very good one.

The Wayshower goes the extra mile for those he is guiding, if one pays close attention to the guidance.

But the help didn't stop there. The Wayshower goes
the extra mile for those he is guiding, if one pays close
attention to the guidance. I had made a commitment
to start the new job in two weeks. This gave us just one
weekend to travel to Portland and find a house to rent.

The first shock came when we opened the newspaper to the rental ads. Most of the houses were beyond
our means. The rest of them were too far from where
I would be working. We finally found two rentals available in our price range and location.

We knew the housing market was tight, so we got
up early Saturday to beat the crowds. Unfortunately
so did everyone else. The first house had been rented
before we even got there. We headed immediately for
the second one, our hopes fading. We arrived to find a
dozen cars parked along the street. A long line of eager,
would-be renters stood at the door. I said to my wife,
"We're here. We may as well get in line."

After a few minutes we got inside. An elderly gentle-
man introduced himself as the landlord. He invited us

to look around with the rest of the crowd. We took a quick look at the house and felt it would be suitable. In any case we were in no position to be picky. But how could we hope to be the chosen ones? We talked some more to the landlord. I saw him knit his brow when we told him we were from out of town. He wanted to gather all of the applications and have the selected renter meet him later that weekend.

Suddenly I got an inner nudge from the Wayshower to talk about gardening. "You have a nice yard here," I said.

Suddenly I got an inner nudge from the Wayshower to talk about gardening. "You have a nice yard here," I said. "My wife and I like to garden. If we rent this place would you mind if we got creative and added some more garden space?"

The landlord's eyes lit up. "Sure, that would be fine." We handed him our application and set out for the three-hour drive home. Shortly after arriving there, the landlord phoned us. The house was ours.

"I'm not sure why," he said. "You just seemed like good, trustworthy renters. And when you said you like to garden, that confirmed my feelings. It showed me you would take good care of the property."

This story illustrates two kinds of inner guidance— one from the dream state and the other from an inner nudge to say something. We live in two worlds: the inner and the outer. Therefore we benefit from both inner and outer guidance.

INNER AND OUTER GUIDE

There are many teachers who can guide us in the outer world through their talks, writings, and training. And there are some who can guide from the "other side." More rare are teachers who have the capacity to do both. Among these precious few, how many can work with all their followers at the same time through the inner presence, as the Mahanta does? There is a special inner communication between the Mahanta and all who look to him.

In Eckankar these two sides of the Master are called the Outer Master and the Inner Master. By the time we have found the Outer Master, we have already met the Inner Master. This often happens in a dream, as it did with me. Usually the encounter is not remembered in our waking consciousness.

By the time we have found the Outer Master, we have already met the Inner Master.

Once the connection with the Inner Master is made, we begin to find our way to the Outer Master. We seem to follow a trail of sparkling diamonds strewn along a path through the forest, until we find our way to the Outer Master who is waiting to greet us. At that point the two sides blend together and are seen to be aspects of one guide. Thus the full title of the spiritual leader of Eckankar is the Mahanta, the Living ECK Master. The Mahanta is the inner side and the Living ECK Master is the outer side. The Mahanta's role as a Wayshower applies to both the Inner and Outer.

THE WAYSHOWER'S APPROACH

The approach of the Wayshower is always respectful. The Inner Master will extend an invitation. It is never forced. The inner bond can only occur through mutual agreement. It requires the seeker to say yes to the invitation. If accepted, the guidance begins and a close one-to-one relationship is established.

It should be mentioned that this is no rash or impulsive decision based on emotion. This is not a conversion, but a transformation. It is the love of God stirring in Soul to find Itself, to set Its feet on the path

to spiritual liberation. It is placing our spiritual interests into the hands of the Mahanta with trust. The
scriptures of Eckankar describe it like this:

> It is merely that he puts his trust in the knowl-
> edge that the Master will take care of his spiritual
> guidance. He accepts the aid and guidance of the
> Living ECK Master over a path which is unknown
> to himself. The Master is the guide, for the chela
> starts out in a wilderness and must be carried out
> into the calm of the spiritual worlds.[2]

*Even though
many people
don't recall the
initial meeting
with the
Mahanta in the
dream state,
when they do, it
can be a moving
story.*

Even though many people don't recall the initial
meeting with the Mahanta in the dream state, when
they do, it can be a moving story.

A man who describes himself as a simple farmer
from North Carolina had a dream one night. In it a
slender man (the Living ECK Master) whom the farmer
didn't recognize told him to dial a certain long-distance
phone number.

When he awoke, he had the urge to dial the number
right away and did so. It turned out to be an information phone for Eckankar. But the farmer hadn't left his
number and couldn't be called back.

The next night he had a similar dream, only this
time the slender man from the first dream was accompanied by a second man who had dark, wavy hair and
appeared to be of Mongolian descent (the Tibetan ECK
Master Rebazar Tarzs). A few days later the farmer
called the number again, and this time someone answered.

The farmer explained how he had been having these
dreams and also out-of-body experiences. He thought
he was losing his mind. The ECKist was able to soothe

his concerns and explain to him that this was a very normal thing and quite a joyful experience once one got used to it.[3]

Soon the farmer was moving ahead on his spiritual journey. He had met the Wayshower on the inner planes in the dream state and then made the direct outer connection. The initial fearful reaction of the farmer illustrates why the Mahanta will often let the dreamer forget dreams. The human consciousness is easily upset by the new and the unfamiliar.

THE INNER JOURNEY

Once the seeker has made conscious contact with the Wayshower, he is ready to begin the spiritual journey in earnest. The Wayshower adapts his methods of guidance to suit the realm in which they are applied. Inner guidance requires different means than outer guidance.

The guidance given by the Inner Master may be perceived as nudges, feelings, or intuition. It can come through the dream state, Soul Travel, or any number of ways. It is rarely, if ever, a booming voice from heaven telling you to do something.

Each person has some way he can receive the guidance. It isn't necessary to be psychic or gifted with unusual abilities. Mainly it requires a loving heart and a willingness to trust ourselves with the gifts of the Holy Spirit.

The Wayshower has walked the path before us. He knows every inch of the way to God. He will give advice, especially when asked. But he encourages us to prove the path for ourselves—to accept any advice with common sense and thoughtful evaluation.

The guidance given by the Inner Master may be perceived as nudges, feelings, or intuition.

You will hear many conflicting reports about the heavenly worlds. It's as if two alien visitors came to earth for a brief visit. One spends his day in the heart of New York City, and the other on a remote tropical island. They would return with wildly conflicting reports about the nature of our planet.

The higher planes are even more diverse. It takes a seasoned traveler to sort out the misconceptions people form after a glimpse or two of some inner world.

A good guide will make a map of the territory he has explored so it will be easier for those who come later. Paul Twitchell left such a map of the spiritual worlds through which the Mahanta guides Soul on Its way home to God in his book *The Tiger's Fang*. It recounts a journey he took through the God Worlds with his Master, Rebazar Tarzs.

Paul's travels took him further and deeper into the unknown as well as going over familiar ground many times. One of the things he discovered in his research was how easy it is to overestimate the heights one has attained. This is partly due to the subdivisions and regions that exist within each major heaven. It can seem to an inexperienced traveler that he has scaled the mountain of God, when he is really still on the lower slopes.

A second factor that leads to overestimation is the sheer brilliance and grandeur of each level of heaven relative to the one below it. The pure regions of just the first heaven can create awe in Soul, as can be seen by reading the many ecstatic reports of people who have touched this plane during a near-death experience.

They simply haven't the training and experience to grasp how such awesome experiences are only the beginning steps.

Paul Twitchell left such a map of the spiritual worlds through which the Mahanta guides Soul on Its way home to God in his book The Tiger's Fang.

Yet there are keys to help people determine where they were on their spiritual journey. The Light and Sound of God are the twin aspects of Divine Spirit which flow through all levels of heaven, from the highest to the lowest. There are certain key sounds which are the predominant sounds of Spirit on each level of heaven. Were Soul to be traveling through a particular heaven, or be attuned to it, Soul would likely hear the key sound of that plane or heaven.

The light on each plane is not quite so easy to distinguish. The first three or four heavens have a certain hue which is like an overtone that may color everything in that region. But beyond a certain point the Light of God becomes so pure there is no predominant color tone.

Of course we can no more get a true sense of what the heavenly worlds are like by looking at a written description of them than we can get a sense of the continent of North America by tracing the line of a highway on a map of the United States. But we can use the map to plan our trip and let our imagination spur our interest in whatever adventures await us.

And after we have driven across America we can later get out the map and use it as a reference when talking with our friends about our journey. We can point to the Grand Canyon or Yellowstone National Park and use the map as a communication tool for organizing our experiences. In the same way Souls must first travel across the heavenly regions under the guidance of the Wayshower before the map becomes real to them. With these limitations in mind, Eckankar's map of the heavenly journey home to God[4] is shown on page 80. I think of this as the Wayshower's map.

The Light and Sound of God are the twin aspects of Divine Spirit which flow through all levels of heaven, from the highest to the lowest.

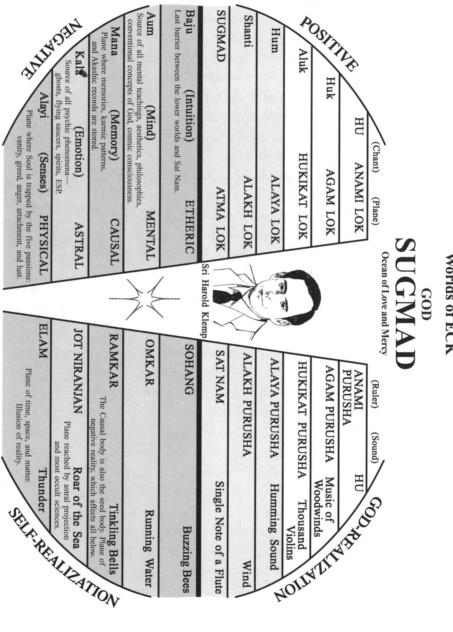

Worlds of ECK

GOD
SUGMAD
Ocean of Love and Mercy

POSITIVE

NEGATIVE

SELF-REALIZATION

GOD-REALIZATION

(Chant)	(Plane)	(Ruler)	(Sound)
HU	ANAMI LOK	ANAMI PURUSHA	HU
Huk	AGAM LOK	AGAM PURUSHA	Music of Woodwinds
Aluk	HUKIKAT LOK	HUKIKAT PURUSHA	Thousand Violins
Hum	ALAYA LOK	ALAYA PURUSHA	Humming Sound
Shanti	ALAKH LOK	ALAKH PURUSHA	Wind
SUGMAD	ATMA LOK	SAT NAM	Single Note of a Flute
Baju	ETHERIC	SOHANG	Buzzing Bees
Aum	MENTAL	OMKAR	Running Water
Mana	CAUSAL	RAMKAR	Tinkling Bells
Kala	ASTRAL	JOT NIRANJAN	Roar of the Sea
Alayi	PHYSICAL	ELAM	Thunder

SUGMAD
Last barrier between the lower worlds and Sat Nam.

Baju (Intuition)

Aum (Mind)
Source of all mental teachings, aesthetics, philosophies, conventional concepts of God, cosmic consciousness.

Mana (Memory)
Plane where memories, karmic patterns, and Akashic records are stored.

Kala (Emotion)
Source of all psychic phenomena— ghosts, flying saucers, spirits, ESP.

Alayi (Senses)
Plane where Soul is trapped by the five passions: vanity, greed, anger, attachment, and lust.

ANAMI PURUSHA

AGAM PURUSHA

HUKIKAT PURUSHA

ALAYA PURUSHA

ALAKH PURUSHA

SAT NAM

SOHANG

OMKAR

RAMKAR
The Causal body is also the seed body; Plane of negative reality, which affects all below.

JOT NIRANJAN
Plane reached by astral projection and most occult sciences.

ELAM
Plane of time, space, and matter. Illusion of reality.

Sri Harold Klemp

Scattered through the writings of Eckankar are many different stories of people's experiences in the heavenly worlds. These can be inspiring and suggest starting points for your own journeys.

The goal is to meet the Wayshower yourself. He will introduce you to the heavenly worlds in a way which is natural for you. He will lead you into a wonderland of love which suits your unique needs as Soul.

Perhaps you will become one of those lucky few who quickly master the art of Soul Travel and have grand adventures aplenty. More likely you will discover something less sensational but just as valuable. Perhaps it will be the gift of a loving heart, the recognition of the constant presence of the Mahanta in your life, or a new talent for learning through your dreams. The path of Eckankar is quite flexible at the individual level so each seeker can find their niche.

The path of Eckankar is quite flexible at the individual level so each seeker can find their niche.

HOW THE INNER GUIDE APPEARS

The Inner Master will usually appear in the form of the Living ECK Master of the times. Often he is surrounded by a radiant light and conveys feelings of deep spiritual love and blessings. A seeker may witness this appearance in dreams, during contemplation, or just by focusing attention upon the inner screen of the mind. Sometimes the appearance is accompanied by melodious sounds, music, or even a fragrance.

There comes a certain stage in the journey when we formally accept the Mahanta as our guide. When we do, the radiant form of the Inner Master becomes established within our inner vision and is always with us. From that point on, the Mahanta's blessings, guidance, and protection rest gently over us like a cloak of divine love.

The Master gently reminds the seeker, "I am always with you, but are you aware of my presence?"

It takes time for the seeker to realize the Mahanta is always with him. The Inner Master does not need to come to the seeker, for he is already there. The Master gently reminds the seeker, "I am always with you, but are you aware of my presence?"

Not everyone will be able to see the Inner Master with them. And those who can may only see him on occasion. Even so he is ever as close as our heartbeat and his love surrounds us. How can this be? How can the Inner Master be with each and every one of his followers at all times? This is the perennial question that perplexes the mind, because the mind stumbles over concepts of space and time which have little relevance in the realms of Divine Spirit.

The Holy Spirit is like a mighty ocean of Light and Sound which fills all the universes, and the worlds of creation are but tiny bubbles floating through its waves.

The Mahanta, in his high consciousness, shares these great attributes of Spirit. As all bubbles float within the embrace of the vast sea, each person who looks to the Mahanta lives and moves and has his being within the spiritual body of the Mahanta. I will explore this aspect of the Mahanta in more depth in a later chapter. But it is helpful to touch upon it here, for it gives the key to understanding.

THE BLUE LIGHT OF THE WAYSHOWER

Another way the Inner Master often appears to people is in the form of a blue star or bluish-white globe of light. The Light of God appears on all planes, but the Blue Star should interest the seeker the most. It represents the presence of the Mahanta and will lead the seeker gently onward through the various levels of heaven into planes of pure Spirit.

The star is greeted by many with rejoicing, for they are glad to have been chosen to witness it. This Blue Star of the Mahanta is vital to the seeker. It is the Wayshower in action. Like the star in ancient times which led the wise men to the birthplace of Jesus in Bethlehem, the Blue Star will lead the wise seeker to the birthplace of his own divine nature.

This Blue Star of the Mahanta is vital to the seeker. It is the Wayshower in action.

The nine-year-old daughter of an ECKist was explaining to a friend of hers, who was from a Christian family, how she did her spiritual exercises. "I'll just show you how to do it," she said to her friend. They sat down together, closed their eyes, and sang HU to start their contemplation.

After about twenty minutes, the young ECKist decided she'd better open her eyes and see what was going on. Finally her Christian friend opened her eyes too.

"What took you so long? What did you see?" asked the ECKist.

Her friend said, "It was really something! When I shut my eyes and sang HU, I saw all these stars. The whole sky was full of stars, and as I watched, they all came together and formed into one huge blue star."[5]

This is an example of how the Wayshower appears inwardly. But the Blue Light of the Mahanta can appear to the outer eyes as well. A friend of mine learned how practical the Blue Star can be in times of trouble.

She went skiing one afternoon and became so absorbed enjoying the experience that she forgot about the time. When dusk arrived she found herself off the familiar trails. It was getting too dark to see clearly. How could she find her way back?

"Mahanta, can you help?" she asked inwardly as she began singing HU.

A shining blue globe of light began to appear before her in the darkness. Moving ahead of her down the mountain, it seemed to beckon. My friend started to follow. As she did the blue globe led the way, painting the snow with a trail of beautiful light.

"All I had to do was ski along this lighted trail," my friend explained. "It was one of the most beautiful sights I've ever seen." In a few minutes she was safely back at the ski lodge.

The Light of God contains, of course, the full spectrum of colors. Blue is emphasized here as it denotes the presence, love, and guidance of the Mahanta. People from other religions may see the Blue Light too, but usually without understanding that it is here to bring them comfort, healing, or guidance.

THE SECRETS OF THE BLUE STAR

When drawn, the Blue Star of the Mahanta has six points. There is a deep significance to this.

When drawn, the Blue Star of the Mahanta has six points. There is a deep significance to this. A six-pointed star made up of two triangles—like the Star of David or the Blue Star of the Mahanta—reflects the creative balance of the spiritual and physical worlds. Harold Klemp says, "It indicates the balance between working in the spiritual worlds and the physical world at the same time. The individual who sees the six-pointed Blue Star of the Mahanta is able to draw on the inner experiences for use in his outer world, and vice versa."[6]

This interplay between the inner and outer worlds, through the matrix of the Blue Star, is a key to our unfoldment as Soul.

Related to this subject is the Rule of Threes. For

example the alert seeker will notice that guidance often comes in threes. This is especially true if it's an important spiritual insight you are being given.

In my experience I've noticed that such guidance may be given in three different ways or in a setting where three key elements are present. By studying each of the three elements as part of an upward or downward pointing triangle, I've often gained a fuller insight into the guidance being given.

I've noticed that such guidance may be given in three different ways or in a setting where three key elements are present.

Allow me to illustrate this principle. One summer weekend I joined my friend Mike to go on a brief vision quest. We hoped to find gifts of spiritual insight by climbing a mountain together. Mike and I are both writers, and writing was much on our minds as we hiked the steep trail toward our destination. The idea for a new book (this book in fact) was on my mind, and I hoped to receive some guidance from the Wayshower about whether I should proceed with it.

After an exhausting climb we reached a peak with a sweeping view in all directions. I turned to Mike and said half in jest, "This is nearly perfect except for one thing—there should be one more person here to make a threesome. Then we would have the Rule of Threes working for us."

While Mike sat down to catch his breath, I walked around the edge of a boulder only to discover a young man sitting there alone. I introduced myself as Mike came over and joined us.

"Hi," the young man said. "My name is Harold." Mike and I exchanged knowing glances, for Harold is the first name of the current Mahanta, the Living ECK Master—Harold Klemp. I saw this as the Wayshower's way of saying, "I'm here with you."

The young man was the third point in the triangle of writers. This became clear as we talked. He explained he was a teacher and was visiting the area to give a writing seminar. As the three of us talked, Harold said some things which, in the context of the situation, were answers to the questions we had brought to the mountaintop that day.

So far we have discussed two ways the Mahanta will appear inwardly: in the form of the Living ECK Master of the times or as a blue light or star. In either case the Wayshower has appeared at the door and is ready to show Soul the way home to God.

THE ASCENT OF SOUL

What is this inner journey for which the Wayshower is to be our guide? And where do we begin?

What is this inner journey for which the Wayshower is to be our guide? And where do we begin? The journey is the gradual ascent of Soul through the many levels of heaven. The beginning point is the doorway of the physical body known as the Third Eye, the inner screen of the mind where the Mahanta awaits our departure. There are hundreds of tested spiritual exercises we can practice to embark upon the journey. A simple and effective one for beginners will be given at the end of this chapter.

One real value of having the Mahanta as a guide relates to the nature of the higher planes. The scriptures of Eckankar make note of this when speaking of Soul's journey:

> The first thing which is noticed here is that all time and space dimensions are different from where It resided in the physical world. The laws are different and the beings and entities all abide by rules unknown upon earth and its respective planes. Soul must again become used to these new

laws, and as It passes through each plane, similar to the time zones and nations of the physical world, It finds different ideas along with new laws and ways of life. Each time It enters into another spiritual world, It finds that the laws are vastly different from those of the area which It has just passed through. It takes adjusting to keep up with the travel from one plane to another.[7]

The nature and laws of all these planes are well known to the Mahanta. Like an experienced scout, he knows the best routes, where dangers lie, and where the safest shortcuts are. He has all the right contacts and connections and has secured all the necessary authorizations to smooth the path of those who have put their trust in him.

The heavenly worlds are vast. They can bewilder the novice traveler. It is easy to be misled by illusions of all sorts, some of our own creation.

One of the greatest of these illusions is the belief that we have reached the pinnacle of our journey, when in fact we are only partway up the mountain. The many levels of heaven are impressive places, filled with awesome sights and grand experiences. It is easy to be swept up in them, and mistake a modest attainment for the higher goal.

The many levels of heaven are impressive places, filled with awesome sights and grand experiences. It is easy to be swept up in them, and mistake a modest attainment for the higher goal.

Many books are written and religious groups founded because someone had an experience on one of the lower levels of heaven, mistaking it for the true realms of God. Outwardly this illusion manifests as a feeling that there is no more to learn or that further attainment is not possible.

There are several major mileposts which the Mahanta encourages us to reach. One is Self-Realization, which is attained on the Fifth Plane. This is the heaven where Soul first tastes the nectar of true spiritual freedom, where It realizes who It is apart from the mind and personality. Below this level Soul is subject to the Law of Cause and Effect and reincarnation.

Another major milepost is when Soul enters into the ninth heaven—the threshold of God-Realization. Soul needs the best guide to reach such heights. It relies upon the Mahanta to take It into the very heart of God.

HELP ON INNER OBSTACLES

The ways in which the Mahanta guides one through the inner planes are as varied as the individual Souls and their stages of spiritual unfoldment.

The ways in which the Mahanta guides one through the inner planes are as varied as the individual Souls and their stages of spiritual unfoldment. Several years ago I felt I had come to a halt in my progress. My spiritual exercises seemed barren. Obstacles would appear in my outer life whenever I attempted to move in a new direction. My dreams presented me with repeated scenarios in which my forward journey was blocked by washed-out bridges, roadblocks, and other impediments.

The resolution to this frustrating state of affairs came one night during an experience on one of the higher planes. I was standing on a broad plateau which was cut in half by a deep chasm about twenty feet wide. I knew the chasm was a barrier set up deliberately by some beings on this plane to prevent those who were not ready from crossing the plateau and continuing to the mountains beyond.

I had gone for miles in each direction trying to find a place to cross, but there was none. I understood the need for the barrier. But I also knew I had passed the tests and earned the right to continue on my way.

At this point I heard the approach of footsteps.

Turning, I saw the Mahanta walking toward me. He was carrying a long plank. When he got to the chasm, he smiled and said, "Help me lay this across the gap." We looked for the narrowest point. Then, together, we placed the plank as a bridge across the span.

"That was the easy part," the Mahanta said. "Your final test is to walk across it by yourself. If you have the courage to do so, you are ready to continue. If not, it is best you wait until you have more faith in yourself."

With that the Mahanta strode across the narrow plank to the other side. He turned to see if I would follow. I was sure if I fell from the plank I would plunge to my death in the abyss. I hesitated a moment, took a deep breath, and walked across the plank, never looking back.

After this inner experience with the Wayshower, things returned to normal in my outer life. My spiritual exercises bloomed once more. The obstacles disappeared.

BYPASSING ILLUSIONS

Another inner experience taught me how easy it is to deceive ourselves without the help of the Wayshower. During an out-of-body experience one night I was walking through a valley. I looked up and saw a magnificent being, clothed in glorious light, moving toward me. He must have been two hundred feet tall, robed in the greatest beauty. I was overwhelmed with feelings of devotion and was about to prostrate myself on the ground when the Mahanta appeared at my side.

"Impressive isn't it?" he asked, gesturing toward the vision. "You built up this deity in your own imagination in a past life, pouring your faith and fervor into it until it became a living reality for you."

During an out-of-body experience one night I was walking through a valley. I looked up and saw a magnificent being, clothed in glorious light, moving toward me.

I looked again at the giant being of light, wondering how something so awesome could be the creation of my own thoughts. As I watched, the apparition began to dissolve into the atmosphere like a morning mist. Soon it was gone.

"How did you do that?" I asked the Mahanta.

He replied, "All I did was help you see through the illusion. You created it. You dissolved it."

TESTING FOR DECEPTIONS

This kind of lesson raises some important questions for anyone who wishes to follow an inner spiritual guide. How reliable is the guidance? How can we know whether the guide is real, whether they are who they claim to be?

The inner worlds are much more changeable and ephemeral than the sluggish physical world—not because they are illusions as much as because they are made of light and volatile atoms which respond quickly to our thoughts and expectations. Beings there can put on masks and deceive with false appearances more easily than they can down here. Even so there are several safeguards for the seeker.

Any spiritual guide of a high order will act with clean ethics.

The first is common sense. Any spiritual guide of a high order will act with clean ethics. They will never encourage anyone to do harm to another or to oneself. True guides are always working for your betterment and everyone else's. And they won't work for your betterment at the expense of others. Sometimes so-called "betterment" is a euphemism for greed or personal advantage.

For example, an ECK Master won't force that girlfriend who left you to come back. He won't support some business scam to help you get rich by fleecing others.

Such acts only entangle the seeker more tightly in the ropes of karma.

A second point concerns the right to privacy. This right applies on the inner planes as well as the outer. The Mahanta will never intrude or force his guidance upon anyone. He comes by invitation, stays by mutual agreement, and leaves when asked. So should any worthy guide.

The Mahanta will never intrude or force his guidance upon anyone.

A third point requires a degree of self-honesty. You may hear people say they are following the guidance and direction of their inner master, then you see them do things which are blatantly selfish, intrusive, or unkind. We all have our bad days and make mistakes. Interpretation of the guidance we are given is our own responsibility.

Finally, if there are still doubts, the Mahanta has provided us with a good test to check the authenticity of an experience with the Inner Master, whether by vision or by voice. You test it by singing a charged word like HU, the ancient name of God, or by using a spiritual word which you may have received from the Mahanta.

If you do this with sincerity, you will usually get different results from the Mahanta than from an impostor. If the guide is really the Mahanta, this technique should leave you feeling calm, loved, and protected. If not, you will likely have a feeling of upset or tension. Often the singing of a spiritual word will instantly change the situation.

THE POWER OF SPIRITUAL WORDS

One night on the inner planes I found myself in an old abandoned warehouse with a friend who also looks to the Mahanta for spiritual guidance. We probably should not have been there, but I don't recall how we came to be in the place. In any case, we heard some noises. Soon a group of malicious people come out of the dark and surrounded us.

My friend and I quickly stood back-to-back in order to defend each other. But we were outnumbered. The aggressors started to tighten their circle like a noose. Suddenly I shouted, "Up with the Mahanta!" The attackers looked startled. A column of blue light surrounded my friend and me and lifted us straight up and into a safe place.

Choosing a spiritual guide is one of the great gambles of life. Some people cling to masters or teachers of bygone eras. Perhaps the legends which have grown with the passing of the centuries have added a luster to these figures from the past. Other seekers decide to wait for some promised messiah who will come any year now, especially if the year ends in zeros, like 1000 or 2000. These people are sitting around waiting for life to begin—or perhaps for life to end at the Last Judgment.

The eager seeker may look around and pick a living guide. Maybe he picks wrong, and he takes a few lumps and bruises and some ridicule from his friends. He may give up and decide all guides are shams.

Divine Spirit, or ECK, will keep sending us guides that suit our capabilities, that fit our state of consciousness.

Or maybe he simply outgrows his guide and decides it's time to look for one who can take him further toward his goal. His search pushes him onward. Divine Spirit, or ECK, will keep sending us guides that suit our capabilities, that fit our state of consciousness.

NO COMPETITION AMONG GUIDES

On the inner planes there is no competition among masters and teachers of different orders. Is the elementary-school teacher any less important in the scheme of things than the college professor? If the school system is to work, the students must be prepared at each level before passing on to the next.

In the spiritual hierarchy of the heavenly worlds, students are passed from one teacher to another in a natural sequence. Each teacher has a mission and works at his appointed task.

It is the mark of any good teacher, including those in the spiritual hierarchy, to pass his students on to the next teacher when the students have learned all they can from him. This transition often occurs in the dream state. There are no petty jealousies, no "my guide is better than your guide" arguments.

In a later chapter we will see how the Mahanta has a number of inner teachers who work with him in the spiritual education of those under his care. The classes taught range from beginner level, for those taking their first steps up the mountain of God, to the very advanced, for those in training for Mastership. Yet these teachers are Masters of high attainment.

To meet the Wayshower in his radiant form on some higher plane and to enjoy his talk and blessings are joyful experiences. The Mahanta's love for the seeker is eternal and unshakable. His only desire is to lift each of his followers into the spiritual heights. So he pours his love, his guidance, and his grace upon them.

SPIRITUAL EXERCISE: MEET THE WAYSHOWER

The grandeur which awaits every Soul is beyond description. The journey begins when the Wayshower appears in the life of the seeker. He stands ready at the door of your inner worlds, awaiting your invitation.

It is the mark of any good teacher, including those in the spiritual hierarchy, to pass his students on to the next teacher when the students have learned all they can from him.

The journey begins when the Wayshower appears in the life of the seeker. He stands ready at the door of your inner worlds.

To open the door, try the following spiritual exercise.

Find a quiet place where you can sit undisturbed for twenty or thirty minutes. Relax, close your eyes, and begin singing HU, the ancient name for God. Pronounce it like the color word *hue,* in a drawn-out sound: HU-U-U-U. Sing it for five or ten minutes.

To open the door, try the following spiritual exercise.

Meanwhile look gently into the screen of your mind, your inner door to the higher planes. Say, "Mahanta, I invite you to show me the way home to God." Look for the inner light. Listen for any sounds evoked by singing HU. Practice this spiritual exercise daily for several weeks or longer. The Light and Sound will eventually become your royal road to heaven.

8

The Dream Master

Sometimes the Inner Master is also called the Dream Master. Inwardly I can teach students of ECK around the world through their dreams.

—Harold Klemp
The Drumbeat of Time[1]

Zan sat across from me in an armchair in my home office. Somehow the presence of this being from the inner worlds seemed so natural that it didn't set off the doubt alarm of the analytical part of my mind. I was telling him, "It's good you dropped in. I'm ready to talk about the Dream Master. Isn't that strange—I was hoping to meet you in the dream state tonight, then you appear here."

Zan smiled and looked around the room, then back at me. "This is the dream state, Jim. That's why your mind isn't shocked to see me sitting here."

The moment he said that I realized it was true. This was a lucid dream. Dreams are so often like that—you don't realize you are dreaming until you wake up. The reasoning faculty gets bypassed, allowing almost any kind of experience to be accepted as real. The trick is to wake up in the dream, turning it into a lucid dream.

"There are two basic principles you must grasp if

Dreams are so often like that—you don't realize you are dreaming until you wake up. The trick is to wake up in the dream.

you are to understand the Dream Master," Zan continued. "The first principle states that dreams are real. The second states that the physical world is a dream. This inverts the usual notion people have about dreams!

"This sounds like nonsense to people who are just beginning their study of the spiritual nature of dreams. Why? The dreams of most people are chaotic, fragmented, and ephemeral. Just the stuff one would expect of illusions. By contrast their physical lives seem to be solid, with reasonable and orderly connections linking one event to the next.

"With the help of the Dream Master a shift begins to occur. The seeker's dreams gradually become more clear and meaningful. The wild symbols and bizarre plots give way to lucidity. The new clarity opens up a whole world of insights and opportunities.

"The seeker's nocturnal wanderings are no longer the confused escapades of yesteryear. In the company of the Dream Master he makes valuable nightly excursions into the higher planes. There he gathers the pearls of the secret teachings along the shores of the cosmic sea.

"Meanwhile the seeker begins to see how much the physical world is a mirror of his own consciousness. Here and there he starts to discover that some of the events in his outer life are waking dreams. At first these are few and scattered. Over time they become more prevalent until a point arrives where the outer life becomes a continuous reflection of consciousness. One day the seeker awakens to realize the inversion is complete."

This last statement caught my attention. Several decades ago, flush with the excitement of having found

With the help of the Dream Master a shift begins to occur. The seeker's dreams gradually become more clear and meaningful.

the teachings of the Mahanta, I had tried to explain a simple form of this inversion principle to my skeptical parents.

My father happened to work in a psychiatric hospital. I had no answer for his comment, which was, "I hear this stuff all the time from my patients down at the hospital. They too think their inner world is real and this outer one is an illusion."

I related this incident to Zan and asked, "So what is the difference between a psychosis and a realization that the world is a dream?"

Zan said, "The psychotic loses control of both his outer and inner worlds. The awakened Soul gains mastery over them both. The average person is caught somewhere in between. He muddles along through life, half-asleep and half-awake. But he is certain he is fully awake. Usually it takes some kind of earthshaking event or trauma to awaken him. This is why so many discover the Mahanta only after life has thrown a bucket of cold water in their face."

Zan stood up, signaling it was time to finish for now. "This should be enough to get you started on this most important aspect of the Mahanta. Perhaps more than any of the twelve aspects depicted on the Rosetta stone of God, the Dream Master is a bridging one.

"This is very fortunate for the seeker, for dreaming is one of the most natural and universal habits of the human race. Dreaming gives nearly all seekers access to the Dream Master. And through the Dream Master they gain access to the other aspects of the Mahanta, such as the Wayshower, the Light Giver, and others. And for those who have difficulty remembering their night dreams, the study of waking dreams as mentioned

Dreaming gives nearly all seekers access to the Dream Master.

above will carry them forward.

"Later, when we discuss the Mahanta as the prophet, I will discuss with you the deeper secrets of dreams. What the human race knows about this subject is but a fragment of a vast and universal science which is at work throughout the cosmos, from the highest planes of God on down.

"The esoteric parts of this study penetrate deeply into the spiritual mysteries. But for the purposes of this introduction to the Dream Master, it is enough to lift the veil and show people some of the immediate and practical possibilities."

I thanked Zan for his instruction as he turned and walked out of the office. Soon I was awake in bed, scribbling down notes like crazy while holding a flashlight. My wife grumbled only a little about the distraction.

DREAMS OF THE ANCIENTS

Dreams are a forgotten portal into the heavenly worlds. Many ancient peoples firmly believed that dreams were a doorway to the spiritual realms. The Mesopotamians looked for spiritual guidance and prophecy in dreams. In the Old Testament spiritual dreams predominate, with God or angels appearing in them to give guidance and messages to the Hebrew people. The Jews also believed Soul could travel in the dream state. The Egyptians, like their neighbors in the Middle East, interpreted dreams as messages from their gods. Similar beliefs were held by the Chinese, the people of India, and the early Greeks.

The ECK Masters have always considered dreams to be central to the life of their students.

The ECK Masters have always considered dreams to be central to the life of their students. As these Masters have brought the ECK teachings out into the open again in the twentieth century, they have elevated dreams to their rightful place in the spiritual life. Their views on dreams are somewhat different from the theories of popular psychology and more like the beliefs of the ancients. The ECK Masters teach that dreams are real and that Soul can leave the body during the dream state to visit heavenly worlds.

The ECK Masters teach that dreams are real and that Soul can leave the body during the dream state to visit heavenly worlds.

THE POSSIBILITIES

Once this basic principle is understood, the seeker will soon discover the many opportunities that await him while his body is sleeping: spiritual instruction from the Dream Master and other teachers, healings, past-life recalls, prophecies, and even service to others.

More down-to-earth are insights into business plans, family matters, and other day-to-day concerns. In the dream state Soul is able to look things over from a higher perspective. It can also draw on a much wider set of resources. These are real advantages.

As a writer I often draw on dream experiences. I will use my own experiences to illustrate some of the ways the Dream Master works with individuals in a way that suits their unique needs and interests.

Though I have had an interest in writing since a teenager, it was the Dream Master who encouraged me to make a serious commitment. One night I dreamed I was sitting in a library when the Dream Master, Wah Z, walked over and sat down across the table from me. Wah Z is Harold Klemp's spiritual name.

He got right to the point, saying, "It would be a real loss if you didn't develop and apply your writing talents in this lifetime."

I answered, "I enjoy writing. But I don't know that I have any special talent for it."

He said, "Let me show you something. Come with me." We walked over to a corner of the library where some files were kept. The Master pulled one from the shelf. "This file contains records of past lives where you have applied yourself to writing." He pulled a sheet out, and as we looked at it, it became a three-dimensional movie.

He showed me several pertinent lifetimes where I pursued writing in one form or another. In one, I was an avid correspondent. In another, an editor. Both lifetimes occurred in England, giving me added ease with the English language.

The next step came one night in a dream when the Dream Master invited me to enroll in a writing class which itself was to be held in the dream state. The main instructor was Paul Twitchell, the former Living ECK Master who had been a prolific writer. The current Living ECK Master, Harold Klemp, was a frequent guest instructor. In my dreams I attended this class perhaps eight to ten times over the course of a year. But in my physical life I had yet to undertake any major writing project.

One night in the dream class a student complained, "It's all very well to talk about writing in this class. But I want to hear from someone who's actually written a book." Harold Klemp was teaching that night. He looked at me and said, "Well, you've written a book, haven't you, Jim?"

I hadn't—at least not in my physical life! But I felt the Dream Master was suggesting it was time. So I began to write. During this phase I had several dreams

Harold Klemp was teaching that night. He looked at me and said, "Well, you've written a book, haven't you, Jim?"

where the Dream Master gave me ideas or images for a book. Within a year the book was finished and accepted by a publisher.

OPENING THE MAGIC DOOR

The above story shows how the Dream Master addresses the unique needs of the seeker. It takes primarily three things to open this magical door to spiritual dreams.

First, invite the Dream Master into your dreams. When you go to bed at night simply say, "Mahanta, I invite you into my dreams tonight. Give me whatever experiences are best for my spiritual growth at this time."

Second, do a daily contemplation of twenty minutes to half an hour. During this contemplation sing HU and fill your heart with love. If possible, obtain a copy of the book *The Spiritual Exercises of ECK* by Harold Klemp. Experiment with the techniques given in it. There is one to suit almost every occasion and temperament.

Third, keep a dream journal and light by your bedside. Discipline yourself to write down your dreams. I know it's hard to rouse yourself out of a groggy sleep to write them down. But the payoff can be handsome. Within six months to a year you will likely have begun a rich record of your dream life.

The Mahanta establishes an individualized course of study for each of his followers on the inner planes.

LIGHT AND SOUND IN DREAMS

The Mahanta establishes an individualized course of study for each of his followers on the inner planes. This study will be partly reflected in the student's dreams. One of the beginning courses is an introduction to the Light and Sound of God.

My initial response to the teachings of the Mahanta was an impatient desire to have an experience with these twin elements of the Holy Spirit. To one who has not experienced them, they can seem abstract and unimportant. I kept asking inwardly to be given the experience.

One night the Dream Master took me on a long journey into the heavenly worlds. We came to the edge of a cliff which overlooked a bright, shimmering sea.

One night the Dream Master took me on a long journey into the heavenly worlds. We came to the edge of a cliff which overlooked a bright, shimmering sea. The feeling of the experience up to that point is best captured in a poem Paul Twitchell wrote. The last two stanzas are:

O'er rough boulders of the falling stars
    I journeyed on wings so swift . . .
And in the haunting vastness of space
    I rounded the trail on God's cliff

In the afterglow of the lingering refrain
    I paused upon some towering hill
Hobbled the steeds upon a quiet windy plain
    And silently watched the golden still.[2]

Looking more closely upon the shimmering sea, I saw it was made of swirling currents of light. "Feel like swimming?" asked the Dream Master. "Yes!" I shouted, and I flew off the cliff and into the sea.

I quickly bobbed to the surface and waved to the Master. The "water" was a perfect temperature. I dove beneath the waves into a realm of light and sweet music. To my surprise and delight I discovered I could breathe just fine beneath the surface. For several minutes I enjoyed the sensation of swimming like a fish in this magical sea.

Then the waters began to flow in a wide circle, like a whirlpool. The light changed gradually from brilliant to dazzling to blinding as I went deeper and deeper. Exhilaration became ecstasy. And the music became louder and more penetrating until the sound was a deafening roar.

Even though I was deep within the sea, I felt like I was standing beneath a giant waterfall cascading from a great height, pounding my head and shoulders. I began to lose myself, to feel overwhelmed. "Help!" I cried to the Dream Master. In a flash I woke from the dream, a little shaken.

"OK," I said inwardly to the Mahanta. "I need to be more patient and go more slowly." Even so, I was grateful for the dream. It had made the Light and Sound real to me. Divine Spirit was indeed a tangible and palpable force as It flowed through the universes of God. It could bring great joy—in moderation. But this current is also the raw, primal force of creation. The Mahanta has his hand on the controls. He can turn them up slowly over time as the seeker adapts to the flow.

SOME VIEWS ON INTERPRETING DREAMS

Another key service of the Dream Master is help in unraveling the meaning of our dreams. Again, this part of his teachings differs from the common notions presented in books on dream interpretation. The first step is to keep in mind that dreams are real experiences in higher planes. What then causes them, at times, to be confusing and hard to understand?

Imagine that your everyday life was lived in a two-dimensional world, like a flat sheet of paper. When you used the words *circle* or *square,* people would understand

The Mahanta has his hand on the controls. He can turn them up slowly over time as the seeker adapts to the flow.

what you were talking about, because circles and squares exist in a two-dimensional world.

Now imagine you had a dream. You went into a three-dimensional world and saw amazing things like spheres and cubes. When you woke up in your ordinary two-dimensional life, what would become of your three-dimensional dream?

Your waking consciousness would have no way of clearly representing the dream images, any more than your three-dimensional mind has a clear way of visualizing a four-dimensional hypercube. You would go to a friend in the flatland of your two-dimensional world and say, "I had this weird dream. It was about something like a circle, only much different. I don't know how to explain it." And your friend would say, "Never mind, you just ate too much pizza before going to bed."

Soul is a multidimensional being.

Soul is a multidimensional being. During dreams we range forth into higher planes where the limitations of space and time as we know them in our physical life do not apply. As the Eckankar scriptures put it:

> The stars of our heavenly world can be contained in the eyes of a swallow. There are also worlds around man that do not respond to our five senses, worlds which are great and small, visible and invisible, and as numerous as the grains of sand on the seashore.
>
> These worlds are levels of consciousness.[3]

According to most dream theories, the confusing nature of dreams comes from not understanding the dream symbols or from some inherent lack of meaning in the dream itself. These explanations may be valid for some dreams.

Yet the fact that dreams can come from multidimensional worlds adds a third explanation which the seeker may find more revealing: His conscious mind is grappling to express in ordinary words or pictures a dream experience of a hypercube or something from another dimension.

A second assumption of common dream theories is that our dreams are in some way a commentary on or mirror of our outer life. Following this idea, the dreamer is instructed to look for the connection between his dream and something happening in his outer life. This is generally good advice and is surely applicable to spiritual dreams at times.

Yet again, an alternative viewpoint may be helpful: The dream experience may have no relation at all to the outer life. Instead, it may be a recall of a real experience on some other plane where Soul is pursuing an interest unrelated to life on earth. In such cases there is no point straining to apply the dream to our outer life.

For example, in a recent dream I traveled to another planet in the inner worlds. The beings there specialized in the healing arts. People visited from surrounding planetary systems to obtain healings and therapy of various kinds. I was visiting simply because I had heard of it and wanted to learn more about the place.

I was met by a friend, a High Initiate in Eckankar, whose interest in healing often brought her to this planet. She showed me around, ribbing me on occasion for the way I gawked at the odd sights and customs. This dream had no particular connection to my physical life. It was simply an adventure in a parallel universe.

The dream experience may have no relation at all to the outer life. Instead, it may be a recall of a real experience on some other plane where Soul is pursuing an interest unrelated to life on earth.

THE DREAM MASTER'S INTERPRETATIONS

Having mentioned these important points about spiritual dreams, there are dreams which do need interpreting and which do relate to our outer life. How can the Dream Master be of help to us with these dreams? What is a good way to interpret them?

One night I dreamed I was standing at the foot of a hill with the Dream Master when he asked me to quickly move back into the shadows. I stepped into the shade of a large oak tree nearby. A moment later an angry mob appeared, marching toward us. I shrank back behind the tree's trunk where I wouldn't be seen, wondering what this was all about.

One night I dreamed a man stepped forward and shook his finger in the Master's face. "I have a complaint against Jim Davis," he said angrily.

The mob halted just in front of the Master. A man stepped forward and shook his finger in the Master's face. "I have a complaint against Jim Davis," he said angrily. Then he proceeded to heap criticism upon my character. The Dream Master listened patiently until the man ran out of steam. "I will have to talk to him about this," he said.

Then an old woman dressed in rags stepped forth and began a similar tirade. I was watching and listening to all this from my hiding place, thinking, *What lies! Who told these people such things?* But it didn't seem prudent to step out and show my face, thinking the mob might attack.

As each member of the crowd had their say, the Master repeated his promise, "I will have a talk with him about this." The crowd finally seemed placated, even tired. One by one they drifted away.

At this point the dream might have ended. I would have awakened wondering how to interpret it. But what happened next demonstrates the value of working with the Mahanta.

I came out of the shadows and joined the Dream Master. We began walking up the hill together in silence. I knew that he knew I was innocent of the offenses the mob had blamed me for. When we got to the top of the hill I asked, "What was that all about?"

The Master looked out over the valley below. "You have suffered from low self-esteem and an inferiority complex in this life," he explained. "Many people do, to some extent. That mob was really made up of all of the personas of your past lifetimes who had some unresolved guilt or self-recrimination.

"This throng of beings are none other than the many parts of yourself as you have played out your roles upon the stage of this earth world over the centuries. These unresolved self-criticisms from many past lives are the root cause of your low self-esteem. A great deal of this karma has been lifted from your shoulders tonight. Over the next year or two, these voices from the past will become silent. There will be an occasional grumble or two, but nothing like before."

This was a case of getting the interpretation of a dream while still in the dream state. Sometimes it is the Dream Master who provides the insights, and sometimes the dreamer. This particular dream also touched upon the Mahanta as healer, a role which will be the subject of another chapter.

This was a case of getting the interpretation of a dream while still in the dream state.

FIVE LEVELS OF DREAMS

There remain the many dreams we wake up with which don't fit any of the above categories. They may need some untangling. When working with them it may prove helpful to keep in mind that according to the ECK teachings dreams originate from five main levels and apply to three main areas of life.[4]

The five levels correspond to the planes upon which Soul dwells and the body It works through on each level.

The five levels correspond to the planes upon which Soul dwells and the body It works through on each level. The following chart is suggestive of some of the clues:

1. Astral Plane—Emotional body
   Dreams with a strong emotional content
   Pink color tones
   Flashy "special effects"
2. Causal Plane—Causal body
   Prophetic or past-life dreams
   Orange color tones
   Insights on links of cause and effect
3. Mental Plane—Mental body
   Dreams containing abstract ideas
   Bluish color tones
   Problem solving
4. Etheric Plane—Subconscious body
   Highly subtle and penetrating insights
   Violet color tones
   Lofty overviews of life
5. Soul Plane—Soul body
   Profound sense of the divine
   Expansive and intensely joyous feelings
   Brilliant gold or whitish light

The Sound Current can be heard in many ways on all of the planes, but in general, the higher the plane of the dream the more refined and beautiful the sound.

There are countless ways these aspects of the various planes can appear in a dream. One night I dreamed I was showing two friends one of the Temples of Golden Wisdom. A great stream of violet-colored light flowed upward into the sky from the peaked roof of the Temple, giving a tint of violet to the surrounding landscape.

Upon awakening from this dream I suspected at once it was from the Etheric Plane. I did some research in the Eckankar writings and found that the description of the Temple of Golden Wisdom on that plane matched the building I had seen in the dream.

The three main areas that dreams can apply to in our outer lives are:

1. Daily life
2. Thoughts and emotions
3. The spiritual life

There is no need to do a methodical analysis from these points. Just keep them lightly in mind when reviewing the dream. See if you can get an intuitive sense of where the dream originated and what it might apply to in your outer life.

HELPFUL PRACTICES

Some people have found it helpful to keep a dictionary of their personal symbols at the back of their dream journal. By observing these symbols when they recur, connections can be discovered between dreams and hidden meanings may surface. This is usually much better than relying on books which give generic interpretations of dream symbols.

Some people have found it helpful to keep a dictionary of their personal symbols at the back of their dream journal.

For example, one year I had three or four dreams of swimming with different groups of people. These dreams were weeks to months apart. Only when I went back through my dream journal later did I notice the common symbol. This led me to compare the dreams as parts of a set, which led to a whole new understanding I had missed before doing this.

While on the subject of dream journals, consider the following helpful hints.

1. With our busy modern lifestyles, it is best to choose one or two nights a week to focus on your dreams. Choose a night when you can get plenty of rest and can take the time at night or in the morning to write down your dreams.

2. Fill your mind with happy thoughts. Dwell on love as you fall asleep.

3. When a dream recall comes, write it in a condensed form, capturing the key feelings and images.

4. Last, try some of the excellent dream techniques which appear in *The Spiritual Exercises of ECK* or *The Art of Spiritual Dreaming* by Harold Klemp.[5]

Don't be concerned if you go through dry spells periodically. This is natural. I may write down twenty dreams one week, and then none for the next month. If you are a person who just never seems to remember your dreams, don't give up. When the time is right, the Mahanta will help you recall something of value.

THE PRECIOUS GIFT OF DREAMS

Dreams are among God's most precious gifts to Soul, flowers of the divine imagination.

Dreams are among God's most precious gifts to Soul, flowers of the divine imagination. For it is Soul's nature to dream, to exercise the powers of creation upon the fertile fields of space and time. Dreams work continuously in our lives, waking and sleeping. They help us learn to walk through the curtain between this world and the inner ones.

Dreams give us insights that could take lifetimes

to gather by any other means. They give us added perception and steady us for the surprises of the day. They yield glimpses of the spiritual life beyond this world and, in the process, soften any fear of death.

This is the mission of the Mahanta in his role as the Dream Master. He is the beekeeper who brings us sweet dreams, honey from the combs of heaven. In closing this chapter, I quote from the scriptures of Eckankar on this great aspect of his work:

> The Divine Dreamer sends out Its dreams to man via the Mahanta, the Living ECK Master in all Its worlds, to arouse individual Souls in their sleep state to seek once again the heavenly kingdom.[6]

May it be your pleasure to invite the Dream Master into your dreams.

9

The Guardian

The Living ECK Master is appointed to his high position and is expected to defend the God power and to defend the works of ECK and the chelas who have put their interest in ECK.

The Shariyat-Ki-Sugmad,
Book One[1]

O ne evening I was watching television with my wife. The episode raised one of the perennial questions of life: Why does God let innocent people suffer?

A drought had lingered over a Midwestern farming community, gradually withering the crops. If rain didn't arrive soon some of the farmers would lose their farms. Driven by the frustration of inaction in the face of this challenge, one of the farmers decided to do something. He began by demanding that the insurance company cover the expense of his lost crops.

"We can't do that," the insurance agent explained. "The drought is an act of God."

"Then I'm going to sue God!" thundered the bitter farmer. The local judge could find no legal reason to block the lawsuit. And in any case he felt it might let the farmer vent some of his frustration.

Why does God let innocent people suffer?

113

At this point, an angel in the guise of a tough older woman arrives to defend God—and the trial is on. The arguments seesaw back and forth with the angel making little headway in winning the jury and farmer to her point of view. Meanwhile, outside the courtroom, the people of the community have been pulling together to help each other through the hard times. Noble acts of self-sacrifice knit together their isolated lives.

As a last stand to save his farm, the farmer suing God holds an auction to sell off some of his essential equipment. All the people of the town surprise him by giving whatever money they can so he won't have to auction his machinery.

The turning point in the trial comes when another angel is put on the stand. She has talked to God and received His answer. "God knows you need water," she explains, "but He knows you need each other more. This hardship has opened your hearts and brought you all together."

"God knows you need water," she explains, "but He knows you need each other more. This hardship has opened your hearts and brought you all together."

This testimony penetrates the hardened crust around the farmer's heart. He recognizes the gift in the hardship and withdraws his lawsuit against God. The story ends shortly thereafter with a crop-soaking rainstorm.

As I went to bed that evening, I kept turning the story over in my mind. Later that night I dreamed of traveling to a farm in the American Midwest. As I walked along a dry, dusty road that went past a wheat field, I heard a tractor coming up behind me. At the wheel was Harold Klemp, the Mahanta, the Living ECK Master. Standing behind him on the back of the tractor was Zan.

They pulled up alongside. Harold turned off the

motor and hopped down, as did Zan right after him. "I'd rather walk," Harold said, dusting off his jeans. "I've done enough tractor driving for one lifetime."

Zan chuckled and added, "It beats riding a yak." This comment hinted as to his cultural roots. Zan was dressed in farmer's overalls. I was surprised at how naturally he fit into this landscape.

The three of us began walking along the road. Little clouds of yellow dust puffed into the air around our feet. "What did you think about the angel's explanation of God's will?" Harold asked, referring to the television show.

"I thought the scriptwriter handled it very well," I answered. "Actually I preferred the angel's answer to one which would have attributed it all to karma. It showed that God's purpose is ever to bring love into our lives—not just assign justice for some misdeed."

God's purpose is ever to bring love into our lives—not just assign justice for some misdeed.

Zan swept his arm in a broad circle. "You can look in all directions out here and see nothing but the horizon. There is not a tree, a fence, or a building to block the view. Such is the vision of the ECK Masters, the Eagle-eyed Adepts. They have cleared all obstructions from their spiritual gaze."

We watched as a lazy breeze sent a straw-colored wave rolling gracefully across the golden fields of ripe wheat. I wondered where Zan was leading with his comment.

"The Mahanta knows God's will and is an agent of it," Zan continued. "One of his great responsibilities is to be the protector of all who come to him. The Rosetta stone of God depicts this aspect of the Mahanta as a man standing with a shield at the ready. I call this role the Guardian. This aspect is one which requires a delicate balancing act with every seeker."

Harold nodded in agreement. "The task is easily stated but must be deftly applied. If not protected from all manner of hidden influences the seeker may flounder in his spiritual unfoldment, at the mercy of his own inexperience. There are predators along the spiritual path looking for unwary victims. Yet if overprotected, the seeker will never learn self-reliance. The goal is to turn novices into masters. But the seeker too often expects to be protected from all the blows and hard knocks which are necessary to sculpt him into that which he longs to become."

The Mahanta's point rang true with me. "I've found that protection from physical harm is the least of your work with me, Harold. Most of the time you seem to be protecting me from complacency—goading me along with frequent reminders to keep alert and keep moving forward."

Zan said, "It may seem so. Yet I would estimate that 90 percent of the protection any seeker gets from the Mahanta slips by unnoticed. Of course the seeker feels he escapes harm because he has become such a skilled mountain climber. He is unaware of the safety ropes provided by the Mahanta to stop his fall should the seeker lose his foothold.

As the Guardian, the Mahanta is ever watchful for anything which may stand between you and God.

"As the Guardian, the Mahanta is ever watchful for anything which may stand between you and God. Yet at the same time, he will stand aside while you run the gauntlet of life. He knows the bruises will heal, and you will be stronger and wiser for your lumps.

"Yes, the drought may come, as the farmer in the television show discovered. The drought may parch your pathway home. But the moment you grasp the point of the lesson and open your heart a little more to

divine love, the gentle rains of heaven will fall to cool
your weary feet."

We startled a pheasant which sprang into the air
squawking. He beat his wings frantically for a few
seconds in a hasty exit, then glided, skimming the
wheat field. "He knew we were coming," said Harold
with a chuckle. "But he wanted to be sure we were close
enough to get an earful of his noisy protest."

The dream scene began to fade, and shortly I awoke
from my slumber. I picked up my dream journal and
wrote down as much as I could remember.

As I lay in bed staring into the darkness, I recalled
a recent incident of the Guardian's protection. Perhaps
the antics of the pheasant brought it to mind. While on
the lookout for a home business opportunity, I had come
across an advertisement in the newspaper which looked
promising. I dialed the number and had a good long talk
with the salesman—a Mr. Segal.

I recalled a recent incident of the Guardian's protection.

The risk was an initial investment of about two
thousand dollars with no promise of recovering it if the
business failed. I was willing to risk the money if the
opportunities were as the salesman had portrayed them.
Even after discounting the overheated sales rhetoric,
I still felt good about the prospects. I decided to give
myself a day or two to mull it over.

Later that afternoon I was strolling through a park
near my home and sat down on a bench to do a brief
contemplation. I closed my eyes and sang HU softly for
a few minutes, when I suddenly got an urge to quickly
open my eyes.

A seagull was flying toward me. He relieved himself
just as he came overhead. Only a quick move to the left
saved me, as his projectile exploded right where I had

been sitting, splattering the entire bench. I instantly recognized that this was a warning from the Guardian. I shouted after the bird, "Thank you for your honesty, Mr. Segal! I decline your business offer." Then I thanked the Mahanta for his timely warning about my business dealings.

To some people this incident would seem a mere coincidence—if they noticed the connection at all between Mr. Segal and the seagull. If the seeker keeps alert, the Mahanta will use any means at hand to pass along a warning. Only by the daily practice of the spiritual exercises can we keep ourselves well-attuned to such messages from the Master.

The seeker is almost always warned. Usually several times. If we keep alert and aware, there is very little that can catch us off guard.

The Guardian sets up road signs and detour arrows to guide us around the dangers. Often we ignore them and stubbornly push ahead, even if we have to kick our way through the roadblocks to get to where we want to go. Then when everything goes awry, we whine, "Why didn't the Mahanta warn me?" The seeker is almost always warned. Usually several times. If we keep alert and aware, there is very little that can catch us off guard.

Even so, the Guardian is on the scene should we be confronted by a dire emergency. A new member of Eckankar had just taken a job working with delinquent youths. One evening he picked up several of them in his van to take them to a movie. He came to an intersection and tried to look left and right, but with the boys all around him, it was difficult to get a clear view. Just as he pulled into the intersection the kids on the left side of the van began to scream. A car was speeding straight for them. A major collision was inevitable.

The boys fearfully braced themselves for the impact—but it didn't come. After a few seconds they began to talk excitedly among themselves. The car had miraculously passed right through the van, like a ghost through a wall, leaving not a trace of harm behind! The ECKist and the kids under his charge had been protected by the Mahanta, who raised the vibrations of the van and all the people in it.[2]

Commenting on such unusual cases of protection, Harold Klemp has written, "The laws of nature can be bent when there is a need for protection or for a spiritual lesson. Usually the experience is given as a way for an individual to learn something that could not be learned any other way."[3]

Does this mean anyone who follows the Mahanta is safe from car wrecks? That's not how it works. The factors which converge upon a potentially harmful episode will vary with every person.

The ECK scriptures point out:

> The ECKist knows that he must steer himself on the path to God, and that not even the Mahanta, the Living ECK Master can give him help unless he works in accordance with the laws of Eckankar. What he requires is restraint, compassion, self-awareness, and wisdom.[4]

Many veteran ECKists have learned the hard way how an uncontrolled burst of anger or sharp criticism has rebounded to them.

It took me awhile to catch on to this. shortly after losing my temper I would inevitably walk into a doorpost, stub my toe, or bring self-injury in some other way.

The role of the Guardian described so far sounds very much like that of a guardian angel. Although there

Many veteran ECKists have learned the hard way how an uncontrolled burst of anger or sharp criticism has rebounded to them.

are many stories among ECKists who have experienced this divine protection from the Mahanta, there is another side to the story. As Harold Klemp mentioned in my dream at the beginning of this chapter, the flip side of the Guardian's mission is to teach self-reliance. Were the Mahanta to pluck us out of every danger and hardship, he would only encourage dependency.

The heart of this concept was imparted to me recently through a few nightmares. In the first nightmare I was being chased by a ferocious Tyrannosaurus Rex. In terror, I ran as fast as I could. But of course my flight was futile. In a few moments the monster was nearly upon me. The quiet voice of the Mahanta broke through my panic and said, "Turn and face him!"

Then the quiet voice of the Mahanta broke in once more. "Just calm your fears," he whispered. Somehow I mustered enough courage to stand my ground.

At that moment I remembered I had a small-caliber pistol in my belt. I quickly spun around, unloading several rounds of puny bullets at the enormous hulk that was about to have me for lunch. To my astonishment the bullets felled my predator as if they were cannonballs. He crashed to the ground at my feet, shaking my dream world like an earthquake.

Two nights later I found myself being pursued by another giant—this time it was an angry man some fifty feet tall who was bent on trouncing me under his feet. Remembering the T. Rex dream, I turned and faced him. I grabbed for the pistol, but it wasn't there.

"Uh oh," I said to myself, "it's too late to escape now!" Then the quiet voice of the Mahanta broke in once more. "Just calm your fears," he whispered. Somehow I mustered enough courage to stand my ground. The moment I did the giant staggered, then pitched forward, falling immobile at my feet. The mere act of standing my ground had felled him.

I awoke from this second dream with a greater self-confidence than I'd felt in years. It completely changed my view of nightmares. I decided that, though often horrifying, they are a very effective way to learn to face our fears.

Hence, one of the benefits of the ECK teachings is how such learning can take place in the dream state. Harold Klemp once wrote, "People who say, 'Please take my bad dreams away,' don't realize that if the dreams were taken away from them and the karma was released in their outer life, it would create hardships that are totally unnecessary in ECK. Instead, they can work it out by giving it to the Mahanta and letting it be resolved in the best possible way. The Mahanta, the Living ECK Master is here for just that purpose."[5]

The nightmares had probably grown from fears of a new and challenging job I had applied for. The job was to start in about a week. After these two initial dreams, I actually invited the Mahanta to send me nightmares for the rest of the week to help me face and overcome any remaining fears.

By the time the week ended I wanted to be ready for any challenge. I looked forward to testing myself this way. A reckless request? Maybe. In any case the nightmares stopped. Apparently I had gained the courage I needed for the time being.

Thinking back over this pair of dreams, I wondered how often we plead for divine intervention to chase away some fleeting obstacle instead of learning from it. It is mostly ourselves, and not God, who must take care of things. And yet the Guardian is always present. He desires to see all who follow him rise to the spiritual

It is mostly ourselves, and not God, who must take care of things. And yet the Guardian is always present.

heights. He pours his love, protection, and grace upon us.

Zan spoke of the symbol for the Guardian on the Rosetta stone of God—a figure with shield in hand. In the works of ECK this shield is called the Shield of Silver Light.

Earlier in this chapter Zan spoke of the symbol for the Guardian on the Rosetta stone of God—a figure with shield in hand. In the works of ECK this shield is called the Shield of Silver Light. Harold Klemp has spoken of this most powerful shield and its purpose in his book *The Golden Heart.* I quote a passage at length, for it is pertinent here:

> It appears as a mighty warrior's shield from medieval times. The Light of God shines down from above, strikes the shield, and comes off in a ray of light so brilliant that it will blind anyone who approaches it with an impure heart. Only the Mahanta can approach this shield, for it is used in his travels on the inner planes.
>
> This Shield of Silver Light stands as a protection for the children of ECK, those who make the commitment to follow the shield of love. No being can approach it except in the spirit of love. And when you can approach the Shield of Silver Light in the spirit of love, you have the protection of the Mahanta with you. Nothing can touch you, nothing can harm you.
>
> When battle must be done to bring protection to Its own, the Inner Master, the Mahanta, will go to the clearing, pick up the shield, and with the sword of the Sugmad he will take the field in battle for you.
>
> If you know and accept this, then you have the love and protection of the Holy Spirit against every psychic attack, against all harm and danger. In times of danger, you have the ability to wrap this

aura of love so tightly about you that nothing can touch you."[6]

This passage reveals the secret of the greatest protection available to any God seeker—a loving heart. With the noble ideal of mastership before him and a pure heart within, the seeker can move forward with confidence toward his goal.

Aside from protection from physical harm, the Mahanta's sheltering love also extends into many other areas of the seeker's life. For example, there is protection from unfolding too rapidly—a state of affairs which could bring major disruption into our life. And there is protection from going too slow due to complacency. These protections remain effective provided we keep an ear inclined to the whispers of Spirit.

The light from the silver shield of the Guardian can pierce illusions, light our way through dark valleys, reveal hidden traps, or surround our homes with a dome of protective love.

One of the subtle tests that faces every seeker at some point along the path is the lure of the half-truth. In the beginning the task is to sift the true from the false. Later the process is refined. It becomes an effort to distinguish the true from the half-true. The Guardian is a key ally at such times.

One of the subtle tests that faces every seeker at some point along the path is the lure of the half-truth.

Some years ago I faced a test like this. I began to take a strong interest in a set of spiritual practices which were being promoted by a certain popular teacher. I had outgrown these methods but didn't know it at the time because they were presented in such a way that they looked like something new and essential.

One night in the dream state I was walking along the streets of a city of the inner worlds. This city exists on the Astral Plane—the first major level of heaven of the inner worlds. The city is a place of exquisite beauty and light. Students of Eckankar visit a Temple of Golden Wisdom in this city during one stage of their spiritual education.

I noticed a poster announcing a workshop to be given by the popular teacher I mentioned above. The poster had all sorts of special effects. It was a colorful hologram and emitted a voice message and soft music when anyone stopped to read it. It happened that the workshop was just a block away and about to start.

I hurried along the street and joined a short line of stragglers entering the auditorium. Since there were no empty seats left, I stood near the door. It was actually a good location, affording a close view of the stage. The guest speaker came onstage to a roaring applause. He surveyed the audience with sure and confident eyes, then began to speak. He was charismatic, articulate, and entertaining. Soon he had me and the rest of the audience enthralled.

About this time I heard a voice behind me say, "What do you think of him?" I turned to see the Mahanta, Harold Klemp. He must have come in just behind me. "Well," I answered, "I'm impressed. He's a good speaker with some valuable insights."

Harold was silent for a moment, then asked, "Is your impression of the value of the speaker's message being distorted by his stage presence?"

Harold was silent for a moment, then asked, "Is your impression of the value of the speaker's message being distorted by his stage presence?"

"No," I answered with a little irritation. "I can tell the difference between the two."

The Mahanta said, "Look again."

In a way which is hard to explain, the Mahanta lifted me in consciousness to a higher point of view. I was able to get behind the facade of the speaker, able to see the inner workings of his technique, to penetrate the essence of his thoughts. The Mahanta was, in essence, reflecting a ray from the Shield of Silver Light upon the situation, stripping bare all illusions.

Possessing this sudden X-ray vision, I was taken aback by what I now could see. As in the fairy tale, the emperor had no clothes. The speaker had no sincere regard for his audience. He was a master manipulator, and his message was a rehash of outworn ideas dressed up in sparkling new garb.

The Mahanta was observing my astonishment. "The Living ECK Master avoids creating this kind of stage-craft magic," he explained. "He will always lose a certain number of his impressionable followers to those teachers who employ it.

"Actually, it's fairly easy to create such an effect. The typical Sunday evangelist on television uses it in a rather clumsy way. People who are more clever know how to enhance the effect with wit, humor, and casual phrasing. It fills auditoriums but brings no deep or lasting change in the listener."

The Mahanta turned and walked out of the building. I noticed the speaker give a darting and nervous glance toward the door as he left. I stayed a few minutes longer but soon tired of the presentation. It had definitely lost its appeal. Soon I too was out the door, continuing my walk along the streets of the lovely Astral city.

Initially I was puzzled by the concept presented in the quote which heads this chapter—that the Living ECK Master is "expected to defend the God power." Why would the God power need defending? Doesn't it do the

The Mahanta was, in essence, reflecting a ray from the Shield of Silver Light upon the situation, stripping bare all illusions.

defending? After contemplating on this puzzle, my new perspective is this: What needs defending is the God power within each individual.

I see the God power as the great current of Light and Sound which flows through Soul. It can be diverted, weakened, or misapplied, from both internal and external causes. The teacher in the auditorium was attempting to use his slick stage persona to redirect the spiritual currents of the audience to his own ends. The Mahanta stepped in and defended this God power within me.

The wonder of the Guardian's protection is that the seeker need not call upon the Mahanta to get it.

The wonder of the Guardian's protection is that the seeker need not call upon the Mahanta to get it. In fact he couldn't in many cases because he is not even aware he needs defending. We may not always be able to understand how and when the protection is working, but we can feel it resting like a comforting cloak around our shoulders.

As the determined seeker climbs farther up the mountain, he comes to appreciate more and more the growth that comes through hardship. His cries for protection from the Mahanta become less frequent as he strives to solve his own problems. This is the testing ground for Mastership. Paul Twitchell put it directly when he wrote, "The ECK Masters did not reach their high state by fleeing from pain, or from finding comfort or sensual pleasures."[7]

The paradox of the Mahanta's protection is that he may step aside to let the seeker go through challenges and difficulties. He knows this is the way to keep the seeker aware and watchful of what life may bring him. Such tests may bring the karma of pain and hardship, for these are often the wellspring of awareness.

At such times the seeker may feel he has lost favor

with the Mahanta. He will curse the problem designed to bring him a blessing. But as he gains more experience he will come to appreciate the wisdom and self-reliance he gains through these tests.

Turning again to the words of *The Shariyat:*

> Man must not think that if he asks the Mahanta's help while facing a serious problem that the Sugmad will remove it to suit man's desires. It works in a different way; the problem itself may remain, but man's approach to it, his understanding of it, will change as a result of his petition. Whereas it may seem a very difficult, even insurmountable battle to face, man will be given the help needed in resolving it."[8]

This is the eternal drama of the Mahanta as the Guardian, armed with his invincible Shield of Silver Light. On one occasion he may step forth and save the seeker with a miraculous intervention. No sooner will the grateful seeker finish spreading the story of this wondrous grace when the reverse happens. The seeker will stumble into a test of pain and suffering that is needed to soften his heart or sharpen his awareness. His loudest cries to heaven will seem to be ignored. Yet all the while the love and blessings of the Mahanta rest upon him.

As with all aspects of his assistance, the Mahanta never forces spiritual protection upon his followers. The role of the seeker is to accept or invite the Mahanta's love and protection into his life. Having done that, the degree of the protection depends upon several factors.

First, as mentioned above, even the Mahanta will not intervene if an individual carelessly breaks the spiritual laws. The door to harm is nearly always opened

The role of the seeker is to accept or invite the Mahanta's love and protection into his life.

by us. Either by drawing ourselves into unsafe areas through misdirected curiosity or through self-centered efforts to harm others, we bring the roof down upon our heads.

There are many such laws we must learn, and they can seem complex at first. But the essential directive is simply to love and respect ourselves and others.

There are many such laws we must learn, and they can seem complex at first. But the essential directive is simply to love and respect ourselves and others. This is nothing new or startling. It can be found in the teachings of all the world religions.

After observing the behavior of many Christians someone once said, "The problem with Christianity is that it has never been tried." The same could be said about many followers of any religion, including Eckankar. It takes real character and patient, lifelong effort to live up to the ideals of unconditional love. Perhaps we need to follow the dog owner's prayer: "Oh Lord, please make me as good as my dog thinks I am."

Harold Klemp has recommended the value of two universal laws of Spirit discovered by researcher Richard Maybury. These appear to be the only foundational laws which all cultures around the world have agreed to. They are: (1) Do all you have agreed to do, and (2) do not encroach on other persons or their property.[9] Maybury describes them at length in his book *Whatever Happened to Justice?* The more lofty and subtle spiritual laws will likely fall into place if we first practice these basic ones.

The second thing we can do to draw upon the Mahanta's protection is keep ourselves spiritually alert and open to his guidance. The best way to do this is through singing or chanting the sacred name of God, HU. When many people hear about this for the first time it seems too simple—almost childish. Yet stories pour in from all over the world telling of the wondrous love and protection people have received by singing this word.

Harold Klemp has written, "In all heaven and earth no name is mightier than HU. It can lift the grieving heart to a temple of solace. A companion in trouble, it is likewise a friend in times of prosperity. And is it any wonder, for HU is Soul's most precious gift from God."[10]

In all heaven and earth no name is mightier than HU.

Finally, you can commit to the daily practice of other Spiritual Exercises of ECK. These daily practices will expand our love and awareness—two traits which will greatly boost our recognition and acceptance of divine protection.

The paradox of the Guardian confronts every seeker: The more we practice self-reliance, the more divine protection surrounds us. It's a restatement of the old adage that God helps those who help themselves. This adage, like much of the greatest wisdom of the world, has lost its power to impress us through overfamiliarity. I believe it is one of the foundation stones of self-mastery. The Mahanta as the Guardian will help us rediscover this ageless truth in a way that makes it active in our consciousness.

10

The Teacher

*What the Mahanta, the Living ECK Master teaches
in words is only a fraction of what he teaches by his mere
presence, his personality, and his living example.*

The Shariyat-Ki-Sugmad,
Book Two[1]

*T*he great religious leaders of history have been
known as excellent teachers. They taught by
example and were good storytellers. The role of
teacher is central to the Mahanta's mission as well.

*The role of
teacher is
central to the
Mahanta's
mission as well.*

Several challenges confront the seeker when such
leaders pass on, leaving behind a body of teaching. First
of all, the interpretation of their works is left to their
followers. Divisions arise because of differing opinions
among them. The followers fragment into opposing
camps over who has the correct understanding.

Second, time marches on. Languages and cultures
change. But the original teachings remain frozen in
time, steadily receding into a past that is ever more
remote from the unfolding consciousness of later gen-
erations. No matter how pure the original truth, it can
never completely escape the confines of its origins.

Some followers, recognizing that their former
teacher may still be accessible inwardly, will rely on

inner guidance alone. Assuming such mystical types are really being led inwardly by their teacher, they will still filter what is received through their own limited viewpoint. Their sense of direction may be confused by a lack of experience and by spiritual immaturity. With no outer teacher to correct the rudder, they lose their bearings and steer off course.

These perennial issues highlight the need for a line of living teachers who can keep the truth alive. In Eckankar this line of teachers is found in the Order of the Varaigi ECK Masters. Their relation to the Mahanta will be explored later.

THE INNER AND OUTER TEACHER

As with many of the other aspects of the Mahanta, the Teacher has two sides to it: the inner and the outer. The inner teachings are given through dreams, contemplation, Soul Travel, and intuition. The outer teachings come through talks, books, monthly discourses, and other media. The two sides support each other, giving a well-rounded whole. The following incident illustrates how this can work.

The inner teachings are given through dreams, contemplation, Soul Travel, and intuition. The outer teachings come through talks, books, monthly discourses, and other media.

One night when I was in college, I stayed up late to cram for a final exam in an accounting course. Hunched over the textbook, I fought to keep my bleary eyes open by sipping coffee and tapping my pencil on the table. The subject of debits and credits and balances was too dry to hold my attention at such a late hour.

At one point I slipped briefly into a sort of dream, though I hadn't actually fallen asleep. It was a shift into one of the hidden dimensions. In that inner world I also hunched over a book. But the location was a temple of the inner worlds, and the book was a spiritual one.

This transition to the inner dimension had been so subtle and natural that I wasn't aware of it for a few moments. As soon as I did become aware, I shifted back to the textbook with a mild shock.

"What was that?" I mumbled to myself as I went back and reread the paragraph I was on. But on the second pass through the paragraph the shift to the inner worlds happened again, only more vividly. I became aware of reading a section in a holy book. The passage went something like this: "The Law of Cause and Effect is a perpetual balancing of accounts. Soul must learn to avoid being immersed in either the positive or the negative currents. Only by dwelling in perfect balance with the forces around and within Itself will Soul discover the narrow passage that leads to freedom."

There before me was the inner principle of accounting! This inner teaching lined up well with what I had read and studied in the outer works of Eckankar.

As the seeker progresses on the path, he finds the inner teacher using every opportunity to enliven him with new insights on life. The lessons come from all directions and greatly accelerate his spiritual growth. Harold Klemp describes this method of teaching in his book *The Eternal Dreamer:*

> Whenever something out of the ordinary comes up—a deviation from the humdrum, routine activities that account for most of your life—it is bringing you a spiritual lesson. It is up to you to take the trouble to try to recognize what this lesson could be. One way is just to say to the Inner Master, "I know you are trying to tell me something. Let me see what it is." Then become still; become the watcher.[2]

As the seeker progresses on the path, he finds the inner teacher using every opportunity to enliven him with new insights on life.

A SPIRITUAL SCHOOL SYSTEM

The Mahanta, the Living ECK Master and the ECK Masters who assist him have established a well-organized approach to the education of the seeker. This approach was one of the unique features of Eckankar that most attracted me in the beginning. It continues to impress me with each passing stage of my unfoldment.

The educational structure consists of a series of schools, called Temples of Golden Wisdom, which have been established on every plane or level of heaven. The key instructors in these schools are ECK Masters of great stature.

The seeker begins his studies in a class appropriate to his level of understanding. After due study, he passes from one school to the next on his gradual ascent up the spiritual ladder into the Kingdom of God. The classes are often attended while the body is asleep and Soul is awake in the higher planes.

The seeker who has taken a serious interest in the teachings of the Mahanta will be met by him in the Soul body.

The seeker who has taken a serious interest in the teachings of the Mahanta will be met by him in the Soul body. The Mahanta will escort the seeker to the appropriate temple.

Upon awakening, the experience may be noted in a variety of ways. Often there is no direct recall at all—just a sense of having been somewhere. Or there may be dream memories of having been in a college or school. The mind may translate this into dream scenes of an ordinary school familiar to the dreamer. On occasion there is a vivid remembrance of actually sitting in a Temple of Wisdom, listening to one of the venerable ECK Masters or the Mahanta give instruction.

But whether the experience is remembered or not,

the teaching is absorbed. It will emerge in the outer consciousness as new ideas, fresh insights, and a clearer understanding of how life works.

I believe these Temples of Golden Wisdom, and the instruction given in them, are the ancient prototypes of all the mystery schools, esoteric societies, and religious educational institutions found on earth.

THE SCRIPTURES OF THE ECK MASTERS

Of greatest interest to the seeker is the source of the teachings given in these temples. I speak of the Shariyat-Ki-Sugmad, the "Way of the Eternal."

A section of the scripture is kept in each temple. Many seekers, myself included, have had the experience of gazing into the pages of one of these books and felt the wisdom and love simply pour into them. One may read words, see holographic images, or have a direct experience with the Light and Sound of God. Anything is possible with these scriptures of the inner worlds.

Two volumes of the Shariyat have been translated by Paul Twitchell from these inner temples into books for the public to read. And though they are excellent writings, no physical book can begin to capture the firsthand experience of reading them in their natural setting in the Temples of Golden Wisdom. The various scriptures of the world are but pale reflections of these heavenly manuscripts.

Book One states, "The scriptures of the Shariyat-Ki-Sugmad can be spoken and written on the lower planes. But in the higher worlds it is only the heavenly white music."[3]

Temples of Golden Wisdom, and the instruction given in them, are the ancient prototypes of all the mystery schools, esoteric societies, and religious educational institutions found on earth.

A group of beings called the nine unknown gods of eternity watch over and guard these golden scripts. They are different than the ECK Masters who teach in the various temples. These nine are the keepers of the divine flame of wisdom.

A group of beings called the nine unknown gods of eternity watch over and guard these golden scripts.

A VISIT WITH YAUBL SACABI

One night during contemplation I tried to reach Zan to have a discussion with him about the Mahanta's role as the Teacher. But my usual method of visualizing him didn't work. After spending most of my half-hour contemplation getting nowhere, I decided to give up for the moment. Maybe the time wasn't right. Later, at bedtime, I drifted off to sleep with my mind filled with thoughts of the Teacher's role.

A few hours later I awoke on the inner planes. I was standing in a narrow hallway built of heavy stones. The ancient ceiling was arched, and the floor was worn smooth by the passage of countless footsteps. Bright sunbeams poured in through tall open windows spaced about every ten feet along the passageway. I stood before a window, admiring the spectacular view: a jagged wilderness of mountain peaks, glaciers, and deep ravines. A cool, pleasant breeze whispered its way in through the windows and along the corridor. The stones themselves seemed to emanate a contemplative serenity.

I recognized that I was in the famed spiritual city of Agam Des. This legendary site, hidden remotely in the Hindu Kush Mountains of central Asia, is the main headquarters of the ancient order of ECK Masters on earth. The only way to see or visit this city is through dream travel or Soul Travel, for it exists in the subtle realm of matter that is above the range of the physical senses.

The leader of this extraordinary city is the ECK Master Yaubl Sacabi. Thousands of years ago, among the early Myceneans, he served as the Mahanta, the Living ECK Master of his day. He laid the foundations for the first Greek mystery schools which helped shape the golden age of Greece. He possesses the secret of agelessness. This has enabled him to continue his mission on earth for millennia.

An elder of the ECK Brotherhood, Yaubl Sacabi is well known to followers of the Mahanta. He teaches at the Temple of Golden Wisdom located at Agam Des. All students of ECK will pass under his instruction there at some stage of their education. As I stood looking out the window, I became aware that I had an appointment with Yaubl Sacabi. I headed down the corridor, which connected the Temple with an auxiliary building.

Entering an outer hall of the Temple, I stood by some heavy blue curtains which provided a separation from the inner hall. I could hear Yaubl Sacabi speaking to a class. He was just closing the session. After a few moments the curtain parted, and he stepped out.

I hadn't been in his presence in the months since I'd been studying with Zan. It struck me immediately how much these two great Souls resembled each other. They could have been brothers.

Yaubl Sacabi greeted me with a smile, shaking my hand as he bowed slightly. "We have an appointment, I believe," he said. "Please come with me." I followed him back through the curtains and over to an altar upon which rested a large, open book. Light shone from its pages. It was a section of the Shariyat-Ki-Sugmad.

I followed him back through the curtains and over to an altar upon which rested a large, open book. Light shone from its pages.

Yaubl said, "I am informed of your research on the Mahanta. Tonight you wish to learn about the role of the Mahanta as the Teacher. Another name for him in this role is the Vi-Guru, or supreme teacher. What does this mean?

The ECK Master turned a few pages of the Shariyat. Putting his finger upon a passage, he read, "Only the Mahanta, the Living ECK Master has the authority to reveal the secret doctrine of ECK in its fullness. To each one of his followers these secrets are imparted in a unique way. One will receive it through the smile of a child. To another it will be given atop a spiritual mountain of the heavenly worlds. It matters not the method, for it will rarely be when or where the seeker expects it."

Yaubl stepped away from the altar and seated himself upon the thickly carpeted floor. I joined him. "When the Mahanta whispers the word of divine love into the seeker's ear, it is often trapped by the mind like a bird in a cage, where it withers and dies.

"This occurs because every seeker, in the beginning, confuses his knowledge of love with love itself. Knowing this, the Mahanta plants the seed of love directly in the heart. There he lets it grow, nourished by gentle sprinklings of the Light and Sound of God.

Eventually the patience of the master gardener is rewarded. The seed in the heart blossoms into a lovely flower, spreading its fragrance abroad.

"Meanwhile, the seeker is oblivious to what has happened. For years, often for lifetimes, he will continue to roam the world in his pursuit of the shoddy goods of the mind. Along the way he will trade away the jewels of love for trinkets, and never know the difference.

"Eventually the patience of the master gardener is rewarded. The seed in the heart blossoms into a lovely flower, spreading its fragrance abroad. The seeker comes to value God's love for Soul. Only then can the real teaching begin."

I said, "Though you are speaking in general terms, you have just narrated a section of my own journey. If I remember correctly, it is at this point that I came knocking at the door of the first Temple of Golden Wisdom. Yet I wonder how things look from your point of view. Let's say the Mahanta has just escorted a group of people to this Temple for the first time. As you look at your audience, what goes through your mind?"

Yaubl answered, "First, I see before me familiar faces. All seekers who find their way to the Temple have worked hard for it over many lifetimes. At one time or another, they have been students of an ECK Master. The record of their long journey is well known to me before they arrive. I am aware of the special needs and strengths, weaknesses and talents of all present.

All seekers who find their way to the Temple have worked hard for it over many lifetimes.

"Second, I see the special protective light and presence of the Mahanta around each of them. It would be impossible for anyone who is unworthy to slip in unnoticed.

"Third, I discern the unique purpose for which Divine Spirit has gathered the group together. The members are usually from diverse cultures and nations around the world. Yet a deep inner connection bonds them together. The class as a whole will serve as a vehicle for the working out of God's plan on earth. Each group that passes through the class carries the divine purpose a step forward. Each leaves some distinctive and valuable contribution to those who will follow.

"In this way, the teaching is ever changing and unfolding. Those who would become teachers in one of the Temples of Golden Wisdom must work hard to keep

abreast of this perpetual renewal. Too many seekers envision the master teachers as all-knowing beings who have nothing to gain by teaching except the satisfaction of helping their students. This is not how it works. The entire creation is alive and unfolding continuously, and the Temples of Wisdom are like buds at the center of this cosmic flower.

"These are things I see and consider as I glance over the class members. The Mahanta, as the Vi-Guru, has an overall mission given to him by God. Each teacher in each Temple of Wisdom has his role to play in supporting that mission. He will carefully consider how his instructions can be adjusted to fit neatly with the Mahanta's mission.

The Shariyat is a testimony of God's divine plan. On the higher planes each Living ECK Master's mission is foretold within its pages.

"The Shariyat is a testimony of God's divine plan. On the higher planes each Living ECK Master's mission is foretold within its pages. The sections of the Shariyat which are kept in each temple have a hidden and multilayered meaning. The teacher there can draw out the meaning which is appropriate to the particular time and mission he is pledged to support. So you see there is nothing static or repetitious in the teaching. The Shariyat is truly a living document."

I glanced toward the altar where the Shariyat rested in a soft glow of golden light.

Yaubl Sacabi continued, "From the point of view of the teacher, the class takes place completely above the worlds of space and time. Depending on the Temple of Wisdom, the students attending the class may be in the Physical, Astral, Causal, or Mental Planes. On all levels the essential instruction involves the passing of the secret teachings of the Mahanta to the seeker in the Soul body.

"As I talk to the class and as discussions take place among the members, the Mahanta is at work behind the scenes. There comes a point when the lesson has been imparted, and the class comes to a natural conclusion.

"Generally, the teaching takes place while the physical bodies of the students are sleeping. Not always. A few realize the ability of Soul to operate on several planes at once. The personality of the seeker can be busy at some task in the physical world, and simultaneously the same individual can be attending class in the Temple. But usually the personality is unaware of the inner activity."

Standing up, Yaubl Sacabi said, "This should give you a foundation for understanding the Vi-Guru. Contemplate on what I have given you and more light will come in." As I got up to go, I said, "Thank you so much for your gift of time. You have given me a lot to think about." He nodded and invited me to return another time.

THE KEEPER OF THE SECRET TEACHINGS

Implicit in Yaubl Sacabi's comments is the unique aspect of the Mahanta as the Teacher: He is the keeper of the secret teachings. Paul Twitchell writes: "The attainment of illuminated insight is the real goal of those training in the teachings of ECK. The word *teachings* is used often, but actually it is a revelation of certain secrets that also show the chela how to use and discover them for himself."[4]

And in *The Shariyat*, Book Two: "Some believe that the scriptures are the highest one can receive from the Mahanta, the Living ECK Master. But this is not true.

Implicit in Yaubl Sacabi's comments is the unique aspect of the Mahanta as the Teacher: He is the keeper of the secret teachings.

The secrets of spiritual practices, which can be known only by the Mahanta, cannot be reduced to writing, nor are they clearly mentioned in any scriptures. There are only vague references to them here and there. They serve only as a testimony in these writings. The complete secret can only be imparted by the Mahanta."[5]

In the early stages of unfoldment the seeker may move from teacher to teacher in an apparently haphazard way. Each teacher will serve him for a while. Then, when the student outgrows that set of teachings, he will move on. The transition may be driven by his own restlessness; or if his current teacher is an honest one, he himself will send the seeker on to another teacher for further lessons. This can be a trial-and-error method of searching for truth.

As mentioned above, the Order of Varaigi ECK Masters have solved this problem for their own students by providing a well-organized method of progress. There is continuity because all teaching is overseen by the Mahanta. Progression from one step to the next comes under his close care and supervision.

This method allows for the ECK teachings to accommodate a wide range of students, from the beginners up to Masters of various initiation levels.

So far we have gotten a glimpse of how the inner teacher works. What of the outer teacher? The Living ECK Master of the times is the voice for the outer instruction. Every year he speaks at major seminars around the world, as well as publishing a number of writings. His task is to put the timeless and eternal truths down into the common language of the day. As Harold Klemp writes:

> All too often we make it a great quest to under-

There is continuity because all teaching is overseen by the Mahanta. Progression from one step to the next comes under his close care and supervision.

stand God with our mind, when we should be putting more attention on issues that we can do something about. Many spiritual answers are found by attending to practical, down-to-earth matters.[6]

The Mahanta, the Living ECK Master avoids intellectual gymnastics. His talks tend toward parables and stories which show how ordinary people can deal with ordinary problems using the teachings of ECK. Hence the focus of many outer talks is on the spiritual aspects of living life here on earth, with all the fullness and richness we can muster. The lessons are about love, self-reliance, how to recognize the guidance of Spirit in our lives, and other practical matters. Through stories and personal examples, the Living ECK Master carries his teachings to the world.

The secret teachings are more often passed from the Teacher to the student, one-on-one, through inner communication.

This approach can be disconcerting to seekers who arrive at a seminar expecting to hear long-winded dissertations and esoteric mumbo jumbo. The secret teachings are more often passed from the Teacher to the student, one-on-one, through inner communication.

THE VIEW FROM THE MASTER'S CHAIR

I thought it would be of value to go behind the scenes and see how the Living ECK Master prepares for and gives a talk. From the perspective of the Master, the seeker can better appreciate the role of the Living ECK Master as Teacher. He will better understand how the inner teachings relate to the outer ones. For in a sense, all of the words of the Mahanta, the Living ECK Master are from the Shariyat. This is called the living Shariyat, the truth which is constantly renewed.

To help create this perspective, I went through the many writings of Harold Klemp, extracting statements he has given to an audience from time to time about this topic. To give a natural flow to this section of the chapter, I have imagined doing an interview with Harold, giving the quotations as though they are answers to an interviewer's questions.

Even though each Living ECK Master will accent the teaching method with his own personal style, I feel the following illustrates the essence of how the Inner and Outer faces of the Master work together to impart the teachings.

Harold, what is the first thing you do to prepare for a public talk?

"My preparation for a talk takes place over a period of months. I look for topics that fit the spiritual needs of the times. I try to find examples that demonstrate spiritual principles. I want to give you a clearer understanding of the psychology of Spirit. In some way, then, you can get an idea of how the ECK and the laws of life operate.

"The material that I accumulate for these seminar talks is not always what I would like to present. It is what is supposed to be given. When the ECK says, 'This is information the ECK initiates need to know,' I put it in a file folder and don't look at it again until I get to the seminar. I use the principle of trusting the ECK.[7]

"Two weeks before a seminar, the ECK, the Holy Spirit, sometimes makes known certain things It wants me to bring out in my talks. Then I wonder how to bring up a subject like that, to make it useful to others.

"As the time draws closer . . . I can hardly wait; I want to find out what's going on too!"[8]

And then a few days before the seminar you get out the material and put it all together?

> "I want to give you a clearer understanding of the psychology of Spirit. In some way, then, you can get an idea of how the ECK and the laws of life operate."

"I used to try to do it a few days ahead of time, and I'd have the talk memorized but it was old news to me.

"And if it was old news to me, it certainly would come across as old news to you. So I put myself on the cutting edge in giving these talks.

"I have certain things I want to mention to you, but until about an hour or two before I actually put the talk together, I often have no idea what the title will be. No idea. So it's always exciting for me too."[9]

That's cutting it pretty close! I've heard from time to time that the Living ECK Master will adjust his talk to fit the consciousness of his audience.

"As I travel to Eckankar seminars around the world, I notice in one location the talk will come out in a serious vein, as if the consciousness of that particular group needs it that way. At the next seminar it may be light and humorous. Sometimes it's dry, without any sparkle or shine. The talk comes out in whatever way that particular audience needs and understands."[10]

That's interesting—how it can even come out dry, if the audience needs it. I have in mind the approach of many speakers who always excite the audience with their dynamic styles and impressive stage presence.

"So much of what passes for truth is a leader playing to the emotions of his followers.

"Even if I wanted to wave my arms and say a lot of emotional things to get people all excited—so we would all have a good feeling, go home, and come back again soon—I wouldn't do it. It's my own contract with you and with Divine Spirit to try to give you things that are useful to you spiritually and also practically."[11]

So the time comes for you walk onstage and face the audience. What happens then?

"It's my own contract with you and with Divine Spirit to try to give you things that are useful to you spiritually and also practically."

"As I give these talks, sometimes I notice that individuals in the audience are not receptive. Everything went wrong as they tried to get to the ECK seminar—the car broke down, the flight was delayed. By the time they finally arrive, they're exhausted from all the problems.

"They may not realize it, but along the way they got a lot of experience. The Holy Spirit softened them up so that they would be a little more able to accept some of the things they heard about truth.

"Only when the hearts are opened can I begin to speak more direct truth."

"Often I start by telling stories because they open the heart. Only when the hearts are opened can I begin to speak more direct truth. If I sense the audience as a group is tightened in consciousness, I continue to talk in stories and parables.

"The New Testament is a fascinating testament that has been misunderstood by so many people. Christ once told his closest disciples that while he spoke in parables to the multitudes, to them he spoke the truth. He was drawing a distinction between the consciousness of his disciples and that of the general audiences."[12]

I have found that the value of stories and parables is they allow each person in the audience to read into them what suits their own level of consciousness. It's hard to argue over or debate about a story.

"There are times I must speak the truth as I see it from a spiritual perspective—when I see things are going very wrong spiritually.

"Up to this point the ECK membership has been used to me telling stories with hints of truth: nice, happy little stories or sometimes poignant stories of some kind or another. They relate this to truth. And as long as I never go out of character and as long as I continue in that vein, then everybody's happy.

"But sometimes I feel there is a spiritual crisis facing either the membership . . . or another crisis in either the United States or the world somewhere. If I mention this, people feel that I've suddenly gone out of character.

"They say, 'These are not the ECK teachings that I was used to. Harold is not teaching it right anymore.'

"People forget that real truth is often not pleasant. Yet the ECK has taken great pains to work with me from my childhood on, trying to make truth as pleasant as possible.

"Onstage, I'm operating and speaking as the Outer Master. But it's your relationship with the Inner Master that is all important.

"There are some things out here that I can never and would never tell you, simply because it would destroy your faith in yourself. Some things the Outer Master must let the individual experience for himself or herself.

Some things the Outer Master must let the individual experience for himself or herself.

"Why? Because this way the person can never come back to anyone, including the Living ECK Master, and say, 'I don't agree with you because you said something about me and I feel it was not true.' If what the Master is saying is true in regard to a shortcoming or a habit you have that is holding you back spiritually, then life will teach you better. And it usually does it through the university of hard knocks. This is how it works."[13]

It must be a real challenge when you are addressing an audience composed of people who cross a broad spectrum of levels of awareness and acceptance.

"I was talking to a group of people, trying to get some ideas across. Most of the people understood, but a few didn't. I worked at this from several different angles, using stories and metaphors, but I'd always hit this blank wall of unconsciousness. So I'd try one more time from another place. And I just couldn't get through—just to a few of the people—because they did not understand, although they believed they understood."[14]

How do you feel when you just can't get through to certain people like this?

"I feel I fail so often. I'll write a discourse and try to give some principle of truth to you as clearly as possible. Then some people will criticize me and say, 'This is too simple.' And other people will say, 'This is too complicated.' On the outside, I am trying to give a teaching to so many different levels of consciousness.

"But on the inside, as the inner teacher, I can custom fit the teachings to you, to give you the experiences that you need in your dreams.[15]

"Out here in the role of the spiritual leader of Eckankar, I am only able to hint at the spiritual truth that exists here and in the other worlds."

"This is often what happens with the Mahanta and you. Out here in the role of the spiritual leader of Eckankar, I am only able to hint at the spiritual truth that exists here and in the other worlds. Part of the fault is mine, because I simply don't have the words. An equal part of the fault lies with the listener, for not having the ability to understand what is being said.

"There is a link that can bridge the gap, and this is known as the inner communication of the Mahanta with the chela. When the Master speaks with the student through the inner communication, sometimes a mere phrase triggers all kinds of memories from the dream state. It can happen when you are sitting in the audience at an ECK seminar or in your own home listening to a tape of the talk. That certain phrase suddenly seems to convey a book of truth to you.

"These are the inner teachings, the secret teachings."[16]

So, when you speak to an audience through stories, you give the secret teachings indirectly?

"These stories will be easy to remember when you go home. Take one story at a time into contemplation, and put your attention lightly on it. This will help you to find its greater meaning.[17]

"The most difficult thing to overcome as I present the teachings of ECK is the misinformation people have about God, about the Holy Spirit, and about heaven. Everything I say is weighed and judged according to what the individual has been taught before.

"It is not my intention to leave someone without a point of reference; therefore I do not get into strong arguments designed to convince them of this or that. Instead, I present examples, images, and spiritual exercises. These may inspire people to try to reach the inner worlds themselves, where there can be no doubt.[18]

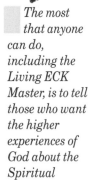

The most that anyone can do, including the Living ECK Master, is to tell those who want the higher experiences of God about the Spiritual Exercises of ECK.

"The most that anyone can do, including the Living ECK Master, is to tell those who want the higher experiences of God about the Spiritual Exercises of ECK. We can encourage them to try these for themselves. All that anyone can do for others, really, is to inspire them to reach out to God themselves."[19]

Just one more question, Harold. I have noticed sometimes that your talk is going along smoothly, when you seem to suddenly stop, and finish up.

"If I seem to end a talk rather abruptly, it's because suddenly I can see that the consciousness in the room is full. I keep going until it fills up, then anything else is like pouring more water into a full glass."[20]

Thank you, Harold. Any final comments?

"The message that I give on the outer is just a link. It is a way for you to connect with the teachings on the inner planes, so that one day you can have a stronger linkup with the ECK flow, the love of ECK.

"Love is the keystone of ECK: God is love, ECK is love, the Holy Spirit is love, and you are love. This is what you are trying to achieve in your realizations. As you rise to the higher states of consciousness, you become not a greater servant of God, but a greater channel of love to all life for the Divinity which is, in whatever way you see or know It.

The teachings of Eckankar are the teachings of love. And with love comes compassion, understanding, wisdom, and freedom.

"The teachings of Eckankar are the teachings of love. And with love comes compassion, understanding, wisdom, and freedom."[21]

CONCLUSION

I hope the above passage gives a sense of what it's like from the Master's chair. We live in an age which admires the mind and intellectual learning. The Master gives a nod to the needs of the mind. Yet the real teachings are given from the heart, to the heart. In their purest form they are the Light and Sound of God which opens the chamber of the heart to the Divine Guest who would come to dwell therein.

This concludes a brief introduction to that aspect of the Mahanta which is the Vi-Guru, the Master Teacher. He has before him the task of teaching us that we are Soul and that Soul exists because God loves It. Along the way he may teach us many other things.

11

The Light Giver

The Mahanta, the Living ECK Master is the Vi-Guru, the Light Giver who lights up the worlds of God when he inherits the spiritual mantle of the title.

The Shariyat-Ki-Sugmad,
Book Two[1]

A s the night flight lifted off from the airport near Los Angeles, I looked down at the beauty of the city's lights. The colorful display stretched to the horizon—a mixture of yellows, oranges, blues, and whites.

Many frequent fliers become habituated to such sights and hardly bother to look out the window. To me, the view made me feel like a space traveler looking down upon a checkered galaxy somewhere in deep space. I gazed at the city lights until the plane was far out over the ocean. Then I leaned back and closed my eyes to take a nap.

ZAN ON THE LIGHT GIVER

Zan appeared on the screen of my mind. He had a way of smiling with just his eyes. "It may seem to you that the steady expansion of light over the face of the world in the modern era coincides with the inner illumination of humanity," he said. "Countless individuals

Zan appeared on the screen of my mind. He had a way of smiling with just his eyes.

151

are awakening to the Light of God as never before in history. Do you remember your vision of this planetary spiritual light several years ago?"

The vision Zan was referring to had been the rarest expression of exquisite beauty I have ever beheld. One night I had found myself hovering in space several hundred miles above the earth. My imagination is sorely taxed to even recall the outline of the vision, so rich was its texture.

For those who have seen some of the computer-generated renditions of fractal geometry, a pale analogy can be contrived. These graphic images are unending spirals and whorls of intricate color, embellished with astonishing symmetry. They seem almost alive, expanding and swirling into an infinitude of microcosmic worlds.

Zan said, "What you glimpsed is the aura of humanity. A glance at this planetary light field tells the story of the growing illumination of the human race."

Now try to imagine such patterns of light in motion, in multiple dimensions, on a scale the size of the planet. Envision them surrounding the earth like an aura, dancing to some blissful cosmic rhythm as they radiate into space.

Finally, listen for a delicate music that sends exquisite shivers through Soul, and feel the aesthetic epiphany that overwhelms the eye as these brilliant wisps of light pass through you on their way into space.

I answered Zan inwardly, saying, "Do I remember? Who could hold such a vision in human memory? But yes, I do carry glimpses of it with me."

Zan said, "What you glimpsed is the aura of humanity. A glance at this planetary light field tells the story of the growing illumination of the human race.

"The Mahanta, in his role as the Light Giver, nurtures the great flame of divine love. On the Rosetta stone of God, the glyph for this aspect of the Mahanta's mission shows a man carrying a torch held high.

"This lonely planet has cried into the cold dark of space for more light, more warmth. Yet the Light Giver has ever been in our midst, reminding us to look within for the holy fire of God. Today the earth is beginning to shine, because more people are finding their way to the Mahanta, the Living ECK Master who lights the divine love in their hearts and initiates them into the Light and Sound of God. Once the initiate is connected with this holy current of Divine Spirit, he becomes a light unto others."

My reverie was interrupted when a flight attendant came down the aisle with refreshments. When I closed my eyes again, the inner screen was blank. Zan had used the distraction to make a graceful exit. I thought about his final statement of how the ECK initiate becomes a light to others.

Harold Klemp has said he can always pick ECK initiates out of a crowd—they have their spiritual lights on. "The spiritual Light of ECK comes through them very strongly,"[2] he says.

THE LOFTY VIEW

With the theme of the Light Giver we enter into the deeper mysteries of the Mahanta. So, before discussing the practical benefits of this aspect for the seeker, I will touch on these mysteries from a lofty viewpoint. In the following passage, the scriptures of Eckankar summarize the key point Zan was giving to me:

With the theme of the Light Giver we enter into the deeper mysteries of the Mahanta.

> The Living ECK Master always brings Light and Love into the world so that all men shall profit by them. Not just his own followers, but the world

of itself. Each of those who follow him should be caught up in the fire of his love. This love begins in each like a tiny flame then begins to consume them until they love all because it is life, and life is God.[3]

Some of the great spiritual leaders of past eras were called light bearers. Buddha has been called the Light of Asia, and Christ, the Light of the World. The Mahanta too carries such titles. In the writings of Eckankar he is called the Light of the Worlds, or the Light of the Universes. These are more than poetic phrases. They describe a real and potent source of cosmic illumination.

The scriptures of Eckankar also speak of the ECK, the Holy Spirit:

> It appears to be simply a great, radiant sheet of blazing light, too great for the human sight, stretching from infinity to infinity, without a beginning, without an ending. It sometimes appears like a great, calm, brooding sea, reflecting a thousand times the light of a brilliant sun. This is the consciousness of the Mahanta, the Living ECK Master.[4]

This vast ocean of heavenly brilliance is the origin of the light which the Mahanta gives to Soul. It comes from the heart of God, sometimes called the Ocean of Love and Mercy.

This vast ocean of heavenly brilliance is the origin of the light which the Mahanta gives to Soul. It comes from the heart of God, sometimes called the Ocean of Love and Mercy. Harold Klemp writes of this role of the Master in his book *The Secret Teachings:*

> The Living ECK Master is called the Light Giver. Some of you have actually seen the Inner Master as a being clothed in light. By his presence, this inner being illuminates Soul and makes a direct linkup with the Audible Life Stream, the Voice of God, which can be heard as Sound and

seen as Light. This is the only way that the true Voice of God can be heard. It doesn't come in an audible manner, such as the way you are hearing me speak now, but in Light and Sound. These are two aspects of God which can lift Soul out of the material worlds, into the high states of conscious-ness here and now, in this lifetime.[5]

How does the Light Giver pass his gift to the seeker? There are three primary ways, and each brings in its wake a sacred moment in Soul's journey home. The first way is through what is called Darshan, an inner or outer meeting with the Mahanta, the Living ECK Master. The second is through the ECK Initiation. The third is through what are sometimes called gift-waves. Let us explore each of these three in more detail and see how they give the seeker a boost in his spiritual unfoldment.

How does the Light Giver pass his gift to the seeker? There are three primary ways, and each brings in its wake a sacred moment in Soul's journey home.

THE DARSHAN

The Darshan is that sacred moment when the Mahanta, the Living ECK Master and the seeker meet in mutual recognition. There are two parts of the Darshan. First, meeting with the Master outwardly and being recognized by him. Second, meeting with him inwardly and traveling with him. This seeing and being seen by him brings the gift of light, or illumination. As Harold Klemp says of the Darshan, "It enlivens Soul, and this is the function of the Light Giver: to give Soul a few more extra watts."[6]

The inner meeting usually comes first, though it is not often remembered. When it is, the memory can be unforgettable. One afternoon many years ago, one of my relatives came to my house for a visit. When she walked into my living room, she was startled by a picture of the Living ECK Master upon the wall. "Who is that man? I dreamed about him a few nights ago!" she exclaimed, a little unsettled.

"He is the Living ECK Master, the spiritual leader of Eckankar," I explained. "Would you like to tell me about your dream?"

"Well," she began, "I dreamed I was a cowboy working on a cattle drive in the old West. We had gathered around the campfire for the evening to drink coffee and swap stories before bedding down for the night. I knew all the cowhands and was surprised to notice a stranger sitting across from me. When my eyes met his, I felt deep waves of divine love just pouring into me from his gaze. I'll never forget the light and love in those eyes."

My relative had experienced the inner Darshan. The dream setting in the old West suggests this may have been woven in with a past-life recall.

In another example, a coworker of mine met the Light Giver under very unusual circumstances. When working with a forest-service crew one summer in my youth, I became friends with this man, whom I'll call John.

Our lunch breaks were like pleasant picnics high in the Cascade Mountains of Oregon. We would sit in the shade of tall fir trees. While we ate our sandwiches, we would swap stories or discuss the meaning of life. I didn't mention my affiliation with Eckankar or talk much about it directly. I thought the subject would arise in a natural way if it needed to.

One day I casually mentioned something about the Blue Light or the Blue Star of the Mahanta, which sometimes appears to people in special moments. John stopped chewing and gave me an odd look.

One day I casually mentioned something about the Blue Light or the Blue Star of the Mahanta, which sometimes appears to people in special moments. John stopped chewing and gave me an odd look.

"Maybe you could explain an experience I had," he said. "Several years ago my relatives pushed me into going to church with them. I didn't really want to, but they insisted. Having got me there, they started pushing me to get baptized. Again I gave in, and the date was set for a certain Sunday. That day I went up to the front of the congregation and knelt before the minister for the ceremony.

"While he began reading something from the Bible, I suddenly noticed a beautiful blue globe of light just off to one side. It radiated a warm and comforting presence. I thought, *Hey! Maybe there's something to this ritual after all.* The blue light stayed for a minute or so then was gone. I asked the minister about it later. To my surprise and disappointment, he didn't have a clue what I was talking about.

"A few days later, I was out in the woods doing a survey. The sun was just coming up over the horizon. I accidentally turned the surveyor's scope directly into the sun. I don't know what happened, but it's as if I was hit by a bolt of intense light so powerful it knocked me flat on my back. When I tried to get up, I couldn't see. I was totally blind.

"I was taken to the best medical specialists, but none of them could explain what happened, or find anything wrong with my eyes. Then one night I had a strange dream. I guess it was an out-of-body experience.

"I was standing on a cloud above the earth. Two men in business suits approached me, as if walking on clouds were as natural to them as strolling down a city street. The taller one said, 'You will be blind for six months. This is a karmic condition you have to endure

The blue light stayed for a minute or so then was gone. I asked the minister about it later. To my surprise and disappointment, he didn't have a clue what I was talking about.

because of a past life when you begged for the Light of God then refused It when It was offered. You will recover full use of your eyes after that time, but will need to wear strong prescription eyeglasses. Sometimes people want the Light of God before they are ready, and when It breaks through, It is too much for them. I have protected you as much as I could, but you must take responsibility for your actions.'

"I asked them, 'Are you guys spiritual masters or something?' The shorter one said yes. I said, 'But masters don't go around in business suits.' They both laughed, and the shorter one said, 'Yes, and only angels walk on clouds.'

"Six months later, almost to the day, I suddenly recovered my eyesight. So I ask you, what was this all about, and what was the tie-in to the blue light?"

I pulled out my wallet and showed John a picture of the Living ECK Master. "Is this one of the men you saw?" John looked astonished. "Yes! That's the taller one!"

I pulled out my wallet and showed John a picture of the Living ECK Master. "Is this one of the men you saw?" John looked astonished. "Yes! That's the taller one!" I explained to him how the presence of the Mahanta often comes in the form of a blue light. We discussed the topic until I had answered John's questions as best I could.

It would have been a nice ending to this story to report that John became an ardent follower of the Mahanta. But he did not. He had a strong attraction to the teachings of the Eastern religions and couldn't accept that real Masters would look and dress like modern businessmen. But that is fine. He received as much help from the Light Giver as he wanted at the time.

This story illustrates a point which Harold Klemp once addressed in a talk:

Sometimes an individual is misled into putting his hand on the curtain that separates this world from the mysteries of the other worlds and pulling it back all at once. We must remember that revelation comes through seeing the Light of God. When the curtain is pulled back all at once, the Light comes full force. It comes too brightly, too suddenly, too soon. And that can cause the individual to become imbalanced.

One is rarely told this by the teachers of the orthodox religions. They don't know about it. When they speak of seeing the Light of God, they mean it figuratively, in the sense that somehow you will become a better person. They do not recognize that when truth comes, there is an actual, visible Light. It acts as the heating element in the crucible in which Soul is tempered.[7]

The Light Giver knows not only when to give the Light, but also when to hold It back until a seeker is prepared to handle It.

The Light Giver knows not only when to give the Light, but also when to hold It back until a seeker is prepared to handle It. It's easy to glamorize the kind of experience like that of Paul in the Bible who was temporarily blinded by the light on the road to Damascus. But when it happens to us, it can be very profound, affecting our physical health and mental stability.

The outer Darshan, or meeting with the Living ECK Master in the physical world, was more common when he had fewer followers. Today relatively few have the opportunity to meet him in person. But when it is possible, the gift of the Darshan is given.

The experience can be a very moving one, lifting the seeker spiritually and deeply stirring his heart. Many have experienced the gift of the Light Giver when sitting in a large audience at which the Master is speaking.

Yet the radiant form of the Mahanta is ever at the door of each seeker's inner universe, standing ready to give him the inner Darshan, as he gave it to my relative in the dream.

INITIATION

A second way the Light Giver passes his gift to the seeker is through initiation. This is of utmost importance, and one of the greatest benefits given to all who look to the Mahanta. *The Shariyat-Ki-Sugmad,* Book Two, says, "The initiation into Eckankar is the true way, and the radiant form of the Mahanta, the Vi-Guru, the Light Giver, lights up every Soul who enters into it."[8]

As with the Darshan, the initiations of ECK have both an inner and outer part. During the ECK initiation, the Mahanta passes on to the initiate a greater portion of the Light and Sound of God.

During the ECK initiation, the Mahanta passes on to the initiate a greater portion of the Light and Sound of God.

This increase in the spiritual flow can have manifold effects. How they are felt or noticed will vary with each individual. Some people will hardly feel different, while others will notice an immediate surge of love and energy, or a wonderful lightness.

Initiations may be preceded or followed by major changes in the initiate's life, as he adapts to a newer and broader view of things. These changes can affect relationships, career, eating habits, thought patterns— almost any part of one's life. What has happened inwardly, in addition to the increased flow of Spirit, is a move upward into a higher plane.

There are twelve major initiations in Eckankar on the way to Mastership, each corresponding to one of the twelve planes of God. As we adapt to the next plane corresponding to our initiation, there is much to learn. Each plane has its unique set of laws, new realms to explore, new areas of service, new beings to meet and learn from, and new responsibilities to master. The nature of each of these initiations is discussed in the writings of Eckankar.

Each initiation is earned. The candidate must pass a series of spiritual tests in the school of life through which he demonstrates his readiness to take the next step. These tests are not designed or administered by any person but come in the form of challenges and opportunities put in our path by Spirit Itself.

The following passages from a talk by the Living ECK Master, Harold Klemp, describe the initiation process:

Each initiation is earned. The candidate must pass a series of spiritual tests in the school of life through which he demonstrates his readiness to take the next step.

> What happens during the initiation is part of the secret practices of ECK. It is only for the individual who has earned it. But to explain briefly, the Mahanta meets with Soul on the inner planes. He comes to the individual in the Light body, a sparkling body of light which is also called the Nuri Sarup. The connection is made. Often the Master will put his arm around the individual's shoulder, or shake hands, or something of this nature. Generally this meeting takes place alongside a river. . . .

> When Soul comes out of the initiation, the individual may or may not have a conscious awareness of what transpired on the inner planes. Nevertheless, the Light and Sound of God has put a greater light to Soul than ever before.

> This is why the Mahanta is called the Light Giver. It is not an empty title at all. Soul is given

a greater amount of the Light and Sound of the Holy Spirit. . . .

On some occasions during the ECK initiation, the Light and Sound comes through so strongly, bringing a feeling of such happiness, that the individual has to just sit and let it balance out for about five minutes. These are the fortunate ones.

Even if you have no awareness of what is occurring on the inner planes, the initiation is still valid. The truth that you need is instilled in your heart. It will now come out as an expression in your daily life.[9]

Some seekers clamor to become initiates of anyone who claims to be a guru or master. They want the ritual as soon as possible, giving little thought to the needed preparation or what the initiation actually entails. They think of obtaining mystical experiences, supernormal abilities, recognition, and other rewards. But they hardly stop to consider that the real purpose of any true initiation is to train Soul to become a Co-worker with God.

Soul will not be given the true initiation by the Mahanta until certain inner preparations are complete.

Soul will not be given the true initiation by the Mahanta until certain inner preparations are complete. Just as those admitted for higher academic education must have the necessary qualifications, so too must the candidate for initiation.

The keynote is service, with the scope and quality of service expanding with each step toward mastership. In the beginning, the word *service* rings in the aspirant's ears as self-sacrifice, and who wants that?

In time the initiate discovers that service is a joy for Soul, a natural and spontaneous outpouring of love for all life. And the initiate even discovers that service is at its best when he is doing what he loves to do. He finds it was his identification with the ego which made it all seem like sacrifice. But each initiation chips away at the crust of the ego, until the full light of Soul shines through.

The Light Giver helps us combine and blend the physical and spiritual. By gently dissolving the barriers between the inner and outer parts of ourselves over time, he helps us develop a much clearer understanding of how life works. Hidden causes become manifest. The heavenly worlds beyond are no longer the "worlds beyond," and sleep is no longer the great amnesia. Very gradually the circle of our awareness expands and clarifies, as curtain after curtain is pulled back. The scriptures of Eckankar describe this unfoldment:

The Light Giver helps us combine and blend the physical and spiritual.

> Proper training under the direction of the Mahanta after initiation will work wonders, and the seemingly impossible becomes possible. The finer senses become active and aware by right use, as directed by the Mahanta. At first the ECK Sound Current is weak, often imperceptible, but variable. However, by continual training, a transformation takes place and the Music of the Spheres is heard quite distinctly. Its divine and delectable Sound is of a sweetness and serenity unsurpassed by any.
>
> This Music draws Soul upward by Its strong power, like a powerful magnet. It purifies all which Soul picked up as dross during Its sojourn on earth.[10]

GIFT-WAVES

This leads directly into a third method by which the Light Giver passes the light of God to Soul. Paul Twitchell calls these gift-waves, a phrase which aptly evokes how the process works in the seeker's life. These stimulating waves of love can be given at the time of initiation, or between initiations as needed. They are waves of spiritual energy sent forth telepathically from the Mahanta to stimulate spiritual development and boost the aspirant seeking enlightenment.

Of the many blessings bestowed by the Mahanta, I have found the gift-waves to be the most precious. For me they can come at any time: during contemplation, while taking a walk, while consoling a friend, or even while doing a task at work. I find their approach is signaled by little ripples of lightness and love. These are followed by a vivid awareness of the loving presence of the Mahanta, the Inner Master. Very quickly the ripples build into large, rolling waves of Light and Sound.

Rebazar says to Paul, "I have given you the cosmic Light. What do you see?" Paul answers, "Waves of Light coming in like breakers on a beach. I feel them so strongly!"

I can't describe the feeling better than Paul Twitchell who described how he felt when he was being given these waves as an initiate in training under the ECK Master Rebazar Tarzs. Rebazar says to Paul, "I have given you the cosmic Light. What do you see?"

Paul answers, "Waves of Light coming in like breakers on a beach. I feel them so strongly!"[11]

Recently my father, who was seventy-eight and in very poor health, entered the hospital for the last time. He lay on his deathbed for several days and couldn't seem to let go. He had been an atheist all his life. Perhaps he feared the nothingness he thought awaited him. I visited him in the hospital one night. He was sitting up in bed, oblivious to his physical surroundings, yet reaching into the air as if to grasp the hand of some beckoning but invisible presence.

I leaned down and whispered in his ear, "Only light and love await you on the other side. There is nothing to fear." At that moment the most deeply loving gift-waves began rolling in from the Mahanta, pouring over me and my father. Joy, comfort, and a tangible brightness filled the room. The waves continued for about fifteen minutes, then subsided. My father peacefully passed on a few hours later.

Harold Klemp wrote the following passage about these gifts of love:

> The changeover from ego to Soul, from fear to love, is done gradually, in such a way that an initiate can remain in control of himself. The Mahanta passes to him a gift of love, which is a burst of spiritual energy. This speeds up the chela's unfoldment. He is able to accept more of the Light and Sound, and the truth contained in them. In this, he becomes a brighter light, bearing the message of the Living Word within him, to all who listen.[12]

The Mahanta, the Living ECK Master bestows the gift of the Light and Sound of God. Through the Darshan, through the initiation, and through gift-waves he lights up the hearts of all who come to him. This is the eternal mission of the Light Giver. He tips the cosmic bowl of heaven, pouring down the living waters from the Ocean of Love and Mercy, filling the cups of the thirsty until they overflow.

The Mahanta, the Living ECK Master bestows the gift of the Light and Sound of God.

12

The Wind of Change

The Mahanta appears again in this world to gather up Souls to return to the true heavenly home. Wherever he goes and whatever he does, the great ECK power clears the way like the whirling winds of a storm.

The Shariyat-Ki-Sugmad,
Book One[1]

O n the Rosetta stone of God the glyph for the Mahanta as Purifier, the Wind from Heaven or Wind of Change, is a small tree bent by the wind, being stripped of its last clinging leaves. It signifies the purifying element of Divine Spirit, which has the purpose of clearing away all unnecessary obstacles along the spiritual path.

The phrase *wind of change* describes Divine Spirit. In the Bible Jesus tells his disciples, "The wind blows where it wills, and you hear the sound of it, but you do not know whence it comes or whither it goes; so it is with every one who is born of the Spirit."[2]

Paul Twitchell wrote of his encounter with this quality of the Holy Spirit in his book *The Tiger's Fang.* He had paused for a rest from his journey through one of the heavenly worlds. He and his guide, the ECK Master Rebazar Tarzs, were sitting on the side of a

The phrase wind of change describes Divine Spirit.

rocky trail near an escarpment that stretched across the black, frozen wilderness of a vast desert. Across it blew a wind that made a strange humming sound.

Soon the two travelers were joined by an ECK Master from ancient Persia, named Shamus-i-Tabriz. He looked at Paul and said, "Do you hear it?" Paul sat motionless, listening to the wind. "Yes," he answered, "I hear the sound of the winds!"

Shamus replied, "There is no wind, young one. That is Akash Bani, the Voice of God!"[3]

THE MAHANTA AS AN AGENT OF CHANGE

The Mahanta is a powerful agent of spiritual change, both in the life of the seeker and in the world at large.

The Mahanta is a powerful agent of spiritual change, both in the life of the seeker and in the world at large. Ironically, he does not seek to bring change or reforms. Yet wherever he goes, he is the vehicle of divine Spirit. My first book, *The Dream Weaver Chronicles,* is an in-depth study of this aspect.

During the years 1989–90, Eckankar built a Temple of Golden Wisdom near Minneapolis, Minnesota. This was an important event in the spiritual history of mankind. It drew a tremendous inflow of spiritual energy. I saw an uncanny, even a precise, correlation between the key events of the Temple's construction and the political and social upheavals that circled the globe at the time. I tried to show how the strong spiritual inflow of Light and Sound swept over the world to cleanse, purify, and uplift mankind.

A hint of what was to come that year was given to me one night on the inner planes in early summer of 1989. In the dream state I was walking through a park on a pleasant and sunny afternoon, with a notebook in hand. Finding a vacant bench, I sat down and pulled out a pen. My intent was to begin a book about the Mahanta's influence in the modern world.

I started writing and was soon oblivious to my surroundings. I didn't notice that very quickly a bank of clouds moved in and a breeze kicked up. Soon the breeze was gusting.

I looked up, startled that the weather had turned so quickly. Peering up at the sky, I saw the clouds starting to boil and turn dark. A sudden powerful blast of wind almost tore my notebook from my hands. A moment later I was being pelted by huge raindrops.

Clutching the notebook to my chest, I jumped up and ran for cover as the full fury of the storm began to hit. Spotting a public building near the park, I dashed inside and hurriedly closed the door behind me.

Turning around I bumped into a certain ECK Master who is not known to the public. He chuckled and said, "Things can get stirred up when you align yourself with the Mahanta's mission. By sitting down to write about it, you innocently tapped into the Wind from Heaven, unleashing a reaction from the negative forces."

Things can get stirred up when you align yourself with the Mahanta's mission.

Later that year Harold Klemp, the Mahanta, the Living ECK Master published an autobiography titled *Child in the Wilderness*. In it he reported a similar account, only his was an *outer* experience—it happened in the very physical world of Las Vegas, Nevada. He had sat down to write about his experience of touching the face of God during his quest for Mastership. He writes:

> The act of beginning to write this story had unleashed a grand wave of positive energy. The mere retelling of a God-Conscious experience has a tremendous impact upon the spiritual community

of the world. It causes the very ethers of creation to tremble.

As I had been pounding out the account on my typewriter, a great spiritual energy was released that ran head-on against the normal, everyday vibrations of Las Vegas. This caused a terrible collision between the ECK and Kal forces. The positive and negative energies. Like a cold front overtaking hot weather, the inner clash of positive and negative forces caused an outer storm to manifest.

Overwhelmed by the splendor of the raging storm, and unable to continue typing anyway, I made a dash for my car. Slowly I drove along residential streets, watching trees bow before the gale.[4]

THE STORMY TRIALS

Soul has forgotten Its true home is in the heavenly worlds. So It seeks peace on earth. It forgets that God sent Soul into these stormy worlds of karma in order to learn to love and to serve.

This clashing of forces can be frightening to the human consciousness. Soul has forgotten Its true home is in the heavenly worlds. So It seeks peace on earth. It forgets that God sent Soul into these stormy worlds of karma in order to learn to love and to serve. The suffering comes from the selfishness in ourselves and in others. If all the people on earth became sufficiently developed to have mastered love, we would have learned the lessons for which we were sent here.

It is, of course, noble to bring as much grace and love into one's life as possible. Gentleness and kindness are virtues extolled by the ECK Masters. They are the attributes of an awakened Soul. But the lower worlds are under the Law of Cause and Effect. They are the training ground, the school of life. If it were God's will to establish peace and comfort here, it would be done in the wink of an eye. But Soul's destiny is spiritual liberation, not physical comfort and worldly security. The trials of the body are the gifts of the Spirit.

There is an upbeat side to this subject. After the storm has passed, there remains a spiritual freshness in the air. The choking dust has been washed away, and all things are renewed. Much old karma is swept away, replaced with the healing influence of the ECK. This leaves room for greater wisdom, love, and happiness in our lives.

THE SWORD AND THE SHIELD

This whole aspect of the Mahanta as Purifier, or the Wind of Change, is very closely tied to his mission as the Guardian. Remember that the Guardian possesses the Shield of Silver Light. It is used to protect and defend those who put their trust in the Mahanta. Related to the shield of the Guardian is the sword of the Sugmad. While the shield protects, the sword cuts a wide swath through the obstacles which stand in the seeker's way. Says *The Shariyat:*

> The Sugmad sends Its messengers into this world as warriors. None come as doves. They are the eagles who must seek food for the young. They are the shepherds who keep the wolves away from the flock.
>
> The Adepts for the ECK are the swordsmen of the Sugmad. Whenever they travel, the pace of karma is quickened.[5]

Harold Klemp expands on this point in one of his books. He writes, "I'd like to be able to say that there

Remember that the Guardian possesses the Shield of Silver Light. It is used to protect and defend those who put their trust in the Mahanta.

will be peace on earth and that it is my mission to bring peace, but it's not, nor was it Jesus' or any other past teacher's mission. The teachers of the past even mentioned that they hadn't come to bring peace, but to set one against another. They didn't mean they would directly be the cause of war. They meant that when the spiritual consciousness goes among mankind, it stirs up the passions of men as they interact, causing them to go to war and fight with each other. This process is what burns off the gross nature of the human condition so that Soul can become a purified entity.[6]

SECRETS OF THE SWORD OF GOD

One evening Zan came to me in contemplation and gave me further insight on the meaning of the Sword of the Sugmad. He said, "The sword is the Sugmad's Word. The handle, the hilt, and the blade are its three key parts, and each has an esoteric significance.

The sword is the Sugmad's Word. The handle, the hilt, and the blade are its three key parts, and each has an esoteric significance.

"You can think of the two edges of the blade as the positive and negative forces in the lower worlds, while the central shaft is the neutral force of the ECK. The blade's point is the focus where all three forces are concentrated.

"The hilt is the dividing line between the lower and higher planes of God. It is where the three forces merge into one, becoming the handle.

"The handle can be gripped and the sword wielded only by one who has reached the state of detachment from all personal motives and urges to power. Such are the Adepts of the ECK."

It's human nature to go the way of power when people get in the way of our plans. It takes much more patience, effort, and selflessness to follow the path of love, to seek a harmonious solution. It also creates more growth and depth of character. Harold Klemp writes: "There is a time to pull the sword from the sheath and wield it in battle, in self-defense or for the protection of the weak and helpless. There is also a time to return the sword to the sheath and try again to work things out harmoniously. These situations go on every day, all the time."[7]

THE CALL OF SOUL

We live in exciting times. The Light and Sound of God, Divine Spirit, is pouring in, washing over the planet in wave after wave, stimulating everyone and everything upon it, clashing with the old and outworn habits that hold humanity back. One evening after contemplating upon this phenomena, I had the following insight and understanding.

A wind from heaven is blowing over the earth. Silent to the ears, its passing is heard by the heart.

Pausing at the threshold of our own life's mystery, it beckons us. Then it moves on, leaving behind in us a yearning to rise and follow. The touch of this wind may be as light as a whisper in a dream, forgotten in the morning. Or it may surge into a storm, a roaring wind of change which sweeps away our old secure foundations.

If one is vigilant and listens closely, he can hear a voice in the wind. It is the call of Soul. When the tame domestic swan hears his wild kin migrating high overhead, he lifts his breast and beats his wings. The spark that has lain dormant inside is fanned, and flames into a bright spiritual desire.

The wind moves on to touch others, and we are left at a turning point in our life. Outwardly, we may be

We live in exciting times. The Light and Sound of God, Divine Spirit, is pouring in, washing over the planet in wave after wave, stimulating everyone and everything upon it, clashing with the old and outworn habits that hold humanity back.

unaware of the significance of the moment. It may come in a quiet way: a chance encounter with a curious stranger, a book borrowed from a friend, a pleasant trip abroad. For others it could come as a rite of passage: the death of a loved one, the trauma of a serious illness, marriage or divorce, a new job. Often it is a spontaneous and unexpected mystical experience, like a prophetic dream or an out-of-body experience.

However the call of Soul enters into our waking consciousness, it begins to break up the routine habits and complacent assumptions of our lives. It instills a restless desire to penetrate more deeply into the mystery of life.

PURIFYING OF SOUL

Often the first indication that the seeker is close to discovering the Mahanta is the wind of change blowing through his life.

Often the first indication that the seeker is close to discovering the Mahanta is the wind of change blowing through his life. And many a seeker may encounter major changes when he invites the Mahanta into his world. This is not inevitable, but it can happen.

What is the cause of this? The same principle that is working on the world stage applies to the individual. The Holy Spirit begins to drill into the old habits and attitudes that have been imprisoning us spiritually.

Harold Klemp writes, "When this purifying of Soul begins, we may find a couple of things happening in our outer life: Things go a little bit on the fast side, and for a while we really have to step along. Spirit will open up new avenues in our life. And if we go along with them, things will go smoothly. . . . There don't have to be hard times. Things will straighten out as quickly as we can pick up the new direction that Divine Spirit is giving us."[8]

He also notes, "Burning off karma means revising the old habit patterns that brought about the conditions that made us unhappy, that held us back from the joy and spaciousness and fulfillment we are looking for in life."[9]

ACCELERATED LEARNING

Before one invites the Mahanta into his life, karma can take a leisurely pace. For example, a burst of anger at someone may not come back around for fifteen or twenty years. By the time it does, the connection between cause and effect is lost. This slows the learning process and weakens our incentive to improve.

When the Mahanta appears, the Wind of Change, the ECK, starts cleaning out our closets very quickly. An angry outburst will likely bounce right back to us within a few hours or less. Though the phrase *instant karma* is tossed around these days in humor, it becomes real to the followers of ECK.

I was given a vivid lesson in this many years ago, shortly after starting on the path of Eckankar. At the time I was playing in a basketball league. The skill level of the players varied widely. In one game I was being guarded by an inexperienced young player. For fun, I decided to play a prank on him. The next time I got the ball, I planned to move quickly toward the basket, dribble the ball between his legs, and—before he knew what had happened—make a basket. This would make me look good at his expense.

A few minutes later the opportunity came. I made my move. But it didn't go as planned. I stumbled and bounced the ball off my foot right into his hands. As I tried to regain my balance, he quickly bounced the ball

When the Mahanta appears, the Wind of Change, the ECK, starts cleaning out our closets very quickly. An angry outburst will likely bounce right back to us within a few hours or less.

between my legs, ran down court, and made a basket. I looked foolish, and the spectators roared with laughter.

This was instant karma. In a sense, it was even faster than instant, because the effect did not come after I pulled the prank. The mere intent to do it brought the reaction. But it also brought instant learning. I got to feel right away what the other player would have felt had my little mischief worked on him. And it wasn't at all pleasant. Since that incident many years ago, I have seen these fast-acting lessons at work countless times in my daily life and in the lives of others on the path of ECK.

THE ECKANKAR SEMINAR EFFECT

One of the most fascinating and illustrative modern-day studies of the Mahanta as Purifier, or the Wind of Change, is what I call the Eckankar seminar effect. Several times a year Eckankar organizes major seminars around the world. Thousands of people come to these seminars for a few days of spiritual sharing, learning, and growth, and to hear the Mahanta, the Living ECK Master speak.

The alert observer will usually see the effects the Wind of Change brings to the area where these seminars are held. Many times the effect is in the form of weather extremes which occur just before, during, or just after the seminar. Again, this is not instigated by the Mahanta. It is the inevitable clashing of forces as the negative energies resist the spiritual vortex created by the seminar.

For example, in November 1982 a regional seminar was held in Hawaii. Harold Klemp noted, "As soon as

One of the most fascinating and illustrative modern-day studies of the Mahanta as Purifier, or the Wind of Change, is what I call the Eckankar seminar effect.

we left, a hurricane blew in. One of the ECKists and his wife had stayed to vacation in the islands, but for nine days straight there was no sun."[10]

Just before a seminar in Sydney, Australia, the city got hit with nine inches of rain in a twenty-four-hour period. The weathermen couldn't believe it. To make its point, the stormed backed off, then hit the city two more times.

Sometimes the weather extremes can be pleasant. In 1986 Eckankar moved its headquarters from California to Minnesota. The winter that year was one of the mildest Minnesota winters in over a century. Some natives called it the winter that wasn't.

Once the new headquarters were established, the Minneapolis area began to feel the effects of the increased flow of Spirit through the area whenever a major seminar was in progress. During a talk in April 1992, Harold Klemp said, "We had snow so early in Minneapolis this winter that even the sparrows left. A big snowfall came right after the ECK Worldwide Seminar [in October], and another came in November after the South Pacific Seminar."[11]

Natural elements like the weather seem to reflect the consciousness of an area as much as the local culture and politics. Thoughts are things, and emotions are real energies. The habitual thoughts and emotions of a group of people saturate the areas in which they live. These give each area its distinctive feel, or group consciousness. Some cities or regions, just like some homes, have a light and happy atmosphere. Others are heavy and depressing.

Natural elements like the weather seem to reflect the consciousness of an area as much as the local culture and politics.

When Divine Spirit moves strongly into a region, such as during the time of an Eckankar seminar, there is more spiritual power than people are used to. It gives a spiritual boost to the inhabitants and the seminar attendees, as well as an opportunity to cleanse themselves inwardly. While big storms rage in the skies, little healing storms may pass through the lives of those in the area.

It's important to understand that the Living ECK Master does not personally cause any of these changes. "When the Holy Spirit is using you as a vehicle," writes Harold Klemp, "things happen around you. It's not that you're causing them, or that you want them to happen, or that you're playing with the forces of nature to affect the natural course of events."[12]

THE HIDDEN WORK OF THE MAHANTA

Actually, in his role as the Guardian, the Mahanta is a secret protective force behind world events. He often halts earthquakes and other disasters, softening the blows of the negative power. This is a grand claim which is easy to make, and nearly impossible to prove. So why state it?

There are many things about the hidden work of the Mahanta which can only be validated by personal experience. Yet I believe some seekers will benefit by being presented with such statements. It will give them food for thought, and an incentive to penetrate more behind the surface of world events.

Through the Spiritual Exercises of ECK, through Soul Travel, through dream travel, and through the tools of the ECK-Vidya, the ancient science of prophecy, seekers will gradually develop the ability to prove or disprove such statements for themselves.

Through the Spiritual Exercises of ECK, through Soul Travel, through dream travel, and through the tools of the ECK-Vidya, the ancient science of prophecy, seekers will gradually develop the ability to prove or disprove such statements for themselves.

A FOUR-STEP FORMULA

How can the seeker benefit from this sixth aspect of the Mahanta, the Purifier? How is the Wind of Change of value to him on the spiritual path? Is there anything the seeker can do to call upon the ECK? Let's turn now to these practical questions.

In a recent discussion about change, some friends and I were exploring why some people embrace it while others resist it. One of the group had a witty answer. She said, "Change is fun when you choose it."

Change is fun when you choose it.

By being proactive, the seeker can make change a choice. He can hoist his sail when the wind blows, and use it to make swift progress. There are several spiritual disciplines with which to take the initiative.

The first is a daily practice of the Spiritual Exercises of ECK. Like the laundry soap which leaves your garments lighter, softer, and fluffier, these exercises will gently scrub and clean the inner bodies, the garments of Soul.

The exercises can be continued throughout the day by remembering to sing the word *HU,* the secret name for God. This can be done inwardly when it would disturb others, or out loud at other times. Singing HU will tune up the vibrations and bring them into better alignment with Divine Spirit. It is sung as a love song to God, and also in times of need.

Second, you can choose one day a week during which to hold yourself to a higher standard, to keep your attention more fully upon things spiritual. For those who look to the Mahanta, Friday is generally the chosen day. By this weekly focus for a day on the Light and Sound, and on holding oneself in an elevated consciousness, the purification started by the daily contemplations is given a boost.

Third, you can write a report of your spiritual progress once a month in your journal. ECKists address their reports to the Mahanta, the Living ECK Master. The report is a time to review progress made for the month, and to surrender to Spirit unwanted habits that are holding you back.

Fourth, at the beginning of each spiritual new year, the seeker can benefit from the spiritual energies flowing into the world at that time. It's a time to review the spiritual lessons of the past and to set new goals for oneself. For those who look to the Mahanta, the spiritual new year begins on October 22. This date and its significance will be explored more fully in the chapter on the Ancient One.

The daily spiritual exercises are the main stage which lifts us into the spiritual atmosphere. The other three stages carry us the rest of the way until we break free of the downward pull of the earthbound consciousness.

Taken together, these four practices give the seeker a daily, weekly, monthly, and yearly boost. Each lesser cycle builds up and feeds its energy into the next greater one. Hidden in these four simple disciplines is a formula of great power. They are like the four stages of a rocket. The daily spiritual exercises are the main stage which lifts us into the spiritual atmosphere. The other three stages carry us the rest of the way until we break free of the downward pull of the earthbound consciousness. For the truly dedicated, there is a fifth stage wherein the seeker reexamines his goals and mission every twelve years.

These disciplines act like sails on a ship, taking fullest advantage of every breeze and gust of the wind of change. If the seeker faithfully adheres to these practices, he will avoid a great deal of the pain associated with the kind of change one does not choose. But

in honesty he cannot avoid all pain. Life and learning
don't work like that.

On the Rosetta stone of God, the glyph for the
Purifier, the Wind of Change, shows a sapling bending
in the wind. This portrays Soul's need to keep flexible
through the stormy trials of life. Whether the weather
is foul or fair, this aspect of the Mahanta always re-
freshes the life of Soul on Its journey home to God.

13

The Healer

*Man is subjected to three illnesses which are mani-
fest and three which are hidden....*
*It is only the Mahanta, the Living ECK Master who
is able to bring about a healing for any of these ills that
man may have, both outwardly and inwardly.*

The Shariyat-Ki-Sugmad,
Book Two[1]

*I*n times of pain and suffering, people have always
turned to God for solace—in hopes of a healing.
In fact, pain is sometimes the only thing which
turns a person to God. Nothing else seems as effective
at getting our attention. Perhaps it is the possibility of
a miracle that draws people to God at such times. Or
it may be an instinct of Soul to recognize that Divine
Spirit is the supreme healer.

Healing is one of the greatest gifts of God passed
to Soul through the Mahanta. But it takes a fresh
perspective to appreciate that aspect of the Mahanta,
the Healer. For example, a good healer seeks to go
deeper than mere symptoms, to get at the root cause
of a disease. The healings of the Mahanta go deep—
very deep—as we shall see.

*Healing is
one of the
greatest gifts of
God passed to
Soul through
the Mahanta.*

THE SIX ILLNESSES

For a start, consider the quote which heads this chapter. It refers to a most unusual list of illnesses. *What are the three manifest illnesses, and what are the three hidden ones?*[2] Not at all what you might expect. Were a random group of people asked to list their illnesses, it is doubtful that any of the following would be mentioned:

What are the three manifest illnesses, and what are the three hidden ones?

Manifest, or outer, illnesses:
1. Constant birth and rebirth
2. The struggle with the mind
3. Absolute ignorance

Hidden, or inner, illnesses:
1. Vanity
2. Anger
3. Lust

One evening I sat down in contemplation intending to talk with Zan about these six illnesses. I frankly had no clear idea of how to present them as a topic. They were far removed from my usual notions of disease. After singing HU for a few minutes, I became quiet and invited Zan into the inner screen of my attention. Soon I saw his smiling face before me.

"The words of *The Shariyat* do not explain themselves," he began. "It takes persistence and insight to penetrate the surface meaning."

I said, "It looks like I need some help here. It's pretty abstract."

Zan said, "I will give you an overview and show how this part of the Mahanta's work fits in with his mission to help Soul return home to God.

"Heading the list of the six illnesses is the ultimate illness, from Soul's perspective—birth and rebirth in the worlds ruled by karma. In any given lifetime, and at any given time within that lifetime, one may suffer from a variety of ills. Aches, pains, injuries, diseases, emotional pains, mental instabilities, and a host of other troubles pester us.

"We seek relief from these troubles; we search for a healing of the particular ill. Yet all of these miscellaneous illnesses are only the symptoms of the deeper illness of karma and reincarnation. We are like a person dying of cancer who is only interested in healing a little cut on his finger.

"Next on the list of outer ills is the struggle with the mind. Except for cases of clinical mental illness, who would put this second on the list of mankind's great diseases? Again, it takes a new perspective to catch the Mahanta's view on this.

"Despite modern civilization's praise and admiration of the mind, the mind is a source of much misery to Soul. In the material worlds, Soul is largely the slave of Its Mental body, not the master of it. The ensnaring tendrils of the mind reach deep into all aspects of our nature. They reach across centuries from past lives, tripping us on the spiritual path. Some of the ill-begotten children of the mind are vanity, worry, doubt, fear, regret, and attachments of all kinds. So struggle we must, wrestling with this powerful opponent until Soul becomes the master of it. The Mahanta's healing assistance in this conflict is a blessing.

"What of the third outer ill? Who would not be indignant at any healer who insulted him with a diagnosis of ignorance? Yet the world is full of people who sleepwalk through life, without a clue as to their life's meaning or purpose.

We seek relief from these troubles; we search for a healing of the particular ill. Yet all of these miscellaneous illnesses are only the symptoms of the deeper illness of karma and reincarnation.

"They chafe against their misfortunes, blaming other people and circumstances for their hardships. They constantly break the spiritual laws, such as the Law of Noninterference, and reap the consequences. Their criticism, judgment, and meddling entangle them in a web of their own making. If told what the spiritual laws are, or even that these laws exist, they laugh with derision at such foolishness. In the next breath they complain about how unjust life is. Among the sleepwalkers are people admired for their intelligence and learning.

The Healer, the Mahanta, has great compassion for those who wander in the dark, oblivious to the divinity which dwells within them. ●

"The Healer, the Mahanta, has great compassion for those who wander in the dark, oblivious to the divinity which dwells within them. With endless patience he lifts veil after veil, until a glimmer of insight penetrates our darkness.

"Even the seeker, alive to the impulses of Soul, sometimes suffers often from his own ignorance. He tends to ignore the hints and guidance of the Mahanta which would ease his pain. We touched on some of these forms of guidance when discussing the Wayshower.

"The three inner ills of anger, vanity, and lust are very much the roots of the outer ills. They create the karma which drives Soul to be reborn again, to struggle with the vanity of the mind, with the lust for power, for possessions, for all the hungers of the flesh."

HELP FROM THE HEALER

Zan paused to see if I was keeping up. "Please continue," I urged him. "This is very helpful."

"Very well," Zan said. "In the chapter on the Wayshower you discussed how the Mahanta often appears to the seeker in the form of a six-pointed Blue Star. When Soul begins to work with the Blue Star of the Mahanta It tunes in to a great healing force. This is the symbol of the eternal Light and Sound of God.

"The Mahanta as the Healer arrives at the hospital to find Soul suffering in agony, praying to be healed of some surface affliction. He examines the patient from head to toe. But this is mainly for the patient's benefit, who believes it is necessary.

"The moment he walked into the room, the Mahanta could see the patient was suffering from the sixfold illnesses of ego. If he sees it will help, the Healer will give the patient something for immediate relief. The patient may even receive a miraculous cure.

"Soon the patient is out of the hospital, thinking the healing is complete. But it has just begun. The patient is still sick but doesn't even know it. The three manifest and three hidden illnesses are still blocking spiritual health and vitality. It will take time to do the deep inner cleansing.

Zan bid me farewell and faded from my inner vision. I continued the contemplation for another fifteen minutes or so, thinking over what he had said.

No Soul can stand before God until It is purified of all Its karmic ills. What healer can bring such a deep cleansing to Soul? It is the Mahanta's mission to do so. It is time now to explore the practical application of these ideas, to see how they work in the nitty-gritty of our daily lives.

No Soul can stand before God until It is purified of all Its karmic ills.

THE VALUE OF PAIN AND PROBLEMS

Perhaps the best place to start is with a few thoughts about the role of pain. As mentioned in the opening paragraph of this chapter, it is often pain that drives Soul toward God.

I have never seen anyone grow substantially," writes Harold Klemp, "who has not gone through a period of suffering or trial."

"I have never seen anyone grow substantially," writes Harold Klemp, "who has not gone through a period of suffering or trial. If you can go through the trials of life and say, 'I wonder what ECK is trying to tell me,' you will be far richer in consciousness than if you say, 'Now who's to blame for this?' Meaning, of course, anyone but you."[3]

The saying No pain, no gain contains a seed of real wisdom. The old must be shed to make way for the new. Before it spreads its wings, the butterfly must strain to emerge from its chrysalis. The chick struggles free of the egg, the baby is pushed from the womb. The gift of freedom is just on the other side of the struggle.

A surprising discovery to many seekers is how the very process of spiritual evolution can sometimes appear to worsen our health. How? As our consciousness shifts to higher planes, old living and eating habits no longer fit our new vibrations. One result is that karmic conditions are pushed to the surface. In the parlance of modern healing, this is a cleansing reaction.

Fortunately there is a flip side to this dilemma. Moving into a higher state of consciousness can also be the action that helps to heal us. We see life more clearly. We become more conscious of the effect of our thoughts and choices on our health. And we can choose more wisely.

In my own spiritual life, these cleansing reactions tend to erupt most noticeably before an ECK initiation. Several years ago I was responsible for supervising my first large project at work. Everything started well, but as things progressed the problems began to pile up. Everything that could have gone wrong, did go wrong. People who had been supportive backed away. They didn't want to be associated with a failing enterprise. Many fears which had lurked unknown within me

began to surface—fear of losing my professional repu-
tation, fear of failure, fear that the project would drain
me of all interest in my work, and so forth. Despite my
fears and a strong urge to just give up, I doggedly
pushed through the obstacles one by one, day after day,
month after month.

But there came a point where I reached my limit.
As I lay awake in bed late one night, I hit my darkest
hour. I felt completely exhausted. "Mahanta," I whispered, "I can't go any further myself. If this project is
to get done, I need help." I rolled over and soon fell into
a sound sleep.

The next morning I awoke and sprang from bed
with complete self-confidence and enthusiasm. I strode
into work as though nothing could stop me from accom-
plishing anything I chose to do. My fears and fatigue
had vanished.

Obstacles which had seemed insurmountable the
previous day fell before me like paper tigers. The remaining several months of the project went smoothly—
the problems weren't gone, but they didn't bother me
anymore.

It so happened that the project, which was a new
computer system, began on October 22, the ECK Spiritual New Year. The gift-waves of Light and Sound
poured in from the Mahanta. A deep healing of fear and
doubt would be accomplished, brought to the surface by
the test of the trying project.

Harold Klemp writes:

> These obstacles give you the opportunity to
> delve into your creative imagination. Constantly
> pushed to the wall, you have to make decisions
> and figure out ways to meet your commitment.

These obstacles give you the opportunity to delve into your creative imagination.

This is part of spiritual unfoldment. Solving these problems expands the consciousness, and as the expansion occurs, you become more able to find solutions to the problems that would have defeated you yesterday.[4]

Life on earth is a school, and a problem or an illness is meant to teach us something. People have their troubles because they made them for themselves. We use them to grow.

When we are in pain and cry out for a healing, Divine Spirit may give one. It also may not.

When we are in pain and cry out for a healing, Divine Spirit may give one. It also may not. If the illness were removed immediately, we could be halted in our growth and lose the gift of a new insight. In this regard I find these words by Harold Klemp worthy of deep contemplation:

> Even as you learn to love more, you will feel the pain of life more because you're becoming more sensitive to the love of God. You're understanding more of how people feel when they are going through their hard times.
>
> What would be easier? To become more unconscious, to not notice when someone hurts. This would make life very easy for you, but you wouldn't be much more than a rock. And this isn't the purpose of Soul.
>
> You, as an individual, are to become more aware of God's love. What makes you aware of this love?
>
> The experiences you have in your daily life.
>
> And the experiences that teach you about love are often those of pain. Pain teaches God's love. We don't like pain, we don't like change, but they are blessings in disguise. They teach us to become more godlike.[5]

THE SELECTIVE NATURE OF HEALINGS

Many years ago I lived near Seattle, Washington, and worked at the Boeing Company. A once-popular song says the bluest skies you've ever seen are in Seattle. Even so, the region is notorious for its gray, soggy winters. One particular winter the clouds seemed nailed in place. Weeks went by without revealing even a spot of blue sky. It had been a hard year for me emotionally, and the dismal weather added to my depression. Nothing seemed to lift my spirits.

One day at work I hit bottom. I felt I couldn't carry on. To shake off the gloom I got up from my desk and took a walk outside. The sky was cold steel. A drizzle extinguished what little spark was left in me. Inwardly I searched for the presence of the Mahanta, asking, "Is there anything you can do to help me through this gloom?"

The words had barely passed my lips when I felt a movement within my heart, like the petals of a flower opening. Then a soft inner rain of golden light began to fall upon me. A passage from Shakespeare came to me: "The quality of mercy is not strain'd, / It droppeth as the gentle rain from heaven / Upon the place beneath."[6]

Joy bubbled up from some deep well within, washing away darkness. My spirits soared like a lark in the rapture of song. By the time I returned from my walk, the depression had lifted.

Back at my desk I felt blessed beyond measure. As far as I was concerned, I had just walked through a miracle. This episode was a major turning point. A week later an advertisement appeared in the local newspaper inviting people of my profession to interview for job openings with a company in Florida—the Sunshine State.

> *Joy bubbled up from some deep well within, washing away darkness. My spirits soared like a lark in the rapture of song.*

Though I had not given any thought to moving, I went to an interview out of curiosity. The people doing the interviewing said I was under-qualified. But they promised to keep my resumé on file and call me if they had an opening "someday." I gave no further thought to the matter. But the clouds of Seattle still didn't budge, and the thought of leaving the area for a sunnier climate began to appeal to me.

About a month later, I arrived at work one morning and noticed my manager's office door was open. On impulse, I walked in and gave the required one-week notice of termination. It happened so suddenly I wondered what made me do it. On my last day of work, I came home and found a letter from the company in Florida in the mailbox. Inside was an offer of immediate employment for 20 percent more than my current salary.

Within two weeks I was living in central Florida, in a cottage adjacent to a lovely park. I entered into a serene and happy period in my life. All this change had come from a plea for divine help in my darkest hour. It had all happened so suddenly and was so unplanned, that it didn't seem real.

I share this story for two reasons. First, it's an example of the kind of miraculous healing that the Mahanta can bring to people. Such stories are common among those who look to the Mahanta. Second, for every story of this kind, there is a contrasting one where someone's cries for help seem to go unanswered— even when the person had done everything humanly possible to first help himself.

Harold Klemp writes:

> It doesn't matter what religion you're in, some
> people have healings and others don't. Some people

On my last day of work, I came home and found a letter from the company in Florida in the mailbox. Inside was an offer of immediate employment for 20 percent more than my current salary.

in ECK have healings, others don't. Sometimes it's not the fault of the particular Soul, the individual. It can be a necessary life experience.

But other times, when it isn't a necessary life experience or you've learned to love . . . a healing can come."[7]

Karmic debts may block the healing process. Some people have accepted the idea of a God who will heal us no matter what we do wrong. They might abuse their bodies for years with poor living habits, until disease catches up with them. Then they pray for a healing, and if it doesn't come, they wonder what is wrong with God. But everything is in order—the school of life is teaching its lessons as intended.

Karmic debts may block the healing process. Some people have accepted the idea of a God who will heal us no matter what we do wrong.

More disconcerting is the illness that appears to strike out of nowhere, from no apparent cause we can trace in this lifetime. There is little comfort in being told that we caused it through past-life behavior if we can't verify it. In such cases, the seeker can ask the Inner Master to show him whether the cause is in a past life. Through a dream, contemplation, or outer guidance, the answer is often given. Such an answer can give us forbearance by letting us see the karmic debts we are resolving.

There is a belief in New Age thought today that we create everything in our own lives, including every illness and disease. Harold Klemp moderates this view with the following observation:

> In more instances than I can name, it is not past karma that has caused the illness, as so many people would like to believe. Many physical ailments are simply a product of the times. Nuclear weapons exploded into the atmosphere since World

War II have changed the very air we breathe. Increased food production has led to the necessity to preserve it for a longer shelf life, which means we now routinely consume a variety of preservatives. It's a catch-22 situation: Science has been able to improve the quality of life faster than our bodies have been able to evolve.[8]

Environmental illnesses of all kinds are an increasing problem. The old slogan It's your karma is too simplistic an answer. It may be karma, but it's the group karma of the entire human race. Any Soul who chooses to incarnate on earth must take what comes with it. Individual karma comes into play with the relative resistance to becoming sick and in the ability to follow the Mahanta's inner guidance toward the best healer for the condition.

Any Soul who chooses to incarnate on earth must take what comes with it.

When a request to the Mahanta for a healing goes unanswered, it is not because he is powerless to help. The Inner Master sees the cause of the problem and knows the proper cure. Harold Klemp describes the picture from the Mahanta's view:

> Some of the letters that cross my desk are truly heartrending. I know the people who are asking for help will be given the help. But it may not always come as quickly as they feel they need it or as quickly as I would like for them to have it.
>
> Sometimes I would like to snap my fingers and say, "Worry no more—you are healed." But the ECK, in Its divine intelligence, may deem that this kind of an instant healing would be a disservice to one who is truly working to return home to God. Instant cures are often temporary healings

which do very little to teach the individual the reason for his illness, sadness, or heartbreak.[9]

To put the key idea of this topic very simply, Spirit will give the healing if it is the best thing for the spiritual growth of the seeker. And if a healing were not in his best interests, the wise seeker would not want it anyway.

Yet we ourselves are sometimes the obstacle to the healing. In some way the Mahanta will give us directions on how to live our life better, how to sidestep a problem—if we listen. Spirit is very patient. It will warn us once, twice, three times. But if we get out of the habit of listening, the voice of the Inner Master becomes harder to hear.

He's not talking more quietly; we have turned down the volume. Who wants to listen to a voice which is suggesting we take action we would rather not take? Eventually the problem gets out of hand, and we find ourselves in a crisis. A good protection against closed ears is the daily practice of spiritual exercises.

In some way the Mahanta will give us directions on how to live our life better, how to sidestep a problem—if we listen. Spirit is very patient.

HOW THE MAHANTA HEALS

When it comes to healing, the seeker may be expecting the Mahanta to use all kinds of miraculous healing powers. The seeker may have in mind the stories of Jesus, walking among the crowds, making the blind see and the lame walk with a mere touch or glance.

We live in an age of great advances in science, medicine, and the healing arts. Some religious groups avoid these basic services because they are not natural enough or supernatural enough! It doesn't occur to them that God may work through the family doctor just as well as It may work through an angel or some kind of miracle.

Much of the time, the Mahanta will simply guide the seeker to the appropriate doctor, healer, or book. If the seeker is open enough to accept this help, the healing can proceed.

Much of the time, the Mahanta will simply guide the seeker to the appropriate doctor, healer, or book. If the seeker is open enough to accept this help, the healing can proceed.

A few years ago I developed symptoms of arthritis in my left shoulder. It developed gradually over the course of about two years, getting steadily worse with the passage of time.

I keep myself informed of the latest knowledge in health and nutrition. I felt there was nothing in my living habits that would lead to an arthritic condition in my body at my age. I went to a medical doctor. He examined my shoulder and said there wasn't much to do but go easy on the joint and take some pain medication. I told him I wanted to think it over.

During contemplation a few nights later I asked the Mahanta, the Inner Master, whether there was a better way to heal my pain. No answer came to me immediately. But a few weeks later I met with a friend I hadn't seen in a long time. He casually mentioned a natural healer he was seeing and how the therapist had cured him of a severe back injury.

I felt a nudge to go see the therapist. During a massage, he asked if I had any particular areas that were painful. "Not really," I answered. "At least nothing that a massage can fix. Just a little arthritis developing in my left shoulder."

"Let me check it," he said. He squeezed and poked around a bit, then said, "You don't have arthritis. Just a few knotted muscles. I think we can take care of that."

"You can't be serious," I said. "Pain from knotted muscles can go on for years and immobilize a joint like arthritis?"

"Exactly," he explained. "You'd be amazed how many chronic aches and pains can be cured with skillful manipulation of the bones and muscles. Unfortunately many healers don't have the touch. I teach courses on this, and I'm always surprised how few students can catch it."

He was right. I walked out of his office an hour later with my shoulder back to normal. A pain that had been getting worse for two years was healed in one visit. What is more, I learned a whole lot about how muscle tension can cause pain that mimics chronic illnesses.

The Mahanta had brought me the healing in a simple, effective way. To have a long-standing pain cured so quickly could be counted a miracle. Yet it is amazing how many people are helped this way and don't make the connection with their request for help from the Mahanta.

The Mahanta had brought me the healing in a simple, effective way. To have a long-standing pain cured so quickly could be counted a miracle.

Say a person writes a letter to the Mahanta asking for a healing. Then over the next few weeks they just happen to find a doctor that cures the problem. They may not see the link between their request and their finding the doctor. In this way many spiritual healings go unrecognized.

The Mahanta may send us to a healer who is not what we think we need. Perhaps the healer is someone too orthodox, too unorthodox, or from the "wrong" school of healing. We let our prejudices blind us to where the Mahanta is leading us. When we don't get better, we think our request for help from the Mahanta went unanswered.

Another healing method the Mahanta uses is based on love. He may see that the real cause of suffering in the seeker's life is a closed heart, even though the surface symptom is some illness or disease. The Mahanta will try to gently open the seeker's heart to divine love, to the Light and Sound of God. This may take more time than a physical healing but goes much deeper.

When someone is suffering acute pain, the healing can be very swift. One girl of ten was suffering intense pain when a filling fell out, leaving the nerves of the tooth exposed. At bedtime the little girl prayed to God to take the pain away. Eventually she fell asleep. The ECK Master Rebazar Tarzs came to her that night and healed her pain. If you have reached your limit or no longer need the lesson of the pain, Spirit will provide comfort in some form.[10]

In reality, it is Divine Spirit that does the healing. The Mahanta, the Living ECK Master is only the vehicle.

In reality, it is Divine Spirit that does the healing. The Mahanta, the Living ECK Master is only the vehicle. Harold Klemp writes:

I don't cure anyone myself. I turn it over to Spirit. Spirit may bring a healing; It may bring an understanding. It may lead the person to a doctor or a source of help that he's never considered before. But of myself, I don't do anything. The quicker I can pass this off into the Audible Life Stream, into the ECK, into Spirit, the quicker I do it. If I think about it or if any part of it stays with me, then I get a health problem. If that happens, I have to get right at it and get myself straightened out. This is a real art, and it's part of the discipline and the training that you will receive on your way to self-mastery as you come in contact with this Master power.[11]

In another place Harold Klemp writes:

Paul Twitchell said that when he took over the responsibility as the Living ECK Master, some of the load that he helped lift from you and me affected his health. Sometimes it is a little bit hard to keep the physical body operating well. Some of the things that an individual goes through in this position—and I speak with a little bit of experience now—are unbelievable. And anyone who takes on the position knows this before they accept it.[12]

As with most of the twelve aspects of the Mahanta, the inner and outer sides of the Master play distinct but related roles. Sometimes people have a healing when they come in contact with the Outer Master. Thinking he is personally responsible, they thank him for restoring their health. But the healing really comes from the Mahanta, the Inner Master. The Outer Master will not take credit for it.

It may seem confusing at this point. The terms *Divine Spirit* and *Mahanta* and *Inner Master* are often used interchangeably. It's difficult to make the big picture clear until the seeker has come at it from many directions. Toward the end of this book, I will draw all the parts together into a vision of the whole.

Another way the Mahanta heals is by raising or lowering the vibrations of the seeker's inner bodies to the right level. Put another way, he adjusts the flow of the spiritual current. Many people suffer and cannot get help because their leader knows nothing about how to do this. This is closely related to the Mahanta's mission as Light Giver. People often clamor for another level of initiation before they are ready. It takes time to condition the inner bodies to the inflow of Spirit.

The effect of a sudden flow of Light and Sound can be overwhelming to one not used to it. Recently I attended

Another way the Mahanta heals is by raising or lowering the vibrations of the seeker's inner bodies to the right level. Put another way, he adjusts the flow of the spiritual current.

a retreat for Initiates in Eckankar. On Sunday morning a young couple happened to be in the same building of the retreat. They had heard a little about Eckankar and singing HU. They asked if they could join us for the morning HU Song.

We welcomed them, and they seated themselves in a pair of vacant chairs next to me. There were sixty or so of us. We all began to sing HU. Barely a minute or two had passed when I heard the young man crying. I opened my eyes and saw tears pouring down his cheeks. The HU Song continued for about fifteen minutes, then we stopped.

I heard the man say to his partner, "Whatever this HU is, I've never felt anything like it before. The love was incredible, almost too much for me." I felt compassion for him. Yet the incident made clear to me the value of gradually adjusting our vibrations as we unfold.

One of the most important factors in healing is often tracing the causes of an illness in past lifetimes. The Mahanta can see the entire history of any seeker. He knows the hidden problems and the best time and place to resolve them. The depth and breadth of his insight far surpasses anything that can be gotten through past-life readings, hypnotic regressions, and other psychic means.

Over a ten-year period some years ago, the Mahanta, the Healer, helped me resolve a very painful chain of karmic events that extended over many lives, going back some five thousand years. He didn't simply remove the problem. His method was to have me face my past, step-by-step, handling as much as I was ready for. It was all done without upsetting my state of mind or emotional balance.

I heard the man say to his partner, "Whatever this HU is, I've never felt anything like it before. The love was incredible, almost too much for me."

In summary, these are some of the ways the Mahanta heals us:

* Guides us inwardly to a healer or to the information we need to correct the problem
* Passes the illness or acute pain into the stream of Spirit
* Opens our hearts to divine love
* Adjusts our vibrations to the level that is right for us at the time
* Releases deep-seated illnesses from past lifetimes

WHAT WE CAN DO

As with all aspects of the Mahanta, he meets us halfway. He does his part, and we do ours. The path of ECK is for those who would become self-reliant masters in their own right. Having said that, what is the best approach? Harold Klemp writes:

The path of ECK is for those who would become self-reliant masters in their own right.

> People would like me to give a certain formula for healing—to do a little dance, mumble the sacred words, go into deep contemplation, and lo and behold, the healing is accomplished. But there is no formula. Healings of a miraculous nature always depend upon the conditions in a person's life at that particular time.[13]

When we need a healing, there are many things we can do to help out. A good starting point is to see if we can find a good doctor or healer who can help us. There is a growing community of excellent healers the world over. Before calling on the Mahanta as the Healer, we can call on him as the Wayshower. We can ask him to guide us to someone who is right for us.

In the meantime we can greatly ease the burden by

Remember the healing power of singing HU as a daily spiritual exercise. It is effective for healings on the physical, emotional, mental, and spiritual levels.

a few simple but powerful habits. The first is to remember the healing power of singing HU as a daily spiritual exercise. It is effective for healings on the physical, emotional, mental, and spiritual levels.

The second is to stop and count our blessings, to realize how much we have to be grateful for. This keeps the heart open to love and all the gifts love brings.

The third is to be grateful for the growth God is bringing to us through the suffering. If we let them, most illnesses will bring new depths of character to us and a greater capacity to love. And these, after all, are what we are here on earth to learn.

The fourth is helpful for one who is crying out for relief from loneliness and emptiness. A very healing activity is to find someone to give love to, someone to serve. Perhaps a person who has even less than you.

All four of these suggestions share a common purpose: To open the heart by turning our attention off ourselves and our illness, and outward toward others.

Another step is to write a letter to the Living ECK Master and ask for a healing. This has two parts to it, the first of which is writing the letter. Address the letter to Harold Klemp at the Eckankar address found at the back of this book. Your request will set in motion the healing power of Divine Spirit. It isn't even necessary to mail the letter. The Mahanta hears your request inwardly. Do not write to him asking for a healing for someone else, unless that person asks you to. The Mahanta always respects the privacy of each person to make his own decisions about asking for help.

The next part of requesting a healing from the Mahanta is often the hardest. It is surrendering the problem or illness to Divine Spirit. So often the cause of our problem is a stubborn resistance to the direction we need to be going. Once we give up the struggle and let go of the attachment that is holding us back, things start to smooth out.

One man wrote for a healing. He was deeply in love with a woman who did not return his love. He felt helpless, on the verge of an emotional breakdown. During contemplation he saw himself sitting on a beautiful old sailing ship. The ship was anchored off a sandy beach, the mast empty of sails.

He knew this dream boat represented his relationship, which was going nowhere. There was a button on the mast which, if pushed, would explode the ship and destroy his lovely dream. He knew he had to push the button if he was to have any peace.

He pushed the button and watched the ship sink into the sea. For a moment he experienced intense sorrow and loss. But in its wake came a release. The burden lifted, and the Mahanta led him into a bright new land. The man was ready to move ahead with his life.[14]

The ECK Masters also assist people in the dream state. On the inner planes they will sit down and talk to those in need of help. The therapy may include bathing the person in light of various colors, reviewing pertinent past-life influences, and a study of cycles. Whether or not such visits are remembered by us upon awakening, they will aid the healing process.

You can employ the spiritual healing effect of colored lights at home whenever you feel the need. Try the following techniques given by Harold Klemp:

The ECK Masters also assist people in the dream state. On the inner planes they will sit down and talk to those in need of help.

> The Audible Life Current is the total wave of Light and Sound, similar to white light before a prism breaks it down into beautiful colors. This

rainbow of light can heal the physical and psychic bodies.

The orange light is for healing the physical body from disease, ailment, or accident. Go into contemplation and visualize yourself on the bed, surrounded by an orange stream of effervescent light waves. Direct the stream of orange light toward an injured or diseased organ—in your own body only. Never do this for another person unless you want his karma. . . .

The Blue Light also heals—but especially the Astral, Causal, and Mental bodies. In the same way as with the orange light, put attention upon this Blue Light during contemplation. Let its cleansing light wash over and around you for twenty minutes before dropping the exercise.

If you have a need for this, let this contemplative aid become a part of your regular spiritual exercises for several weeks. It takes discipline to hold the inner channels open while the healing is to take place.

Experiment with these techniques until you find a tailor-made approach that fits you, for everyone is different.[15]

The Mahanta, as a vehicle of healing for Divine Spirit, is a great comfort to us in the hour of suffering.

CONCLUSION

The Mahanta, as a vehicle of healing for Divine Spirit, is a great comfort to us in the hour of suffering. He pours upon us the healing balm of the Light and Sound of God. Yet his greater purpose is to heal us of the primary illness of Soul—the burden of karma and rebirth. And this links his mission as healer very closely with the next role of the Mahanta—the Redeemer.

14

The Redeemer

The Master's greatest role is that of redeemer—
liberator of all Souls from the eternal wheel.

Paul Twitchell
The Spiritual Notebook[1]

O ne night in the dream state I walked beside the Inner Master, Harold Klemp, down a city avenue. It was a workday, and most of the people seemed intent on getting to their destinations. As we strolled along, I noticed something very subtle passing between the Mahanta and the people as they walked by. I wasn't sure, at first, if it was just my imagination. So I looked more closely. My Spiritual Eye began to open, and soon I detected what was happening.

Wrapped around each person we passed were nearly invisible karmic threads which made them look as though they were walking balls of colorful string. As the Master passed, he untangled many of the karmic threads in a way which was imperceptible to the recipients of this gift. A sadness was lifted here, a self-doubt there. It wasn't that the Master somehow reached over and pulled them out. Rather, it was the spontaneous effect of his spiritual presence.

Wrapped around each person we passed were nearly invisible karmic threads which made them look as though they were walking balls of colorful string.

After the people passed by, they stepped a little lighter. Shaking my head I said, "I marvel at how you do that!"

Harold had given me a tiny glimpse of the Redeemer, the name for that aspect of the Mahanta which lifts Soul up to spiritual liberation. A few days later I invited Zan into my daily contemplation to discuss this aspect of the Mahanta. He appeared after a few minutes, radiantly filling my inner screen.

"On the Rosetta stone of God," he explained, "the glyph for the Redeemer is a man setting a bird free from its cage. This is a symbol for the emancipation of Soul. Spiritual liberation is the great treasure to be won by the steadfast seeker. With it comes all things: Self-mastery, freedom to roam the heavens at will, and the capacity to be of real service to all life.

"Freedom and service walk hand in hand with the liberated Soul.

"For centuries Soul has struggled to learn the seemingly opposite lessons of detachment and love. Freedom is a child of detachment, a release from the craving for worldly things. Service is a child of love. He who can mingle and blend love and detachment within himself is reaching for the crown of Mastership.

"Let me see if I can make these clear and simple.

FREEDOM

Spiritual law:	The Law of Economy.
The ideal:	I am the master of my destiny.
Sample qualities:	Detached, self-reliant, independent, creative, resilient, a zest for life.
Sample motto:	I do my best and I am being my best.

Freedom is a child of detachment, a release from the craving for worldly things. Service is a child of love.

Sample image: A soaring eagle.

SERVICE

Spiritual law: The Law of Love

The ideal: I use my talents to serve all life.

Sample qualities: Giving, helpful, patient, kind, trustworthy, reliable, empathetic.

Sample motto: I do what I love, and I do it for love.

Sample image: A golden heart.

"It is a worthwhile spiritual exercise to contemplate on love and detachment," Zan said. "The seeker can visualize a warm, golden stream of love flowing into him, and also a cool, silver stream of detachment. Feel them mingle inside, blending to form a perfect balance, which then issues forth to the world in all the seeker does, says, and even thinks.

"How does the Redeemer help us gain these noble attributes? This aspect of the Mahanta is almost entirely hidden from public view. The scope of his mission is beyond the belief of many. The sacrifices made by the Mahanta for his followers and for the world exceed what many people consider possible. Nor does the Living ECK Master often speak about the subject."

The sacrifices made by the Mahanta for his followers and for the world exceed what many people consider possible.

THE SEEKER'S REFUGE

I said, "I've found that people have some very strong opinions about this subject—both within Eckankar and in other religions. I'd rather not write about it!"

Zan waved a hand, as if brushing aside the concern. "God has bestowed upon the Redeemer the authority to wield the law in all Its creations. This is the seeker's refuge. At the Redeemer's approach the rulers of the planes open their gates, the Lords of Karma bow, the Angel of Death retreats, and the Judge of the Dead stands mute. Yet not through wielding power but through sacrifice does the Redeemer lift Soul into the secret place of the most high.

"This is the profound mystery of the incarnation of the ECK in the worlds of matter. In the tradition of the sun gods and saviors the world over, the Redeemer descends from the celestial world, appears on earth as the Word made flesh, and brings universal redemption.

"A key distinction of the Mahanta is his continuous presence on earth in his outer form as the Living ECK Master of the times. The world is never without the Redeemer. This is the great historical secret which is being revealed in this age. There is no need to wait for some millennial return of a past spiritual leader.

"The bird in the cage sings its song of longing for freedom. The Redeemer hears its melancholy notes floating upon the air. He follows the sound to the cage and opens the door, setting the bird free. As the little one flutters away into the clear blue sky, it hears the beautiful melody of God calling it home. The Voice of God and the song of Soul meet and kiss in midheaven, and the rapture of spiritual liberation is born."

Zan smiled a good-bye, then faded from my inner screen.

The world is never without the Redeemer. This is the great historical secret which is being revealed in this age.

THE MEANING OF REDEMPTION

The main subject in this chapter is loaded with explosive religious connotations. This is the idea of redemption. I believe it is helpful to defuse it by starting with a careful definition. In theology the word *redeem* means to deliver from sin and its consequences by means of a sacrifice offered for the sinner.

If the word *sin* is replaced by the word *karma,* the definition fits the Mahanta a little better. A first try at a better definition could be, "To deliver from karma and its consequences by means of a sacrifice offered for the seeker."

This still misses the mark somewhat. As Harold Klemp has put it, "The difference between the Mahanta in Eckankar and a savior of another religion is this: A savior tries to save you from yourself; the Mahanta tries to help you to help yourself."[2]

The Mahanta helps Soul in many ways through the twelve aspects of his mission. But in his role as the Redeemer there is a stronger element of sacrifice. Harold Klemp writes, "The Mahanta, the Living ECK Master accepts suffering and cares in secret for the spiritual welfare of his beloved ones. But his concern is largely unknown to them."[3]

The above quote was written in the spring of 1984. During this time I met the Mahanta in the dream state. He looked trim and fit in a new blue suit. As I shook his hand I said, "You look very well, considering the heavy responsibility you have on your shoulders lately."

He replied, "Things are not always what they appear on the surface. But why make an issue of it? Divine Spirit will have Its way."

I said, "What do you mean?"

He removed his jacket, then carefully removed his shirt. I could see him wince as he did it. Then he turned and showed me his back. It was covered with deep open sores. I understood they were caused from karma he was passing through his inner bodies to help some of his own followers.

The Mahanta helps Soul in many ways through the twelve aspects of his mission. But in his role as the Redeemer there is a stronger element of sacrifice.

"It is necessary that this be done now, or many innocent people would be knocked off the path to God," he explained. "Most who will be helped by this sacrifice will never know it was done for them."

I was shocked. I didn't know what to say. When I awoke from the dream, I wondered whether this was a literal picture of the Mahanta's inner bodies, or just a symbol of the burden he was carrying for his followers. After thinking it over I decided it didn't really matter. The point was the same in either case.

About nine years later, in 1993, Harold Klemp described some of the adverse effects that carrying the mantle of Mahantaship had had upon his health. After describing these effects he wrote:

> All this is necessary for a transformation to lift the consciousness of people around the world (and everywhere else) to a new level.
>
> The Master endures suffering because of his love for Soul.[4]

In July 1971 Paul Twitchell wrote a letter to his followers discussing the Mahanta's sacrifice. The following excerpts are from that letter:

> His sacrifice comes in the form of an overwhelming love for all things of life, man and the subspecies, beings and entities on all planes. Not only does he serve mankind, but each individual Soul and Its fellow Soul from the earth plane to the Ocean of Love and Mercy. He sacrifices his time, health and anything which would have a hold upon his mind and interest in this world. . . .
>
> The supreme sacrifice for all chelas goes on constantly. And more than this, he constantly makes the supreme sacrifice for the varied nations who

Most who will be helped by this sacrifice will never know it was done for them.

are at one another's throats constantly over political problems threatening war, the constant sacrifice against dictatorship, and the turmoils which shut off the freedom of the individual. . . .

The Mahanta may suffer for the karmic debt which the nation and its people have created. He may have to go through a prolonged suffering for some reason which is mainly for the purpose of removing the karma of the nation and its people. He might develop illness which baffles medical authorities and certainly his own followers, for they do not believe that if he is a perfect channel that he could become ill. Such illnesses are not of the common causes of mankind but the karma which he has taken upon himself to remove a nation's debt and solve its illness, perhaps economically, political, health, and spiritually. When he does take on such karmic loads he might have a whole siege of problems to work off, which has been accepted as the karma of that nation, and he struggles to get it into the ECK stream to be completely resolved. This can often make him physically ill, or some other catalyst can trigger a chain of events which has the same results.[5]

This is not to say the ECK Masters are martyrs. They look upon martyrdom as a form of suicide or self-destruction, and shun it.

I suggest a key distinction lies in the nature of the Mahanta's sacrifice, especially when it applies to the individual seeker. The notion in Christianity, for example, is that all sins are forgiven, all responsibility for our actions is dissolved in the blood spilled by the savior. In contrast, the ECK Masters aim to teach their students to be self-reliant and responsible.

The notion in Christianity, for example, is that all sins are forgiven, all responsibility for our actions is dissolved in the blood spilled by the savior. In contrast, the ECK Masters aim to teach their students to be self-reliant and responsible.

I feel the sacrifice of the Mahanta is this: He will go to almost any length to help the seeker gain self-mastery. On occasion this includes the sacrifice of taking on some of the seeker's karma, to soften a blow, to ease a heavy burden, to shield him from the attacks of the negative forces. This is only done when it will help the seeker move forward—not merely to ease his burden.

I feel the sacrifice of the Mahanta is this: He will go to almost any length to help the seeker gain self-mastery.

Imagine two travelers on a journey being led by the Mahanta. They come to a swift river (their stream of karma) which blocks their path. The first man turns to the Mahanta and says, "Please, carry me across," by which he means, "take my sins away." This is a person who expects a savior to take all responsibility for his debts to life. He hasn't learned much about responsibility. The Redeemer turns away from him, knowing the first follower is not ready for the pursuit of Mastership.

The second follower takes the initiative. He immediately puts his creative faculties to good use and sets about looking for a solution. He gathers some driftwood and improvises some crude cord to rope them together into a raft. He finds an old board to use as a paddle. Inviting the Mahanta along, he bravely pushes out into the white water of the rapids.

Nearly across the river, the raft strikes a submerged rock, causing the seeker to pitch headlong into the water where the current pulls him under. Quickly the Mahanta dives into the cold water (takes on some of the man's karma) and rescues him. He knows the man was doing his best. He knows that this sacrifice on his own part will keep the man moving forward on his journey, yet without robbing him of self-reliance.

So, the following might be an improved definition of *redeem* as it applies to the Mahanta: To deliver from unnecessary karma and its consequences by means of a sacrifice offered for the seeker. I believe this definition captures the spirit of the Redeemer's role as he helps Soul return home to God. This redemption, or deliverance, is very much a gift of divine love. It leads to spiritual liberation in this lifetime, which is the ultimate redemption the Mahanta offers the seeker.

The Shariyat-Ki-Sugmad says of spiritual liberation, "This is the deliverance, the disappearance of the illusion of servitude, because of man's unhappy conduct toward man. This freedom takes away his blindness and opens his eyes. It takes away his deafness and opens his ears."[6]

This redemption, or deliverance, is very much a gift of divine love. It leads to spiritual liberation in this lifetime, which is the ultimate redemption the Mahanta offers the seeker.

HOW THE MAHANTA HELPS US RESOLVE KARMA

According to the teachings of the ECK Masters, there are two different ways a person's karma is administered. For the bulk of people, it is done by the Lords of Karma. These beings see that all people meet in the right place and time, and under the right circumstances, in order to gather the consequences of their actions.

Authors Whitton and Fisher speak of this first kind of administration in their book *Life between Life*. Drawing on the technique of hypnotic regression, Dr. Whitton regressed people to the time between incarnations and asked them what their experiences were. The authors write, "Nearly all . . . have found themselves appearing before a group of wise, elderly beings—usually three in number, occasionally four, and in rare instances as many as seven—perceived in a variety of guises. They can be of indeterminate identity or they may take on the appearance of mythological gods or religious masters."[7] In their book they called this group of beings a board of judgment.

The authors go on to write of these judges, "Their role is to assist that individual in evaluating the life that has just passed and, eventually, to make recommendations concerning the next incarnation."[8]

Even in Betty J. Eadie's bestselling book, *Embraced by the Light,* which is the record of her near-death experience from a Christian perspective, we find a similar board of judges. She calls them the Council of Men. Her guide, Jesus, escorts her into a room where she is presented to a council of twelve beings. They lead her through an evaluation of her life and deeds, and make recommendations that she must return to Earth, as her incarnation is not finished.[9]

When a person becomes a disciple of the Mahanta, the administration of his karma is transferred from the Lords of Karma into the Mahanta's keeping.

When a person becomes a disciple of the Mahanta, the administration of his karma is transferred from the Lords of Karma into the Mahanta's keeping. *The Shariyat-Ki-Sugmad* states, "The Mahanta is the distributor of karma in this world and what he says is the word of the Sugmad. All the Lords of Karma are under his hand and must do as he directs. Hence, Eckankar is the spiritual refuge for all Souls."[10]

A handicap for people who do not have the Mahanta's help is that their karma may come in any scattered order, so the links between cause and effect are obscured. When the Redeemer receives the individual's karmic accounts from the Lords of Karma, he first adjusts them. Harold Klemp says that the Mahanta "arranges the chela's karmic debts into some semblance of order. Karma due for repayment is fed back to his charges in accord with the Law of Economy."[11] I suggest that one benefit of this reordering is that the links between cause and effect are much more clear. The result is a faster learning process.

He also gets beneath the symptoms of the seeker's hardships, tracing them back to their root causes. Then he presents the needed resolutions to the seeker to work out as he is able to.

For many years I was highly claustrophobic. Since I could not trace the cause of this fear anywhere in my current life, I presumed its cause lay in the past. One night in a dream the Mahanta took me on a journey back in time to the period of the Inquisition in Spain. I had done some things that put me out of favor with the Church. The local hierarchy turned me over to a small mob to do their dirty work for them. I was wrapped and bound tightly in a blanket so only my head could move. Then I was hauled out to the edge of the town and stuffed into the crawl space beneath the floor of an abandoned building. They left me there to die a slow death.

And slow it was—taking many days. The fear, the nibbling rats, the darkness, and the immobility combined to gradually drive me into raving insanity. As the Mahanta and I hovered over this scene, witnessing the last struggles of life in that incarnation, he told me, "You need to go back into that body now." He knew it was the only way to erase the terror that lingered in my unconscious.

With extreme reluctance, but knowing it was necessary, I slipped back into the last hours of that incarnation. Only this time I was conscious of the Mahanta's presence and of what I was doing. I stayed in that dying body just long enough to overcome the sheer terror and panic. Once I was able to calm myself, I slipped into the observer position.

This dream accomplished two things. First, it erased my claustrophobia. Second, it engendered a resentment

I slipped back into the last hours of that incarnation. Only this time I was conscious of the Mahanta's presence and of what I was doing.

in me against the Catholic Church. I had solved one problem only to succumb to another—the human tendency to blame someone or something else for my misfortunes. No doubt the Mahanta foresaw this result. For he said, "This is all for now."

I wondered what he meant "for now." Hadn't I overcome the karma of that lifetime?

It was more than ten years later that the Mahanta revealed the second half of the story to me. Once again he met me in a dream and took me on a journey back in time. The destination was ancient Egypt. The scene we hovered over this time was of a group of slaves toiling on a pyramid under the whip of a harsh slave master. It only took a moment for me before I recognized myself as the slave driver. He became irritated with one of the slaves. With cruel indifference, he forced the poor man into a cramped hole in the pyramid and had a heavy slab of stone moved into place, burying him alive.

From my perspective in the dream, I watched with shame and remorse as the slave died a very slow death, going completely insane by the time he died.

The Mahanta in his role as the Redeemer had sequenced the recall of these two past lives in the order which would bring me the most clear understanding. He had also spaced the recall of them ten years apart in order to give me sufficient time between the first recall and the second to process and resolve the karmic issues.

The goal is generally to work out as much karma as possible without greatly upsetting the person going through it. If we can handle it, the karma will be fed to us at a fast clip.

The goal is generally to work out as much karma as possible without greatly upsetting the person going through it. If we can handle it, the karma will be fed to us at a fast clip.

The seeker is blessed with a third benefit when the administration of his karma is passed into the Mahanta's hands. A great deal of the karma begins to be worked out in the dream state. This may result in an occasional nightmare. But it's a lot better to go through the ordeal in a dream and be done with it than to meet the karma in the physical world. There are fewer lingering after-effects—such as crunched car fenders, broken bones, hospital bills, lost jobs, and so forth.

As always, the seeker makes the best progress when he takes the initiative and does his part. The daily practice of the Spiritual Exercises of ECK acts like a road-repair crew, keeping one step ahead and filling in the karmic potholes before we hit them. The experienced seeker who slacks off on this discipline will quickly feel the road getting rougher again.

The daily practice of the Spiritual Exercises of ECK acts like a road-repair crew, keeping one step ahead and filling in the karmic potholes before we hit them.

The Mahanta's role as the Redeemer is closely linked with his roles as the Dream Master, the Light Giver, and the Healer, as he lifts the seeker into the heavenly worlds.

As the Light Giver, the Mahanta links Soul up with the Light and Sound of God. This is essential for spiritual liberation. As the Healer he begins to mend the bumps and bruises of our many lifetimes. As the Dream Master he eases our way by resolving as much karma as possible in the inner worlds while we are asleep. As the Redeemer, he takes custody of our karmic accounts and adjusts them for our greatest spiritual benefit. And when necessary, he helps us release unneeded karma by passing it through himself and dissolving it into the stream of Divine Spirit.

"Man is not saved," says *The Shariyat-Ki-Sugmad,* "but Soul is redeemed by the Mahanta, the Living ECK Master."[12] The Mahanta can give Soul true spiritual freedom after Its multitude of incarnations spent on earth.

15

The Godman

Everything in the universes of the Sugmad takes its greatness from the ECK, and of this, the Mahanta, the Living ECK Master is the human symbol. He is the Godman who, through the earth and heavens, connects all of us with the ECK.

The Shariyat-Ki-Sugmad,
Book Two[1]

I had been in a good mood all day. The Light and Sound hummed merrily in my awareness as I settled down to do my evening contemplation. On such days I dispensed with the usual preparations. Simply closing my eyes was enough to slip effortlessly into the inner worlds. There I found Zan ready with another discourse which he began immediately.

"The legends and myths of the human race abound with tales of gods who became men and men who became gods," he began. "They are mostly entertaining fables, but all veil a deep underlying truth: When Spirit and matter meet and balance upon the fulcrum of the human consciousness, a potential godman is born.

"Speaking of fables, there was once a certain Soul assigned to the school of the lower worlds. It began Its lessons as a mineral. So everyone would recognize that

When Spirit and matter meet and balance upon the fulcrum of the human consciousness, a potential godman is born.

It was a mineral, It wore a rock costume. Whenever somebody chanced by, they would say, 'Oh, what a lovely rock.' This made that Soul proud and happy.

"After a few million years It learned all there was to learn about being a rock. It moved ahead to the next lesson, studying the ways of plants. There were a lot of new things to master: responding to sunlight, sinking roots into the ground, handling photosynthesis, and so forth. The Soul was issued various plant costumes as time passed so everyone on earth would recognize It as a plant.

"Next, It progressed into the great classroom of the animal kingdom. It tried hundreds of different costumes, changing species whenever It needed to learn further lessons. But whatever costume It wore, no one ever doubted It was an animal. The costumes fit the part very well. After a long cycle of adventures the Soul had learned enough to become a human being.

"The tests and challenges of playing the role of human were very trying, but the Soul never gave up. It kept at it, and after thousands of tries, wearing every size and shape and color of human costume, a very special day arrived. God informed the Soul that It was now ready for the next big step: to become a godman.

"The Soul asked God, 'What new costume do I get to wear now?' God answered, 'There isn't any special costume for a godman. Just keep using the human one.'

"The Soul was puzzled. 'Then how will anyone know I'm a godman?' God smiled and replied, 'Those who know their own divinity will see the god in you. Those who don't will see only the human.'"

Chuckling, Zan said, "The human race longs to believe in saviors and the incarnations of gods. At the

God informed the Soul that It was now ready for the next big step: to become a godman.

same time most people are never quite convinced any person they know personally could be one. After all, such people eat and sleep, walk and talk, get hurt and sick, just like they do. Yet I tell you the kingdom of the God-Realized is as distinct from the human kingdom as the human is from the animal. It is a fundamentally different level of life."

"It seems there is always a small group of seekers who think the Living ECK Master is a god," I said, "and another who thinks he is an ordinary person. I feel that both of these groups run into trouble at some point along the way.

"The ones who think he is a god are shocked when they discover one of his human qualities, or that he has an interest or hobby which is not godlike enough in their minds. This knocks them off the path.

"The ones who think he is not so different from themselves fail to see past the human costume. They can turn into cynical critics who impute their own selfish motives to everything the Godman does.

"The more successful seekers seem to appreciate the meeting of the human and the divine within the Godman. They can accept his human nature and personality, yet they have the perception to see the face of God in his countenance."

Zan replied, "Well said. The Godman becomes a mirror who reflects the seesaw battle within each seeker. Of the twelve aspects of the Mahanta, the Godman's role is to be a living example to others. The Living ECK Master is both the Outer and the Inner Master. It's never easy to be a role model, and the task is even tougher to be a spiritual role model, for people carry all sorts of misconceptions about what the Godman is.

The Godman becomes a mirror who reflects the seesaw battle within each seeker.

"His followers will waver back and forth in their faith in him, according to the faith they have in their own spiritual potential. The point where seekers quit the path in disillusionment is the point when they have lost the realization of their own divinity. They have looked in the mirror of the Godman and found only the reflection of a man looking back.

"The Godman knows this. When doubts and accusations are hurled his way, he does not take them at face value nor try to refute them. He recognizes that the seeker is waging a battle within himself.

"But if the seeker stays with it and passes the tests, he becomes ever more grateful to have a living example. Despite what some people think and say, it is very difficult to reach the stage of God-Realization. Having a living example bolsters one's faith when the going gets tough. The seeker sees that he, too, can one day become an ECK Master. Each and every one of the ECK Masters have gone through the very same tests of doubt about the Mahanta and about their own worthiness.

Each and every one of the ECK Masters have gone through the very same tests of doubt about the Mahanta and about their own worthiness.

"The beauty of God's plan is that it doesn't matter. Soul cannot escape Its destiny to one day join the God-Realized. Of course, God-Realization does not apply to men only. Every man and woman has the opportunity to set this high goal for himself or herself." Zan signaled the completion of the discourse by fading slowly from the screen of my inner vision. I opened my eyes and pondered his words. An incident from my early years on the path of Eckankar came to mind.

A friend and I had journeyed to our first Eckankar seminar in the mid 1970s. We were both new to the teachings and were curious to see what kind of people we would meet. One afternoon we were sitting in the audience when the MC brought on the next speaker. He was a man named Harold Klemp and was introduced as a Higher Initiate in Eckankar. This was several years before he became the Mahanta, the Living ECK Master.

A slender man with black-rimmed glasses walked onstage. He began to speak in a quiet voice, telling some simple stories. My friend was not very impressed. He turned to me and said, "If that guy can become a Higher Initiate in Eckankar, anybody can!"

Years later, after Harold Klemp had gone on to become the Mahanta, the Living ECK Master, my friend and I were Higher Initiates in ECK. One day I reminded him of that first seminar and asked him what he thought about it now.

He replied, "Now that I have an inkling of how challenging it must be to reach God-Realization, I have tremendous respect for Harold Klemp and his example. He is a real inspiration for me."

FALSE IMAGES OF ECK MASTERSHIP

My friend and I had carried outdated images of mastership to that seminar. Harold Klemp didn't match the image in our minds. Fortunately, by the time this man became the Living ECK Master we had done some revising and updating of our images. This problem of false expectations is an old one for the God-Realized. It is something they must contend with right from the start of their missions.

Harold Klemp writes,

> History is filled with errors simply because it is reported by fallible human beings. The qualities of divine love are usually defined by people who do not have divine love. This, to me, is ironic. But

My friend and I had carried outdated images of mastership to that seminar. Harold Klemp didn't match the image in our minds. Fortunately, by the time this man became the Living ECK Master we had done some revising and updating of our images.

these people are often gifted in writing, they are the reporters of history. They are the ones who presume to determine what divine love is, how it emanates from a certain person who especially inspires them, and whether such a person is or was a high spiritual being."[2]

Many of the myths about masters can be dispelled by taking the time to read the biographies of the great spiritual figures. All the trials, illnesses, hardships, and personality quirks of humanity can be found in their lives.

Many of the myths about masters can be dispelled by taking the time to read the biographies of the great spiritual figures. Not the ones where the grit is painted over with twenty coats of legends. But real cases of known historical people. All the trials, illnesses, hardships, and personality quirks of humanity can be found in their lives. Some of the common myths which we can rub from our eyes are:

1. Real masters don't need sleep.
2. Real masters can't eat meat.
3. Real masters never get sick or hurt.
4. Real masters never need glasses, go bald, use hearing aids, or whatever.
5. Real masters are not subject to human emotions.
6. Real masters only wear robes or some other distinctive clothing.
7. Real masters always walk and talk and act with great dignity.
8. Real masters never do ordinary things like watch television or play sports.
9. Real masters know everything, from planetary secrets to household plumbing.

The list could be extended indefinitely, adding items from all the differing religious and metaphysical viewpoints.

The Shariyat-Ki-Sugmad says,

Many seekers of God make their own image of

what they expect a Master to be, and, learning that the Mahanta does not fit this image, they become disappointed.[3]

The Shariyat states further,

No one should require the Living ECK Master to fit into that person's image of what a spiritual giant might be. Few ECK Masters will ever fit the popular image of what the masses think is a Godman. ECK Masters act too independently of the general social concept, doing as they wish, and usually living a life of their own and never bothering anyone."[4]

What then are Masters really like? They are often family men. They tend to be low key and have a fine sense of humor. The way they spend their spare time, what little they may have, is not so different than you and I. They mow the lawn, go grocery shopping, take out the garbage, walk in nature, visit with friends, and enjoy all the other normal activities of life.

GOD-REALIZATION DOES NOT CONFER HUMAN PERFECTION

Perhaps all of the misconceptions about Mastership are offshoots of the main one, which is the belief that a Godman is humanly perfect—as if the human part of anyone can be perfect. This belief can be a crutch which encourages the seeker to lean on and worship some perfect being rather than take the initiative to develop their own qualities.

When I first started on the path of Eckankar, I made a god out of the Living ECK Master. I imitated his personal mannerisms, speaking style, and so forth, thinking this would make me more spiritual. But I ran into

Perhaps all of the misconceptions about Mastership are offshoots of the main one, which is the belief that a Godman is humanly perfect—as if the human part of anyone can be perfect.

trouble when the next Living ECK Master came along, because he had a whole different personality and style.

Some ECK Masters are gentle and soft-spoken. Others are direct, no-nonsense kinds of people. Some are full of fun, while others can be rather serious. They represent the full spectrum of humanity. Yet all ECK Masters share a viewpoint of life from the spiritual mountaintop.

Having not learned this lesson, I began to try to fit myself into the mold of the new Living ECK Master. It wasn't working very well. Then one night I had a dream with the ECK Master Fubbi Quantz. He cleared things up for me, saying, "When I was following my own Master, I did much the same as you. I tried to synthesize all his personal qualities and embody them in myself. It proved to be a step backward. Then one day I caught the secret. I began to match his point of view! That was the turning point for me."

In other words, Fubbi was telling me to emulate the god part of the Godman, not the human part. Whoever the Godman of the times may be, he will embody the principal elements of spirituality which are the subject of this chapter.

The Living ECK Master never claims to be God. The ECK Masters teach that it is impossible for any human being to become God, despite the interpretations of some Eastern scriptures.

"Soul realizes that It is part of the whole of ECK, not with God," says *The Shariyat*. "As a divine spark of the ECK, It can have a realization that It is the ECK Itself. No man or Soul has ever, in the true state, felt that he or It was whole with God."[5]

There may well be a vast spiritual gulf between the

Soul realizes that It is part of the whole of ECK, not with God. As a divine spark of the ECK, It can have a realization that It is the ECK Itself. No man or Soul has ever, in the true state, felt that he or It was whole with God.

stature of a Godman and that of most other people. Even among those who have attained Mastership, there are degrees of attainment and consciousness. The journey of Soul never ends, and Mastership is but one more step in an eternal pilgrimage.

The journey of Soul never ends, and Mastership is but one more step in an eternal pilgrimage.

Harold Klemp points out that whether Master or initiate, we simply follow Divine Spirit's will the best we can. Even the Master at times must make peace with that will. Not because of any disagreement with it, but because he knows the reluctance some of his followers will have to go along with the directed changes. When Eckankar built its first Temple, a number of followers protested that this was too churchy, and some left. Presumably they felt the inner temples were fine, but somehow having an outer one upset them. The same reaction occurred among some ECKists when formal worship services were introduced.

Despite any limitations experienced by the human part of the Godman, there is a relative perfection that hinges on the god part. Soul is not bound by worldly limitations. "Man becomes perfect when he lives as the ECK," says *The Shariyat*, "when he makes the journey that all ECK initiates make to arrive at the goal of God-Realization, which is becoming the ECK of Itself." There will never be perfection in the human consciousness, but in my mind, this is as good as it gets.

QUALITIES OF THE GOD-REALIZED

It takes a fair amount of presumption to write a book like this one without being a Master, and perhaps no more so than in a discussion on God-Realization. I am even playing the fool a bit to list some of the attributes of the God-Realized. "There is no checklist of the traits of God-Realization that would apply to every-one," writes Harold Klemp. "This is simply because each of us works within our own individual world."[6]

Yet unless this is to be a chapter of blank pages, some attempt must be made. All I can do is ask the reader for empathy and patience as I draw on those who speak from experience.

So far in this chapter, I have mostly described what a God-Realized person is not. Now I will attempt to describe what a God-Realized person is. But first, as a transition to God-Realization, I will discuss Self-Realization. Most everyone assumes they know them-selves. Yet having once stepped outside the human consciousness completely and observed it from the viewpoint of Soul, this assumption crumbles.

Self-Realization, like the higher state of God-Realization, is a uniquely individual experience. For me Self-Realization feels like a light cloak of knowingness around my shoulders which never lets me forget, even for a moment, that I am more than my body, feelings, thoughts, and impressions.

There is constantly a part of me which stands back and observes everything as would a hawk circling over a summer meadow. With a little effort, I can shift into that other viewpoint and know I am Soul, an immortal spark of God. Perhaps an example will make this clearer.

In a recent dream some assassins captured me and dragged me to the top floor of a high building. They took me to the window and threw me out. As my body hurtled toward the ground, I, as Soul, never lost my perspective. "No use staying in this body any longer," I observed. "I better exit before it hits the ground."

As easily as the thought came, I slipped out of that

Self-Realization feels like a light cloak of knowingness around my shoulders which never lets me forget, even for a moment, that I am more than my body, feelings, thoughts, and impressions.

body and moved into a higher plane. A few minutes later I awoke from the dream.

To someone who identified with their body, this could have been a terrifying nightmare. But my feeling in the dream and upon awakening was calmly objective.

Of course, I would have been a lot less calm had this incident occurred in the physical world. The physical body has an instinctive urge to survive which can be very strong in moments of danger. Even so, the dream reflected the perspective of Soul.

To illustrate from another experience, one day I Soul Traveled above the lower worlds. I had recently become a Fifth Initiate on the path of Eckankar, and it was time to explore Self-Realization firsthand. Next to me was the ECK Master Rebazar Tarzs. Both of us were little more than viewpoints in a world of being. Looking "down" through the planes to the earth world, we observed a certain experienced Higher Initiate in ECK whose life was in disarray as he dealt with a number of problems.

In a moment the Higher Initiate popped up above the lower worlds and joined us. He joked about how his little self had lost its perspective, amusing Rebazar and me with his banter. Then he said, "Well, time to get back!" and in a moment he was back down in the theater of his little self, but with a calmer and more confident attitude.

Rebazar pointed out that I, too, could get this high perspective of Self-Realization at any time, provided I kept a fit awareness through the Spiritual Exercises of ECK.

To one who has not experienced this point of view, these are empty words. How much more so, then, when the God-Realization view is being described!

Rebazar pointed out that I, too, could get this high perspective of Self-Realization at any time, provided I kept a fit awareness through the Spiritual Exercises of ECK.

"Man confuses self-knowledge with the knowledge of his conscious ego-personality," says *The Shariyat*. "One who has any ego-consciousness at all takes it for granted that he knows himself. But the ego knows only its own contents, not the psychic self and its contents. Man measures his self-knowledge by what the average person in his social environment knows of himself, not the real spiritual facts which are for the most part hidden from him."[7]

The reality of this was made vividly clear to me one day on a college campus. I was taking a course in psychology. The instructor wished to help us gain some self-understanding by listing ten things about our personal identity.

When we finished, each student took a turn reading their list. The other students had written things like I am a student, I am a mother or wife or daughter, I am an American, an athlete, a businessman, a Christian, and so forth. These are exactly the kinds of identities *The Shariyat* described as "what the average person in his social environment knows of himself, not the real spiritual facts." The listed items were little more than social roles and personality characteristics.

When it came my turn to read, I fidgeted in my chair. "Well? What did you write?" prompted the instructor. "I could only think of one thing," I answered. "I wrote 'I am Soul, a spark of God.'"

The room was totally silent for a minute as everyone stared at me like I was an alien creature. I wish to emphasize that the answer I had written down was a sincere and spontaneous response to the question. I wasn't trying to impress anyone.

"The realization of God," Harold Klemp tells us,

"Well? What did you write?" prompted the instructor. "I could only think of one thing," I answered. "I wrote 'I am Soul, a spark of God.'"

"begins as Soul makes the transition between the Eighth and Ninth initiations in ECK, increases through the Ninth and Tenth, and reaches fulfillment at the Eleventh."[8] *The Shariyat* says it is not always a shattering experience that tosses the pieces of one's life to the four winds. But more often it comes without startling drama, stealing over one with a strange subtleness. Not being something the mind can easily grasp, the seeker may fail at first to recognize the realization that is being born within him.[9]

Of the new Ninth Initiate *The Shariyat* says, "Of course, he cannot understand what this means at the stage of development in entering into the Ninth Circle, but it isn't long before his intellectual senses grasp the full significance of it."[10]

Now his consciousness embraces the universe, his inner vision sees the vistas of the higher realities, his speech expresses divine truth, and his body becomes an expression of the ECK. He becomes a full citizen of the Kingdom of God and prepares himself for Mastership.

What does this transformation mean in practical terms? It means he is no longer the seeker. Now Soul is the knower.

When asked to describe some of the attributes of God-Realization, Harold Klemp has said,

> I would say harmony is among the best of them. Harmony in this sense is not necessarily something that shows out here. It means working toward integrating my personal mission with the greater mission, so that it fits together for the benefit of everyone.
>
> The ECK Masters have two missions as they support the Living ECK Master. There is a personal

What does this transformation mean in practical terms? It means he is no longer the seeker. Now Soul is the knower.

mission that keeps them interested in the microcosm; and when they are working in the macrocosmic
state of consciousness, there is the greater mission
of helping with the teachings of ECK. So besides the
service you give to ECK, it is important to have your
own life, your own goals, to plan your vacations, and
to pursue your own ambitions. You need both for
balance.[11]

*The macro-
cosm and
microcosm are
married within
the Godman. He
is the Inner and
Outer Master.
His mission is
to show Soul the
way home
to God.*

THE GODMAN'S MISSION

The macrocosm and microcosm are married within
the Godman. He is the Inner and Outer Master. His
mission is to show Soul the way home to God. Harold
Klemp writes, "There are just a few people who can
really recognize the gift of the Inner and Outer Master."[12]

The Outer Master teaches us through his talks,
books, and discourses. And when we take his outer
image into contemplation or the dream state, we more
easily make the connection with the Inner Master.

Over the years I have heard a certain story told
many times, but the plot is ever new to the person
telling it. A person will arrive at an Eckankar class,
seminar, or ECK Worship Service and see a photo of the
Living ECK Master. "Oh, I've met him before, in a
dream! Who is he?" Or if not in a dream, in a vision,
or during a crisis, or from a chance encounter somewhere.

Occasionally a seeker will show up at an ECK center
and say, "My inner guide (or guardian angel) told me
to find out about this teaching."

They may even discover that their inner guide was
one of the past ECK Masters whose picture is hanging

on the wall of the ECK center. Many ECK Masters serve as guides to lead people to the Living ECK Master.

As another aspect of his mission, the Godman sets a living example and ideal for the seeker. *The Shariyat* states, "All people find in him inspiration for the development of noble character." And, "The Living ECK Master is, therefore, the divine man; a real son of God. Yet every man has in him the latent possibilities for the same expansion to mastership. He only requires the Living ECK Master to help develop it."[13]

Throughout the ECK teachings can be heard the refrain: Your mission is to become numbered among the God-Realized, to become a Master in your own right.

Having studied a great deal of literature about successful people in all walks of life, I have found most had one or more role models who became an ideal for them. When everything seemed to be going against them, the image or life story of their ideal inspired them and they turned the tide in their favor.

Luck, circumstance, and the favors of our upbringing seem to have very little to do with whether we succeed. It's our determination, hard work, the greatness of our aspirations, and a noble ideal which count.

These are the very qualities which shine forth in the life stories of those who have become ECK Masters. Their lives cut through the myths and tell us what we really have to do to become one of them.

They all shared a burning desire to touch the heart of God. They all maintained a relentless, tireless persistence which refused to surrender to any setbacks on their long journey to the goal. They all looked past their own limitations, pushed aside their self-doubts, and chose the identity of Mastership.

Throughout the ECK teachings can be heard the refrain: Your mission is to become numbered among the God-Realized, to become a Master in your own right.

The Shariyat states,

> The idea of the Mahanta as representative man appears sometime to be quite startling to the traditionalists of religions. It need not be, though the eternal and essential Godman does involve seeming contradictions. The incarnation of the Mahanta in every age is not only a showing forth of the divine drama being played out, but also a continuing portrayal of the human drama. This gives the only true promise of salvation, the liberation of Soul from the world of matter.[14]

Understanding how Soul combines the attributes of human and god is the question posed to every serious seeker. The answer is found in the heights, yet also in the depths of life. It is the marriage of heaven and earth which recurs every time another Soul discovers the answer to the eternal riddle of Its true nature.

16

The Prophet

The Mahanta, the Living ECK Master, is the prophet for all the works of Eckankar. When he gives prophecy it is under the possession and influence of the ECK.

Paul Twitchell
The ECK-Vidya,
Ancient Science of Prophecy[1]

P rophecy is one of the most ancient and influential of the spiritual arts. Our own era, which bridges the second and third millennium of the Christian calendar, is flooded with prophecies and predictions. Many center on geological and social catastrophes, contact with extraterrestrial civilizations (benign or not), fantastic and rapid spiritual transformations of the entire planet into higher dimensions, and the return of past saviors. The claimed sources of these prophecies range widely. Almost anyone who can gain an audience adds to the hodgepodge.

In general, the prophecies of the Mahanta speak with quiet and restraint in this hubbub of excitement. But not always. Startling prophecies can be found in the writings of Eckankar.

Paul Twitchell wrote *The ECK-Vidya, Ancient Science of Prophecy*. He made a number of prophecies in that book

Startling prophecies can be found in the writings of Eckankar.

and in his talks and other writings during his term as the Mahanta, the Living ECK Master. Since he passed from this world in 1971, he has been a frequent inner teacher for me. Rather than visit with Zan on the subject of this chapter, I decided one evening to invite Paul into my contemplation to discuss it.

I felt a key to understanding the Mahanta's role as the Prophet lies in a statement from *The ECK-Vidya*. Paul writes, "It is said that prophecy is a matter of telling forth, and prediction is that of foretelling. The prophecy is of course the more prominent of the two."[2]

It is said that prophecy is a matter of telling forth, and prediction is that of foretelling. The prophecy is of course the more prominent of the two.

KINDS OF PROPHECY

Before sitting down to contemplate, I went to take a shower. While soaping and singing like a bathroom baritone—or more accurately, like a terrible tenor—Paul suddenly appeared on the inner screen of my mind and launched into a discourse on prophecy. Apparently he wanted to get started immediately.

"There is an old saying," Paul began, "that the best way to know your future is to create it. Imagine a young woman who feels it is her mission in life to be a healer. She studies hard in college with hopes of getting into medical school. A safe prediction at that point in her life is that she will become a medical doctor. But unforeseen circumstances come up which block her from medical school. The prediction fails.

"Holding true to her dreams of becoming a healer, she adjusts her plans and finds acceptance in a school of alternative medicine. This approach proves successful, and the woman goes on to a career in healing.

"Now here is the point I am illustrating. The telling forth of this woman was her intent to be a healer. This was the design and purpose of her life, emanating from the Soul level. The foretelling is that she would become an M.D. It was her personality responding the best way it could to Soul's intent. But medical school was only one of many ways to reach her ideal of being a healer. The foretelling proved to be wrong, but the telling forth was accurate.

"Lift this analogy to the high spiritual planes. The best way to know the future in broad terms is to know God's plan and purpose. When the Divine Being establishes Its great plan, the lower creation is set in motion and must ultimately conform to that plan, as the carpenter builds a house to the blueprint of the architect.

"When the Mahanta is telling forth in his role as the Prophet, he is communicating to the lower creation the cosmic blueprint of the divine purpose. This kind of prophecy is highly accurate, except in the inevitable limitations of language and human thought.

When the Mahanta is telling forth in his role as the Prophet, he is communicating to the lower creation the cosmic blueprint of the divine purpose.

"How will mankind or the lower creation respond to this plan? This is where the lower form of prophecy comes in, the foretelling or predictive mode of prophecy. These are what I call if-then prophecies. If the human race follows this course of action, then such and such will happen. These prophecies can never be completely accurate. There is wide latitude in the free will of people to respond to God's will. They may conform to the divine plan in a variety of ways, and the timing may come sooner or later than expected. But the ultimate destiny cannot be escaped.

"Take another example. It is part of God's plan of creation that each and every Soul will one day become a Co-worker with God, a master of Its own destiny, a God-Realized being. Soul cannot escape this destiny, even if It wanted to. Though few would consider it so, this is one of the great telling-forth prophecies given by all Mahantas in history. How and when and under what circumstances each individual Soul will achieve this high destiny is a matter of foretelling, of if-then prophecy.

The high prophecies based on God's purpose establish lasting foundations, long-range trends, and broad themes.

"The high prophecies based on God's purpose establish lasting foundations, long-range trends, and broad themes. They lack the glamour and excitement of flashy, near-term predictions like those given by psychics."

As I turned off the shower and reached for a towel I said inwardly to Paul, "I don't think I can remember any more right now."

He chuckled and responded, "I gave this to you in the shower because you needed a clean, fresh viewpoint on the whole subject! Good night."

DREAMS OF DESTINY

Having duly noted Paul's helpful comments, I turned first to the consideration of what he calls the telling-forth prophecies. I went through the works of ECK looking for any that fit the definition. I feel it is best to get the view on these foundational prophecies before examining the foretelling ones.

The word *dream* has an interesting double meaning in the English language, which pertains here. First, it means to build the future in our imagination. Second, it refers to our nocturnal adventures. Both meanings are variations of the principle that all creation happens first on the inner levels and then on the outer.

As mentioned in the earlier chapter on the Dream Master, the high spiritual view of dreams is the reverse of the ordinary one. That is, physical life is the dream, and the inner life is the awakened state. The further one moves outward from the center of the Divine Being, the more he enters into a dream world and a state of sleep.

Putting these ideas together we can see how the process of creation, whether cosmic or personal, is a matter of dreaming from the inside outward. So there is a connection between prophecies and dreams. We know the future through creating it, and we create it through dreaming.

Applying these insights, we can catch a glimpse of the major outline of the telling-forth prophecies as given by the Mahanta. These may be thought of as the cosmic dream, the world dream, the dream of a great era, and finally the dreams of the time periods of specific Living ECK Masters.

We know the future through creating it, and we create it through dreaming.

We shall see how these mighty dreams cascade from God into ever smaller parts until they reach the dreams of the individual seeker. Let's look at these dreams of prophecy now, from the macrocosm to the microcosm.

"In the beginning," reads *The Shariyat,* "the Sugmad rested quietly in Its abode in the Ocean of Love and Mercy. Outside Itself there were no other planes, universes, nor worlds. Not a Soul, being, nor creature existed. Only the Sugmad lay dreaming in Its eternal realm. And while It dreamed, there began the formation of the worlds inside Itself."[3]

Here begins the first prototype dream of all dreams. This first act of creation may be called a cosmic dream. *The Shariyat* continues with a description of the progressive manifestation of the entire creation, all unfolding in a series of ten cosmic dreams of God.

Each stage in the ten-dream set is described as occurring because God was not yet pleased with what It had created. Isn't this how Soul creates Its own universe? It creates a life for Itself through dreaming and imagination. Yet once the dream is attained, It is not satisfied and dreams some more, improving upon it.

Isn't this how Soul creates Its own universe? It creates a life for Itself through dreaming and imagination.

Next we descend a step from God's cosmic dreams to what we may call the world dream. The ancient records of the ECK Masters trace their lineage back to a being named Gakko, who is said to have come out of the heart of God into this world some six million years ago.[4]

Paul Twitchell wrote, "It is found in the Shariyat-Ki-Sugmad, the holy writings of Eckankar, that the world dream was created by Gakko, the first Mahanta, the Living ECK Master."[5] Paul gives little more than this fragment of history about Gakko.

I think we are helped by the way Paul worded this tidbit—the world dream was "created" by Gakko. This is using the word *dream* in the sense of manifesting a vision, rather than in the sense of the musings of slumber. I believe this dream established the telling-forth prophecy dream for the spiritual destiny of this planet and all the future Mahantas who would play a part in it.

I believe the vision includes the root races which were destined to play out their roles in world history. The prophecies about these races are classic examples of telling-forth prophecies. At our present point in world history, we are currently in the time of the fifth, or Aryan, root race. The previous four root civilizations vanished long ago. The others lie far in the future.

Paul wrote about the coming root races, even giving the names of future Mahantas who will lead a few of them spiritually. I feel it would be missing the mark to call Paul's writings about these races "predictions," or foretelling. My impression is they are part of the world blueprint, part of the major scaffolding upon which the details of planetary history will be built.

At the close of the eras of the past two root races, the Lemurian and the Atlantean, ECK Masters stepped forth and warned the people of the imminent destruction of their continents. Pronouncements of this scale are a telling forth.

Descending yet another step in the ladder of great dreams, we come to the dreams of certain key ECK Masters who have a great and enduring destiny to play out in world history. Yaubl Sacabi is one. Paul Twitchell states that Yaubl Sacabi heads up the order of the ECK Masters on this planet, is in charge of their capital at the spiritual city of Agam Des, and is of an age beyond human conception. He served as the Mahanta, the Living ECK Master among the Myceneans, who invaded Greece during the period between 2000–1700 B.C.

The dream was given to Yaubl by Sat Nam, the great manifestation of God on the Soul, or Fifth, Plane. Yaubl Sacabi's dream extended over a ten-day period. In broad terms, the dream prophecy of Yaubl Sacabi revealed the destiny of America and the world in our own times, and into the twenty-first century.

The fourth descending step in the cascade of dreams brings us to each individual Living ECK Master and his mission. If the particular Master's mission is global in scope, then to read his mission is to get a glimpse into the spiritual mission of the world. How?

At the close of the eras of the past two root races, the Lemurian and the Atlantean, ECK Masters stepped forth and warned the people of the imminent destruction of their continents.

"The words of the Mahanta alone can change the world, completely and irrevocably," states *The Shariyat*. And, "If he so desires, the Living ECK Master can make spiritual contact with the whole of mankind or all beings in any country at any time, regardless of language barriers."[6] In my book *The Dream Weaver Chronicles* I illustrate how this works through the example of the global mission of Harold Klemp.

This brings us finally to the fifth level of prophecy-dream, that of the individual seeker. This dream does not unfold in isolation. It is encompassed within a series of expanding concentric circles of the four higher dreams discussed above.

THE BOOK OF LIFE

I feel one of the most profound statements about the interdependence of our personal dream with God's cosmic dream is found in *The ECK-Vidya* where Paul Twitchell is discussing the scriptures of the Shariyat.

He gave a number of prophetic readings for people using the method of the ECK-Vidya. He found that, "so many times the life of every Soul is dictated by these strange books [the Shariyat-Ki-Sugmad]; and that many times the readings might be found in Soul records [Fifth Plane records] almost identical with the works of ECK, for ECK Itself is life."[7]

Imagine a scripture which, on the higher planes, merges into the very Light and Sound of God, which is so vast in Its scope that It encompasses the very lives of the countless Souls unfolding throughout creation. In other words, God's cosmic dream is embodied within the Shariyat-Ki-Sugmad, and it enfolds the seeker's dreams in a grand symphony of divine purpose moving

Imagine a scripture which, on the higher planes, merges into the very Light and Sound of God, which is so vast in Its scope that It encompasses the very lives of the countless Souls unfolding throughout creation.

onward to some great and unfathomable destiny.

One night many years ago I had a powerful prophetic dream. At the time, in August 1982, I lived in the state of Kansas. I dreamed I was kneeling in the center of a circle—a zodiac mosaic which was inlaid on the floor of a small stone building. The only light came from an aperture in its south wall.

I knew I was awaiting the fall equinox. At precisely the equinoctial moment, a sunbeam shot through the aperture and illuminated a point on the circle where was written "September 22."

The voice of the Mahanta, the Prophet, said, "Between September 22 and October 22 your life will take a totally new direction. This is the last month in the annual calendar of the ECK Masters. It wraps up the old year and sets the stage for the new. Be prepared to align yourself with the new spiritual year."

A few days later, I was suddenly laid off from my job when the company lost a major contract. I drove to Oregon to spend a few weeks visiting my parents on their farm. I kept busy for several weeks helping with chores and repairs around the property.

When September 22 came, I thought, *How in the world can my life take a totally new direction when I'm sitting on a farm in rural Oregon? I guess I'll have to make something happen.*

I packed my few belongings into my Volkswagen bug and told my parents I was going to hit the road. Just as I was backing out of the driveway my mother came running from the house to tell me I had a long-distance phone call.

I hurried in to the phone. On the line was a job agent. He said, "I was just cleaning out some old files

The voice of the Mahanta, the Prophet, said, "Between September 22 and October 22 your life will take a totally new direction."

and found your resumé at the bottom of the drawer. It seems you have some skills needed right now by a company in Israel. Would you be interested in applying for a position there?"

Of course, I assured him, I was, and I would apply for a passport immediately. He laughed and said, "Don't get your hopes up yet. They've been very selective about who they would take."

"Don't worry," I assured him, "I'll get the job." He phoned back a couple of days later to tell me I had indeed been accepted.

One month later, on October 22, I landed in Tel Aviv, Israel. My life took a whole new direction, as the Mahanta as Prophet had said it would. This major new cycle in my personal life was exactly in sync with the cycle of the new spiritual year.

It so happened that the contract in Israel ended under strange circumstances on October 22, 1986, precisely four years later. Even that termination was given to me in a form of prophecy called a waking dream a week in advance. I was standing at a bus stop waiting to catch my ride to work when my attention was drawn to an incident across the street. Without going into the details, it was made clear to me that some kind of important ending was to take place that day.

Shortly after I arrived at work, my employer surprised me with a dismissal notice. He had always been pleased with my work, and the sudden firing didn't make sense. "What is the cause?" I asked.

My boss said, "You visited a religious seminar in Europe during the summer. Upon returning to Israel you went through a routine security debriefing because of the sensitive nature of the work you are doing for us.

Shortly after I arrived at work, my employer surprised me with a dismissal notice. He had always been pleased with my work, and the sudden firing didn't make sense.

During the interview you were asked by our agents whether you met with anyone from the Communist Bloc. You explained to them that there were people at the seminar from all over Europe, and that you had talked with some who were from behind the Iron Curtain.

"I'm sure you are innocent of any wrongdoing, but our security people always play it safe in these situations. The only thing I was able to do was get a one-week extension of your employment. So your last day will be October 22."

In the next chapter I will relate the deeper reason and ancient roots which led me to the historical landscape of Israel. But for the moment I feel this story exemplifies the way our individual destinies and prophetic dreams are centered within the greater circle of the higher dreams.

Our individual destinies and prophetic dreams are centered within the greater circle of the higher dreams.

The following passages from *The Shariyat* summarize the key points made so far.

> The Mahanta, the Living ECK Master is not one who merely gives predictions of the future, but he is the ECK prophet. There is a vast difference in the two. Those who give predictions are merely the readers of the psychic files from the lower planes, generally those of the Astral world. But the Mahanta, the Living ECK Master gives divine utterance from the Sugmad. He is the channel for the Voice of the Sugmad, and in this case nothing comes from the mind, but directly from the heart of the Almighty.

And:

> This is part of the works of Eckankar known as the ECK-Vidya, and the Mahanta, the Living ECK Master is often the only one who

can give this type of telling forth. Again there is a
difference between telling forth and foretelling.
Telling forth comes from the central spiritual region above the Anami Lok, in which the Sugmad
dwells. Foretelling is merely prediction which is of
a psychic nature. The ECK chela will soon come to
know the difference between the two and will give
up anything of any psychic nature which might be
a detriment to himself and his spiritual unfoldment into the heavenly worlds.[8]

THE PROPHET AND THE SEEKER

*The role of
the Prophet
in the seeker's
life is generally
more indirect
than most of the
other aspects of
the Mahanta.*

The role of the Prophet in the seeker's life is generally more indirect than most of the other aspects of
the Mahanta. He knows the past, present, and destiny
of the human race and all people. He knows God's
design and purpose in the large sense, as well as for
each era and generation.

First of all, this enables him to help all seekers
align themselves with the current direction of the Holy
Spirit. When this Wind of Change sweeps over the
planet, many people are slow to sense Its direction.

People have accustomed themselves to the way
things are. They may cling to spiritual notions and
practices which no longer suit the times. As the course
of the river changes, they are left on dry land, far from
the main flow of the Light and Sound of God.

Second, the Mahanta can use his high and clear
perspective to guide the seeker along the best path. He
can help us anticipate problems which are yet over the
horizon. There is no need to consult the Outer Master
for an ECK-Vidya reading. The direction comes through
our dreams, waking dreams, intuition, contemplation,

and other forms of guidance. Harold Klemp's book *A Modern Prophet Answers Your Key Questions about Life* shows how this works.[9]

"The Living ECK Master is above time and space," states *The Shariyat*. "He is God's essential expression and is never separated from the source of true wisdom and reality. He is able to see the past, know the future, and give healings, happiness, and create miracles for those whom he loves and those who believe and can accept his gifts."[10]

Recently the Wind of Change, the ECK, began blowing through my personal life again. This was evidenced by a deep sense of restlessness in my job and a strong feeling to define some new goals for myself. One Friday I took a day of vacation from work to have some quiet time to ponder my future.

During contemplation the Mahanta suggested I write down my new goals very specifically, so I did. Then I spent several hours revising them until I was satisfied they were what I wanted for myself.

During contemplation the Mahanta suggested I write down my new goals very specifically, so I did.

About 11:00 p.m. I went out into the backyard to gaze at the stars. Years ago in a dream, the Mahanta had told me to anchor myself to the North Star. This was a way of telling me to keep my spiritual compass pointing to the goal of God.

On an impulse, I recited my goals aloud to the sky, then reached up and "touched" the North Star as I said a blessing of gratitude. At that moment a shooting star arced across the sky and burst into a colorful fireworks display right at the North Star. I took it as a promise from the Prophet that my goals were sure and true.

The following Monday when I arrived at work, I

was immediately approached by my supervisor. "While you were gone Friday, the whole division was reorganized. Our department has been dismantled and absorbed into other groups. You can choose which of the new groups you want to join."

Hmmm, I thought, *synchronicity.* I phoned my wife to tell her the news. As we talked I said "This may be my signal from the Mahanta that it is time to leave the company and move on to something new." The moment the words were out of my mouth there was a power outage in the building, just for a few seconds. I laughed and said, "There's my answer!"

Things moved along very quickly over the next few days. The path to a new job came about through a remarkable series of perfect coincidences. After settling into my new job I told the story of how it happened to a fellow member of Eckankar who also worked for the new corporation. When I finished he said, "This all sounds familiar. About a year ago, didn't you tell me you had a dream of someday working in this company?"

Almost exactly a year before, I had indeed recorded the prophetic dream in my journal.

I went home that evening and reviewed my dream journal of the previous year. Almost exactly a year before, I had indeed recorded the prophetic dream in my journal. The friend who reminded me of the dream had also been in it. In the dream he had showed me around the corporation as a new employee. I had also written, "This is the way all corporations should welcome their new employees."

The list of qualities I had written down as goals matched the new job very closely. Some aspects of the job were even better. I could say this transition was all due to my own efforts, but I know better. The Prophet gave valuable assistance at every stage. I have found this to be true for each major transition I have made over the years.

Some who look to the Mahanta will receive dramatic guidance. Others will not. It all depends on each person's unique needs, on his own relationship to the Inner Master, on his ability to recognize the guidance when it comes, and on his willingness to follow it.

THE LIVING PRESENT

Whenever exploring the subject of prophecy or past lives I feel it is valuable to end on a reminder that Soul always lives in the present moment. A friend once said, "So many people want to be somewhere else, with someone else, doing something else." This philosophy of life is expressed in America on the ubiquitous bumper sticker which begins with "I'd rather be____," and ends with sailing, fishing, or whatever. How much of our lives do we spend reliving the past with regret or longing, wishing we were somewhere else, or worrying about the future?

Even if we were able to know all about the future, would we choose to? Some who have gained the ability to do so, like Paul Twitchell and Harold Klemp, choose not to. They feel it robs life of adventure.[11]

A good friend of mine had a near-death experience in which she was shown details of the rest of her life, should she choose to return to earth. She chose to come back, but she asked not to remember the future, because it would spoil the surprise.

Soul lives ever in the moment. If the Mahanta gives us a glimpse into the future, knowing the future is not the main point. It is really to help us live better today.

Soul lives ever in the moment. If the Mahanta gives us a glimpse into the future, knowing the future is not the main point. It is really to help us live better today. When Soul is able to scan the lower worlds from the lofty position of Self-Realization, all time seems to collapse into a wondrous searing moment of infinite possibility. Yet as long as we dwell here below, life unfolds sequentially.

The ECK Masters are the prophets of old who travel from the regions of the Absolute. They bring the messages of the Almighty. They keep alive the urge toward spiritual freedom and the memory of Soul's divine origin. Leading the way is the Mahanta, the Prophet, for all who follow the path of the Light and Sound of God.

17 — · —

The Ancient One

The Mahanta is the Godman, the Ancient One who reincarnates again and again in the world of matter. He comes in every age, every lifetime, to gather up those who have failed to accept him in the past.

The Shariyat-Ki-Sugmad,
Book One[1]

I n this chapter we near the climax of our story. This aspect, the Ancient One, involves one of the most vital currents in the spiritual destiny of the human race. To trace this influence is to reveal the hand of God at the controls throughout history.

My thoughts stood mute before the challenge of a testimony to this aspect of the Mahanta. I turned to contemplation in hopes that Zan would give me a start. After a lengthy HU song, I fell silent and awaited his appearance. Instead, the image of a giant oak tree began to form in my imagination. It was one that stood at the entrance to the farm in Oregon where I grew up, serving as an anchor in the stormy seas of my adolescence.

I moved forward into the picture until I was standing by the tree. I reached out and ran my palm over its rough bark. The trunk was some six feet thick. A forester once

This aspect, the Ancient One, involves one of the most vital currents in the spiritual destiny of the human race.

estimated that the tree was about five hundred years old. I used to fantasize that the acorn from which this huge tree grew had sprouted when Columbus discovered America.

"The tree of heaven extends upward to great heights," said a familiar voice. I turned to find Zan just behind me. "To be stable against the buffeting winds of change, its roots must be anchored deep into the bedrock of the earth. The great religions are among the most enduring of institutions in this world, extending over thousands of years. Yet, even these are as the passing daffodils in springtime compared to the ageless nature of the Ancient One.

"His presence is the only tangible thing Soul can fasten upon to keep from wandering about aimlessly during Its incarnations in this world."

I said, "On Columbus Day, 1962, when I was eleven years old, a powerful windstorm swept up from California, through Oregon, and on to Washington. It felled thousands of trees, tore roofs off houses, and created havoc everywhere. Such storms are almost unheard of in this part of the country. I remember that the hefty branches of this old oak tree hardly swayed during the storm."

Zan nodded, eyeing the beauty of the tree's old gnarled branches. "This tree began its growth during the time when the Mahanta, the Ancient One, was embodied in the ECK Master Rebazar Tarzs. Part of his mission was the inner guidance of Columbus in order to reunite the two halves of the world which had been split in two with the sinking of the lost continents of Atlantis and Lemuria.

"It is rightly said that few if any Souls succeed in reaching God on the first try. Many who discover and look to the Mahanta in any age are trying for the

The great religions are among the most enduring of institutions in this world, extending over thousands of years. Yet, even these are as the passing daffodils in springtime compared to the ageless nature of the Ancient One.

second, third, or more times.

"Soul is like a seabird that spends much of its life upon the ocean. Periodically, Soul will dive beneath the waves into the lower worlds in search of food for growth and experience. Then It will appear again on the surface.

"Soul comes to earth in many bodies, many personalities. Yet every time, hidden inside each form is the same eternal spark of God. On the higher level, the Mahanta is the same. He may be embodied as the Living ECK Master of the times. Yet it is ever the one Mahanta, that same state of God Consciousness, which manifests in the Master."

Soul comes to earth in many bodies, many personalities. Yet every time, hidden inside each form is the same eternal spark of God.

"This has always confused me," I said. "Who is the Ancient One?"

Zan sat down upon the grass and picked up an acorn, rubbing its smooth surface between his fingers. "Men live immersed in profound wonders all their lives, but fail to see them. The acorn slumbers and dreams of becoming a mighty oak. No one notices how the dream unfolds, for it does so very gradually over the centuries. It is much like Soul's dream of God-Realization, slowly emerging over many lifetimes. The Ancient One is he who plants the acorns, tends the seedlings, and watches over the growth of the trees.

"He hovers above time. He sees the end from the beginning. Yet he is also the stream of God's Light and Sound which enters into the flow of history, focusing Itself in each Living ECK Master of the times. The flow is not equally strong through every Living ECK Master. Sometimes It runs quietly, and the Master of the time will have a minor mission. At other times It floods through a certain Living ECK Master into the world, and the fullness of the Mahanta walks the earth.

"These flows are cyclical, and in harmony with the spiritual needs of humanity. The human race is now in a great transition. The Ancient One's presence is strongly felt. To recognize him in the face of the Living ECK Master is a great blessing. It can happen in a flash of recognition."

Zan pushed his index finger into the soil, making a small hole. He tucked the acorn in and covered it. As I watched, the scene faded from my contemplation.

As I thought of the Ancient One, I recalled an encounter about fifteen years ago when the Mahanta came to me one night on the inner planes as the Dream Master. He had a scheduling book with him and showed me that I had an appointment for my next initiation in three months. As he turned to leave he said, "You will need to reconnect with where you left off before."

This visit by the Dream Master to discuss my next initiation set in motion a chain of events which would reconnect me with those lost memories.

I knew what he meant. The earlier initiations in Eckankar in this lifetime were not new to me. They felt familiar, and I knew I had been through them before in a past life. But something had gone wrong. Whatever it was, it caused a big setback in my progress. This visit by the Dream Master to discuss my next initiation set in motion a chain of events which would reconnect me with those lost memories. Along the way, I would learn the value in the seeker's life of the Mahanta as the Ancient One.

TRACING LOST MEMORIES

The first part of my reconnection with the past happened at night on the inner planes. A quest had taken me far into the wilderness of a dream world. At the apex of the quest, I was lifted out of the dream world into the Soul Plane.

There I beheld a being of intense light and love. Its presence was as familiar as the depths of my own being. Whoever he or it was, I had known him forever. He began to speak to me in the language of Soul, impressions of Light and Sound.

"I have always been with you," he said. "I was there when you first descended into the lower worlds millions of years ago, to begin your cycle of incarnations. I have watched you grow, loved you, nurtured you. And I will be with you still, until the last wave of God's great music rolls through the universe. Delay no longer! Know that you are Soul, the immortal one!"

It is hard to convey in words the effect of this dream. I awoke with a feeling of absolute comfort and security. I knew that I could never be truly lost or abandoned in this world, that the Ancient One would always be with me.

I knew that I could never be truly lost or abandoned in this world, that the Ancient One would always be with me.

This meeting stirred in me a deep desire to trace my spiritual roots. What had happened in the past that still haunted me? I had a burning desire to find out. And the discovery would not be long in coming.

In the chapter on the Prophet, I told the story of how the Mahanta led me to a four-year stay in Israel. The purpose of the visit was to work there for several years as a consultant. But my spiritual mission was to reconnect with a broken past from several thousand years before.

As soon as I settled into my new job in Israel, I spent any spare time exploring that famous historical landscape. Some of my coworkers planned a trip to Egypt one weekend, but I didn't want to go. "It's only thirty dollars for a bus ticket," they explained. "Would you come all the way to the Middle East and pass up a chance to see the Great Pyramid and other wonders of Egypt?"

"I don't know why, I just feel a strong resistance to going there," was my feeble explanation. My friends would have laughed off any reasoning about past lives, so I let it go at that. They shrugged and went without me.

One afternoon, in contemplation, I suddenly and unexpectedly found myself in the midst of a vivid past-life recall. I sensed the era was around 1000 B.C.

One afternoon, in contemplation, I suddenly and unexpectedly found myself in the midst of a vivid past-life recall. I sensed the era was around 1000 B.C. I was standing with a group of about two dozen other students in a temple. We had gathered for a graduation ceremony, and our several teachers were standing before us on a platform.

The school was organized into three levels—beginner, intermediate, and advanced. At the conclusion of each level, a ceremony was held and announcements made as to who would pass on to the next level. Those who didn't pass were not given a second chance. The etiquette of the day was to express gratitude for having gone as far as one did and to return to a normal life in the community.

The group I stood in had passed the first level several years ago. We were now finished with the intermediate training and were gathered to see who would pass on to the final level.

Torches cast flickering lights upon our expectant faces. I looked around the group, sizing up my classmates. Usually only one or two from any group failed to pass into the final level of training. I had no doubts that I would be among those promoted, so I occupied myself speculating on who would be the excluded ones.

The man who would become our new teacher at the advanced level stepped forth and gathered our attention. Though I hadn't known it at the time, during this recall I could see he was the Living ECK Master of the times. He congratulated all of us on our excellent achievements, taking time to compliment everyone for their unique contributions. Then he held up a scroll and began reading the list of those who were to continue on to level three.

As each name was read, the student stepped up on the platform and joined the teacher. I was surprised at some of the names announced, for I thought the students unfit. My reverie was broken when the teacher announced there were no more on the list. All had passed except me. For a brief moment I was shocked, then I flew into a rage. I accused the teacher of passing over me for personal reasons and of being incompetent to judge my fitness for the next level.

My very behavior proved he was right in passing me over. Denouncing the entire school as a charade, I stormed out of the temple in a huff. The rest of that lifetime I used every opportunity to defame the school and belittle the students and teachers. I made fun of the secret teachings I had been taught.

I was discreetly warned of the karmic implications of my actions. But as time passed and nothing adverse happened to me, I became all the more emboldened and began to ridicule the foolishness of anyone who believed in such notions as karma and reincarnation.

The past-life scene began to fade from my consciousness. But as it did, I caught a fleeting message from the Inner Master. "It took you a thousand years to recover from your actions in that life," he said, "and to regain the ground you had lost."

Today, when I see people turn against the Mahanta and start to follow a course similar to the one I did in

I caught a fleeting message from the Inner Master. "It took you a thousand years to recover from your actions in that life," he said, "and to regain the ground you had lost."

that distant past, I feel like shaking them awake, saying, "Do you have any idea what you are doing to yourself?" But of course they would be no more receptive than I was back then. It's a learning process some people just have to go through.

Now I knew why I had been reluctant to visit Egypt. A few months after this past-life dream, the second part of this long-forgotten story revealed itself.

Now I knew why I had been reluctant to visit Egypt. A few months after this past-life dream, the second part of this long-forgotten story revealed itself. One of my favorite places in Israel was down along the Dead Sea near the old ruins of Qumran where the Dead Sea Scrolls were found. I went there often, just to sit among the ruins or walk along the cliffs. It felt more like home than any place I'd ever been.

One hot afternoon I found a shady spot near some boulders to sit down and have lunch. After eating a few sandwiches, I leaned back and closed my eyes. Soon I fell asleep and found myself viewing another past lifetime.

I was a seeker in the time of Jesus. This was about a thousand years after the Egyptian-school lifetime. I had grown up in Jerusalem, going to any teacher I could find. I had been in the crowds several times when Jesus passed through, but I didn't feel strongly drawn to him. I longed to join a stable community—not follow an itinerant teacher.

When I heard about the Essenes, I was very interested and decided to make the journey to their community. I journeyed on foot from Jerusalem to the Dead Sea. At nightfall I joined a small encampment of travelers. After eating, I wandered around. I felt drawn to a little cluster of three men who invited me to join in their conversation.

One was clearly the leader, a lean and elderly man with graying beard and black eyes. After chatting informally for a few minutes, he suddenly looked at me very intensely and asked, "Have you learned anything in these last thousand years? I believe you have. Join the Essene group. This is the right path for you now. If you prove to be trustworthy, further doors will open."

Then, as though nothing had happened, he continued the light conversation. I felt I knew this man but could not recall where. After awhile I left the trio and went to find a place to sleep.

As I awoke from this dream and squinted out over the Qumran ruins, I knew immediately that this was Zadok, the Living ECK Master in the time of Jesus. He had a small group of followers who had broken from the Essenes.

As I awoke from this dream and squinted out over the Qumran ruins, I knew immediately that this was Zadok, the Living ECK Master in the time of Jesus.

I still had not fully earned the privilege, in that Essene lifetime, of studying the ECK teachings again. Or perhaps I was not yet ready. But I did recognize the Ancient One in the face of Zadok.

I joined the Essene community at Qumran and made good spiritual progress in that lifetime. It would be yet another thousand years or so before I again made contact with an ECK Master. It would be in Tibet, with the famous saint Milarepa. In this ECK Master I would recognize the ancient truth that had shone through the countenance of Zadok.

Even after meeting Milarepa I had a lot of back-and-forth motion on the path. This is not uncommon in the long journey of Soul. I tell these stories because, with the short perspective of a single lifetime, it is hard to appreciate the value of the Mahanta in his role as the Ancient One. Most seekers have no need to go back and trace this connection with the Mahanta. The important thing is the recognition.

The Shariyat says of the Ancient One, "During each incarnation he takes on another body and personality. Those who have followed him in the past and have reincarnated again will always find the Mahanta."[2]

THE LINE OF LIVING ECK MASTERS

Every Living ECK Master is a member of the Ancient Order of the Vairagi. The word vairagi *means one who has mental detachment from worldly desires and things.*

The history of the Ancient One is the record of the lives and deeds of all the Living ECK Masters who have ever lived on earth. These are chronicled in the Kadath Inscriptions, which are kept in the remote and hidden Katsupari Monastery. Every Living ECK Master is a member of the Ancient Order of the Vairagi. The word *vairagi* means one who has mental detachment from worldly desires and things.

The line has been unbroken since it was first founded millions of years ago. Each Living ECK Master has passed the mantle on to his successor. The whole line can be traced clear back to Gakko who came out of the heart of God into this world some six million years ago, as mentioned earlier in the book.

And the line is pure; it has not mixed with other lines of masters or teachings, although some ECK Masters known to history have worked within the traditions of their time. One example is Milarepa, who is revered within the Tibetan Buddhist tradition. Another is Pythagoras, the famous Greek philosopher. But even in such cases, their secret mission dealt with the ongoing work of the ECK Masters.

A continuous line of teachers is very important. It means the teachings will not be lost, they will be kept true and accurate, there will be an ongoing stability upon which the seeker can rely, and there will be a natural progression and unfoldment of the path over time to meet the changing needs of each generation.

Much is revealed about any formal line in the way the position is passed from one leader to the next. It may be through the democratic process, through heredity, by selection among peers, or many other ways.

Candidates in training for the position of spiritual mastership in ECK are chosen in their childhood and trained by the ECK Masters through youth and into maturity. At any given time a number of people are in training. But ultimately, God selects who among the candidates will be the chosen one to serve as the Living ECK Master.

Mankind has improvised many props and symbols for the passing of the mantle on down a line. The king passes his crown, the bishop his scepter. But these are symbolic only. The Living ECK Master inherits far more than a title or symbolic object. He is passed the living mantle of the Light and Sound of God. This is called the Rod of ECK Power. It is a potent and concentrated column of Light and Sound connecting him directly to God.

The Living ECK Master inherits far more than a title or symbolic object. He is passed the living mantle of the Light and Sound of God.

Writes Harold Klemp:

> The Sugmad alone gives the initiation of the passing of the Rod of ECK Power. The hierarchy carries out its role in making plans for the transition from one Master to another. The hierarchy, reflecting the will of the Sugmad, makes the decision as to who is the most qualified being within the order to become the Sat Guru, the leader of Eckankar. The Living ECK Master, or sometimes an appointed Master, does the final phase of training, but all the Masters have a close interest in the candidate's spiritual education.[3]

It is during the ritual of the passing of the Rod of Power that the full force of Divine Spirit descends into the new Living ECK Master. From this moment he possesses the power of the Word of God.

Paul Twitchell describes this most sacred occasion:

It is during the ritual of the passing of the Rod of Power that the full force of Divine Spirit descends into the new Living ECK Master.

The departing Master always leaves on our calendar date of October 22, and in turn his successor always accepts the Rod of ECK Power on the same day, at midnight, in the Valley of Shangta in northern Tibet near the Katsupari Monastery. The ritual takes place at the site of the ancient Oracle of Tirmer under the direction of the ancient sage Yaubl Sacabi, whose age is beyond the imagination of the normal senses.

The Adepts of the Ancient Order of the Vairagi meet at the time of the handing of the mantle of spiritual power from the departing Master to his successor. These are the well-known ECK Masters who are the guardians of the Shariyat-Ki-Sugmad in the Temples of Golden Wisdom. . . .

All the rulers of the various inner planes send their chief representative to this ceremony to greet the Living ECK Master who takes the Rod of ECK Power and the spiritual title of Mahanta. Afterward the Living ECK Master is greeted by each of these rulers within the worlds of God, as he makes his first official journey through them.

Besides these, the nine secret ECK Masters who are responsible for the hidden knowledge of the spiritual worlds pay homage to the new Living ECK Master. These Masters are responsible for the collection of the secret knowledge and its placement into the greatest of sacred books, the Shariyat-Ki-Sugmad.[4]

The new Living ECK Master gives his oath before all these past ECK Masters—the Nine Unknown ECK

Masters, and his own Master—that he will fulfill the duties of the Mahanta, the Living ECK Master so long as he wears the title.

Having accepted this mission, he is now recognized by all the other Vairagi Masters as the key vehicle for the primordial Mahanta, the Ancient One. This is the sublime ECK, that part of the Mahanta which is the same in every individual who becomes the Living ECK Master and inherits the title. In other words, he is now the head of the Vairagi Order and the spiritual hierarchy.

"Through Its Chosen One," writes Harold Klemp, "does Sugmad administer Its will in creation."[5]

Unfortunately, even some of the Living ECK Master's own followers do not understand. With every passing of the Rod of ECK Power, a number of seekers fall away from the Path of ECK. They are unable to see or recognize the Ancient One within the new Living ECK Master, which means they likely did not recognize It within the previous Master either. They have attached themselves to the "man" part of the Godman.

This discussion of the Ancient One shows why the Mahanta has nothing to do with such ideas as the Christian belief in the return of Christ or the Buddhist return of the Maitreya. The Mahanta is eternally present on earth, and in this great truth the seeker's hopes find rest.

The Mahanta is eternally present on earth, and in this great truth the seeker's hopes find rest.

THE CYCLES OF THE ANCIENT ONE

Though each spiritual leader of Eckankar wears the title of the Mahanta, the Living ECK Master, not all embody the Ancient One in full measure. Harold Klemp writes:

> There are four main divisions in the line of ECK Masters:

1. The Mahanta, the Living ECK Master, who ushers in a new spiritual age about every five years to one thousand years;
2. The Mahanta Maharai, who is the Living ECK Master working in the Mahanta Consciousness;
3. The Maharaji, the Living ECK Master who is not yet the Mahanta; and
4. An ECK Master, one of the countless, and generally unknown, spiritual Adepts who help the spiritual leader of Eckankar in his mission.

Many degrees of power are allotted to the beings in each division, depending upon whether or not they hold the Rod of ECK Power or wear the spiritual mantle of the Mahanta.[6]

There have been and will be many Living ECK Masters of lesser degree interspersed among the embodied Mahantas.

As Harold Klemp notes, there is a subtle but important distinction between a Living ECK Master who is the embodiment of the Mahanta, and one who is not.

As Harold Klemp notes, there is a subtle but important distinction between a Living ECK Master who is the embodiment of the Mahanta, and one who is not. The Mahanta has more initiations (fourteen versus twelve) and thus more spiritual power.[7] But perhaps most important, according to *The Shariyat* he inherits the Rod of ECK Power, while a twelfth initiate is only *appointed* to his position. In other words, the Mahanta "is the true representative of the Sugmad manifested within the worlds of God Itself," says *The Shariyat*.[8] For most seekers these distinctions may seem esoteric, even inscrutable. But for the world as a whole they carry profound spiritual significance.

Prior to the modern era, the last embodied Mahanta was Rebazar Tarzs. Paul Twitchell ushered in the present era of Mahantaship when he accepted the Rod of ECK Power in 1965. Harold Klemp comments on this new cycle, referring to Paul Twitchell by his spiritual name, Peddar Zaskq, in the following passage:

> In 1965, there was a dramatic change in the Mahanta consciousness during the transition from Rebazar Tarzs to Peddar Zaskq. This present era of Mahantaship will continue two hundred to five hundred years, more or less, until the next greater change in the Mahanta Consciousness takes place. During the current era, as always, whoever accepts the Rod of ECK Power becomes the Mahanta. Regardless of who the present Living ECK Master is, the Mahanta Consciousness continues to evolve as It derives from the pure, positive God Worlds, where creation continues.
>
> The Mahanta is not a personality. The greater change in the Mahanta Consciousness in 1965 had little to do with the personality of Paul Twitchell, who was merely the physical vehicle chosen by the ECK for the Mahantaship.[9]

We have been blessed with the rare presence of two embodied Mahantas in our own brief era—Paul Twitchell and Harold Klemp. The two of them have wrought great spiritual changes in the world. Where do we stand now, and what lies ahead? Writes Harold Klemp, "The coming of the next Mahanta of the fourteenth circle depends upon spiritual need. All Souls, in all universes, determine that need, for as the group entity their spiritual progress is the final key."

In the first few years following the building of the Temple of ECK in 1989, things looked bright. The collapse of the Berlin Wall and the Iron Curtain—icons of the Cold War between East and West—opened new horizons for

We have been blessed with the rare presence of two embodied Mahantas in our own brief era—Paul Twitchell and Harold Klemp.

the human race. We witnessed what seemed to be the birth of a new world as one totalitarian regime after another toppled, to be replaced by fledgling democracies. Would humanity seize the day? Would we turn away from our endless national, ethnic, and religious feuds? Would we build a new self-reliance and responsibility on the failed ruins of the Communist empire?

It was a momentous turning point in history. Many gave it their best. Even so, collectively we chose to stop and rest. "Current events since then," writes Harold Klemp, "have seen a gradual slow-down of people's spiritual drive as evidenced in a renewed interest in warfare and social welfare. Until these Souls are ready to shoulder their own responsibilities again, they'll rest."[10]

The pace has slowed, by our own free will. But the horizon still beckons.

So rather than the imminent appearance of a third modern-day Mahanta, there will be five to seven Living ECK Masters of the twelfth circle before the next embodied Mahanta. The pace has slowed, by our own free will. But the horizon still beckons. The future Mahantas will come, when the time is right.

We can contemplate the overarching mission of these future Mahantas. I believe each one will have a special role to play in the harvest of eons of spiritual unfoldment on this planet—each embodying the work of the Ancient One.

The Shariyat-Ki-Sugmad states that the ECK Masters are embodiments of Sat Nam, ruler of the Fifth Plane, while the Mahanta, the Living ECK Master is the embodiment of the Sugmad, or God.[11]

It is now time to turn to the final and most sublime aspect of the Mahanta, and to a summation of all that has been presented in this book.

18
The Living Word

Only in ECK is there a renewal of the divine Word of the Sugmad, or God. The Mahanta is the Living Word who gives the ever-new truth to the seeker.

Harold Klemp
The Living Word[1]

*T*he Rosetta stone of God is completed with this aspect of the Mahanta. As mentioned at the beginning of this book, there are no real divisions between any of the aspects. Each is but a perspective or viewpoint on the whole. The Living Word envelops them all in one radiant sheet of Light and Sound.

The spiritual body of the Mahanta is the ECK Itself. This is the Living Word, the cosmic Spirit which pervades the universe. *The Shariyat* sings this theme in eloquent poetry:

> He is the beginning, the life span, and the end of all mortal creatures. He is the radiant sun, the wind, the stars of the night, and the moon. He is the king of heaven, of the sense organs, of the mind, of the consciousness of living. He is the spirit of the fire, the spirit of the mountains, leader of all priests, the ocean's spirit, the greater seer; the sacred syllable ECK, the tree, the ant, the thunder in the heavens, and the god of fishes and

The spiritual body of the Mahanta is the ECK Itself. This is the Living Word, the cosmic Spirit which pervades the universe.

sharks. He is time and the eagle, the lion and bear, the rivers of the world, the sustainer, the newborn babe, and the old man preparing to die. In all things is his face, and in all life is he the divine seed. In this world, nothing animate or inanimate exists without him. This is the Lord Sugmad in action, and one atom of Its body sustains the worlds upon worlds."[2]

One evening my wife, an Israeli, and I attended a concert by a popular folk singer from her native country. The event was held in a large synagogue. The singer introduced herself and explained she wished to focus on the theme of love songs. Not just romantic ones, but love of nature, of friends, of family, and of God.

As she began her series of songs, I settled back into my seat. Looking up, I noticed the high ceiling of the synagogue was graced by a large, blue, six-pointed Star of David. It reminded me of the Temple of ECK near Minneapolis, Minnesota. Above that Temple's sanctuary shines a large, blue stained-glass star of six points. This represents the radiant form of the Mahanta as he appears in the seeker's inner worlds.

As I listened to the gentle music, I closed my eyes and soon was drifting off. Quite spontaneously, and without conscious intent, I found myself inside the Temple of ECK. This was a subtle Soul Travel experience, where a mere shift of attention can transport one's viewpoint to a distant location. I was in the Temple sanctuary beneath the Blue Star, and Zan was standing nearby in his Light body.

"Tonight I will tell you about a key principle," he said, communicating through soft impressions. "The path over which the seeker travels home to God—and

Quite spontaneously, and without conscious intent, I found myself inside the Temple of ECK. This was a subtle Soul Travel experience, where a mere shift of attention can transport one's viewpoint to a distant location.

the One who shows him the way—are essentially the same. How can this be?

"It is an ancient tradition in the spiritual mysteries that the universe is a living being—the external body of God.

"This divine and living reality is like a wondrous fabric of many layers woven from particles of Light and Sound. Each layer veils another, and the innermost veil is woven of the purest atoms in creation. I call this multi-layered garment of planes and galaxies the cosmic robe of God.

"Yet God is also immanent in Its creation through the Mahanta, the Living Word. It is God Itself who leads Soul home to the Ocean of Love and Mercy. The mystery is that the Mahanta is both the path and the guide. He is both the cosmic robe and the wearer of it. Come with me now."

We floated up through the Temple roof and into the night sky until we were high above the Temple. Zan continued. "The Mahanta is the threefold body of God. Look now, and see." Zan hung a sort of giant movie screen in space. The outlines of a ladder appeared upon it, reaching from heaven to earth, with twelve steps representing twelve major planes of creation. It reminded me of a very simplified version of Eckankar's Worlds of ECK chart (see p. 80). On the top rung or plane there appeared a pinpoint of light, so brilliant it hurt the eyes.

"This represents the first part of the trinity of God, the absolute primordial, or the eternal Mahanta," explained Zan. "It dwells always in the Ocean of Love and Mercy, in the very heart of the Supreme."

Next there appeared a beautiful oval of white light which stretched from the Ocean of Love and Mercy

We floated up through the Temple roof and into the night sky until we were high above the Temple. Zan continued. "The Mahanta is the threefold body of God. Look now, and see."

down to the golden light of the Soul Plane. In the center of the oval shone the Star of ECK as an electric-white star of six points.

Zan said, "This represents the second aspect of the trinity—the body of glory, the ECK. It is Cosmic Spirit, the Sound Current which is in all life. Above the Soul Plane the Mahanta is entirely without form and is omnipresent. This represents that part of the Mahanta which is with all Souls everywhere at all times.

Then there appeared another beautiful oval of golden light. This one extended from the Soul Plane down to the Physical Plane. Shining in its center was an electric-blue six-pointed star.

This Blue Star represents how the Mahanta may be perceived in the worlds below the Soul Plane.

"This Blue Star represents how the Mahanta may be perceived in the worlds below the Soul Plane. It is here the Mahanta wears the fivefold bodies described in *The Shariyat* as the Quintan. This is the third part of the trinity, the Word made flesh, the historical Mahanta."

"Each of the twelve aspects of the Mahanta bears a special relationship to one of these twelve planes," he said. "For example, the Wayshower is the first aspect and has its focus on the First, or Physical, Plane. The Wayshower operates on all the planes but starts the seeker on his homeward journey in this earth world.

"The Dream Master has the focus of his work on the Second, or Astral, Plane, the main plane of dreams.

"The third aspect of the Mahanta on the Rosetta stone of God is the Guardian. He protects the works of ECK and the seekers under his care from the karmic forces which find their most ready access on this, the Causal Plane.

"The fourth aspect is the Teacher. The spotlight here is on the Fourth Plane, that of the mind. The goal of the Teacher is to teach the seeker to yield his mind to the guidance of Divine Spirit and the heart.

"The fifth aspect, the Light Giver, finds its main home on the Soul Plane, where the Light of God illuminates Soul as It steps forth into the pure sunshine of the worlds of Spirit.

"The sixth aspect, the Purifier, gains its momentum from the Sound Current of this plane which is like a great, cleansing wind.

"The seventh aspect is the Healer. The seventh plane is that of the bhakti initiation, which is love. This is the true healing force in all of life.

"And so it continues up through the planes unto the aspect of the Living Word which emerges from the Twelfth Plane, the Ocean of Love and Mercy.

"You can think of the trinity as the living body of God, and the planes as the cosmic robe of God in which all is clothed.

"Therefore, the Mahanta is the Wayshower, and he is also the way. He is the Light Giver, yet he is also the Light. He is the Teacher, and yet that which is taught. He is the Dream Master, as well as the dream. You see? The Mahanta is an expression of the Spirit of God that is always with you.

"Fortunate indeed is the Soul who has glimpsed a vision of the Mahanta, clothed in the cosmic robe of God, as he strides across the fields of immortality. Yes, all this you see on yonder screen is but an image for the mind's eye. Only the eye of Soul can see the true vision, and only the heart of Soul can beat in rhythm with the holy sounds of ECK."

Zan dissolved the vision of the screen and bid me farewell. After a few moments I opened my eyes and listened to the Israeli singer as she sang a Hebrew love

The Mahanta is an expression of the Spirit of God that is always with you.

song to God. As she sang, I pondered what Zan had given me about the Living Word.

Later I found this passage in *The Shariyat* which clarified what Zan had shown me:

> All life springs from its origin in God, but manifests in the perfect body of the Sugmad via the Mahanta. This is the living Quintan (five), or the fivefold bodies of the Mahanta. This is the greater part of the Sugmad which is the Word made flesh in the lower worlds. The Mahanta thereby has a body which functions as an instrument of God upon each plane throughout the worlds of Spirit, including the true spiritual planes.
>
> Therefore, the Living ECK Master has existence on every plane in the lower worlds in a body; the Physical, Astral, Causal, Mental and Soul. At the same time, he also exists in the nonbody form which is the ECK. Above the Atma world (the Soul Plane), he is entirely without form and is completely omnipresent. While living in the five lower planes he is omnipresent, while at the same time existing in the Mahanta state in each world and administering to those entities and physically-embodied Souls as deemed necessary, as well as to his own chelas and initiates of Eckankar.[3]

We now stand at the peak of the spiritual mountain we have been climbing. From here we have panoramic vision. We can look down and see the entire path by which we made the ascent.

What more can be said in human language about this final aspect of the Mahanta? Only the God-Realized can know it firsthand. We now stand at the peak of the spiritual mountain we have been climbing. From here we have panoramic vision. We can look down and see the entire path by which we made the ascent. Let's see what the Rosetta stone of God has revealed.

A Walk through the City

Divine imagination is one of the great faculties of Soul. There is an old saying that one who lives from his memory is earthbound, but one who lives from his imagination soars with the eagles.

One of my favorite contemplations is to mock up a scene in my imagination, then step into it and see what happens. It may at times be cut entirely from the cardboard of a personal fantasy. At other times, I believe it is composed of the finest materials of creation and leads straight into an adventure in some higher reality. The ECK Masters teach that imagination is really just seeing a different part of the whole of life to which Soul has access through Its inner eye.

One evening, a few days after the vision at the Temple of ECK, I closed my eyes in contemplation and followed a nudge to take an imaginary walk through a large city. Soon I was caught up in the picture and found Zan falling right into step alongside me. "Nice transition," he said. "Very smooth and seamless."

We were walking along a city street. It was a beautiful spring day. We walked along in silence for a few minutes just enjoying the sights and sounds. Then Zan said, "Let's see what Divine Spirit has to teach us while we enjoy the stroll this fine day."

A moment later a car pulled up alongside the curb, and a woman on the passenger side rolled down her window. "Excuse me," she said, "we're looking for the art museum. Are we headed in the right direction?"

"Yes, it's just three blocks straight ahead on the left side," answered Zan.

"Oh, thanks!" said the lady, as the car pulled away.

Zan said, "Did you catch the message from Spirit in that little episode?"

The ECK Masters teach that imagination is really just seeing a different part of the whole of life to which Soul has access through Its inner eye.

"No, Zan. What message are you referring to?"

"That life on earth is a journey, and for this God gives us the Wayshower."

We walked a half block or so and passed a man sleeping on a bench at a bus stop. Zan smiled and said, "Life on earth is a dream, and for this God gives us the Dream Master."

Just then we heard a screech of brakes. I quickly turned to see a man barely miss getting hit by a taxi. "Life on earth is a risk," Zan observed, "and for this God gives us the Guardian."

We continued walking on, through a university campus. It must have been between classes. Students— with books under their arms or backpacks slung over their shoulders—were hurrying about. "Let me see," I said. "Life on earth is a school, and for this God gives us the Teacher."

"Exactly," he replied. Then he stopped at a floral shop. Under a little canopy were neatly arranged bouquets in vases and baskets. A white bucket filled with many colors of roses sat on the sidewalk absorbing the sunshine. Zan lifted a long-stemmed rose from a bucket, inhaling deeply of its sweet scent, then purchased it from the vendor. "Life on earth is unfoldment," he said, gently stroking the petals of the rose, "and for this God gives us the Light Giver."

Further along we passed a large, run-down lot with a high fence around it. A few people were standing there, watching a crane with a large wrecking ball knocking down what remained of an old brick building. I ventured a guess. "Life on earth is growth and renewal, and for this God gives us the Purifier."

"You're seeing the picture now!" Zan said.

"Life on earth is unfoldment," he said, gently stroking the petals of the rose, "and for this God gives us the Light Giver."

Suddenly he turned down a narrow side street which passed between two large warehouses. The bright sunlight gave way to shadows. Halfway down the alley the smell of garbage wafted through the air.

A homeless lady was digging in a dumpster. She turned as we approached and asked for money. Zan said to her, "Noble Soul, please accept this rose as a symbol of God's love which is with you even now, in these hard times." She looked suspicious for a moment. Then suddenly her weathered face broke into a broad, toothless smile, and she reached out and accepted the gift. As we continued our walk, Zan said, "Life on earth is a struggle, and for this God gives us the Healer."

A few moments later I saw a thin man sitting on some steps which led into a vacant building. He drank from a bottle of wine, indifferent to our passing. I felt a twinge of sadness as I said, "Life on earth is a bondage, and for this God gives us the Redeemer."

A few steps later I felt relief as we passed out of the alley into the bright sunlight again. Zan stopped and looked upward toward the top of a skyscraper. I followed his gaze and saw, way up near the top, a windowwasher. He stood upon a small platform suspended by a couple of ropes. I said to Zan, "Isn't it amazing how those guys can work every day at such heights?"

Zan said, "With experience they do it as a matter of course, giving it no more attention than you would walking down this street. Life on earth is an aspiration, and for this God gives us the Godman."

A young man walking by absentmindedly bumped into Zan. "Oh, excuse me. I wasn't paying attention," he apologized.

Zan asked, "What were you thinking of just now,

"Life on earth is an aspiration, and for this God gives us the Godman."

young man, that so absorbed you?"

The youth looked at Zan quizzically, scratched his head, and said, "Oh, I'm majoring in physics at the university, and I just had the most wonderful idea about how to solve a problem I'm working on."

"I'm sure it's a good solution," Zan commented. "Good luck with it."

The young man said thanks and continued on his way. Zan said, "That student has an important mission to fill for science in this lifetime. Life on earth is a destiny, and for this God gives us the Prophet."

We came to a park with an expanse of green lawn and a small lake in the middle. There were some picnic tables under a large oak tree. About thirty people of all ages were mingling around, and a sign said, "The McKenzie Family Reunion."

"Look at the grandmother holding the baby," I said to Zan. "Despite the great difference of their ages, they actually look alike to me." Zan laughed at my perception. "It is Divine Spirit which causes you to see the face of the grandmother in that of the child. What is the message in this, do you suppose?"

"I don't really know offhand," I said.

Life on earth is a triumph of love and joy, and for this God gives us the Living Word.

"Life on earth is enduring," he explained, "and for this God gives us the Ancient One."

We walked along the lake and sat on a bench to rest. A young couple were rowing by in a little red boat. They held each other in their gazes, speaking in soft tones and teasing each other playfully.

"Hmmm," I said. "Life on earth is a triumph of love and joy, and for this God gives us the Living Word. Only in the ecstasy of the great current of divine love, as it pours into the heart, does Soul find fulfillment."

Zan nodded slowly, then pulled a slice of bread from his coat pocket. Pulling off little pieces he tossed them on the ground. Out of nowhere a flock of sparrows converged on the feast. Chirping with pleasure and camaraderie, they quickly gobbled up the crumbs and looked at Zan to see if there was any more.

Seeing there wasn't, all but one launched into the air with a whoosh of wings and disappeared. The one that remained sat looking patiently at Zan.

"Ah, a seeker!" he said. "You have come for more than just the material food. Very well, then you shall have it. What is your wish?" The sparrow chirped two or three times. Zan nodded and said, "Done!" Then the sparrow flew away. He turned to me and winked. "Our little secret."

It was time to go. I thanked Zan for the wonderful stroll through the city. Shortly, the scene faded from mind as I returned from the divine imagination of my inner worlds.

THE SEEKER'S CHECKLIST

I thought about the twelve aspects of the Mahanta and realized they give the seeker all the help he needs to fulfill his spiritual mission of becoming a Co-worker with God.

The twelve aspects of the Mahanta give the seeker all the help he needs to fulfill his spiritual mission of becoming a Co-worker with God.

The Seeker's Checklist

Can show me the way home to God.
    The Wayshower.
Can work with me in the dream state.
    The Dream Master.
Can provide spiritual protection.
    The Guardian.

Can give me the secret teachings.

The Teacher.

Can link me to the Light and Sound of God.

The Light Giver.

Can clear away unneeded obstacles.

The Wind of Change.

Can heal my spiritual ills.

The Healer.

Can help me gain spiritual liberation.

The Redeemer.

Can be a living example for me.

The Godman.

Knows the will of God.

The Prophet.

Will always be there for me.

The Ancient One.

Is a true vehicle for Divine Spirit.

The Living Word.

As promised by the old saying, when the seeker is ready, the Master appears. But this begs the question— what must the seeker do to become ready?

As promised by the old saying, when the seeker is ready, the Master appears. But this begs the question—what must the seeker do to become ready? He can bring his own efforts to the divine equation, matching the twelve gifts of God with his own twelve labors. I suggest that the following efforts will bring these aspects of the Mahanta into one's life.

To prepare for the Wayshower, study the map of the God Worlds of ECK (see p. 80). Learn where you are going, then set your spiritual goals. The Mahanta is always on the lookout for anyone seeking the way home to God.

To prepare for the Dream Master, value your dreams and see them as real. Expand your dream life! Show up, be ready, and bring a sense of adventure.

To prepare for the Guardian, keep alert. Be aware. Watch for his warnings about illusions and traps along the path. Listen to the still small voice within.

To prepare for the Teacher, be eager to learn and willing to change long-held opinions. Apply what you learn and pass it along.

To prepare for the Light Giver contemplate upon the Light and Sound of God. Open your heart to love. Sing HU, the ancient love song to God.

To prepare for the Wind of Change, keep flexible. Trust in Spirit and bend with the wind. Be willing to let go of attachments and keep moving forward.

To prepare for the Healer, be grateful for all things in your life, however small. Look for the gift of growth in all hardships which must be endured.

To prepare for the Redeemer, love God with all your heart. Do your best and be your best, then leave the rest in God's hands.

To prepare for the Godman, look for Soul in the eyes and countenance of all you meet. Remember that your destiny is to become a Co-worker with God.

To prepare for the Prophet, contemplate upon your mission in life and upon your understanding of God's plan. Know your life has purpose and direction, no matter how things appear otherwise.

To prepare for the Ancient One, remember what brought you to the path. Rest assured that you have earned it through many lifetimes of effort. He is always with you.

All life, all creation, exists for the sake of love.

To prepare for the Living Word, know that Soul exists because God loves It. All life, all creation, exists for the sake of love.

These can be the twelve offerings which the seeker lays upon the altar. They show his sincerity and his readiness to take the first steps toward mastership.

The lazy seeker expects God or the Mahanta to do it all for him. But Masters are not made this way. As Paul Twitchell used to say, the Mahanta does not run a spiritual welfare program. But for those willing to make the effort, Spirit will respond in greater measure.

As Paul Twitchell used to say, the Mahanta does not run a spiritual welfare program. But for those willing to make the effort, Spirit will respond in greater measure.

"The aim and purpose of Eckankar," states *The Shariyat,* "has always been to take Soul by Its own path back to Its divine source. The successful devotee is he who, by practice and use of the Spiritual Exercises of ECK, lifts himself as Soul to Its real abode with the help of the Living ECK Master."[4]

If you are a serious seeker it will repay you many times to study and contemplate upon these twelve gifts of God. They are the greatest treasure in the vaults of heaven. The Rosetta stone of God unlocks the vault and puts this spiritual wealth in your hands.

FAREWELL TO ZAN

As I finished composing this last chapter in my study, I wondered how to close it. It seemed best to do a short contemplation to thank Zan for sharing his time and insights.

During my evening spiritual exercise, I invited him into my thoughts. After a few moments he appeared, and we talked inwardly for a few minutes.

"Zan," I said. "We have covered a lot of material over the past year. If you could sum all of it up into a single statement, what would you say is the most important thing for the seeker to remember?"

He paused, then said, "Write these five words upon

your heart: *Stay close to the Mahanta.* Here I refer to the Inner Master.

"When everyone else abandons you, when nothing goes right, when you feel you will never reach your goal—stay close to the Mahanta.

"When your life is full of joy, when the crowds applaude and all is well—stay close to the Mahanta.

"Whether taking your first steps upon the path or whether you be in the final stages of training for Mastership—stay close to the Mahanta.

"Perhaps one day the Nine Silent Ones, those who watch over the secret teachings, will see fit to reveal more. But this is all for now. The serious seekers of this age are ready for the direct approach to God. They shall find it. May the blessings be!"

The serious seekers of this age are ready for the direct approach to God.

Glossary

Words set in SMALL CAPS are defined elsewhere in this glossary.

ARAHATA. *ah-rah-HAH-tah*   An experienced and qualified teacher of ECKANKAR classes.

CHELA. *CHEE-lah*   A spiritual student.

ECK. *EHK*   The Life Force, the Holy Spirit, or Audible Life Current which sustains all life.

ECKANKAR. *EHK-ahn-kahr*   Religion of the Light and Sound of God. Also known as the Ancient Science of SOUL TRAVEL. A truly spiritual religion for the individual in modern times. The teachings provide a framework for anyone to explore their own spiritual experiences. Established by Paul Twitchell, the modern-day founder, in 1965. The word means "Co-worker with God."

ECK MASTERS.   Spiritual Masters who can assist and protect people in their spiritual studies and travels. The ECK Masters are from a long line of God-Realized SOULS who know the responsibility that goes with spiritual freedom.

GOD-REALIZATION.   The state of God Consciousness. Complete and conscious awareness of God.

HU. *HYOO*   The most ancient, secret name for God. The singing of the word HU is considered a love song to God. It can be sung aloud or silently to oneself.

INITIATION.   Earned by a member of ECKANKAR through spiritual unfoldment and service to God. The initiation is a private ceremony in which the individual is linked to the Sound and Light of God.

LIVING ECK MASTER.   The title of the spiritual leader of ECKANKAR. His duty is to lead SOULS back to God. The Living ECK Master can assist spiritual students physically as the Outer Master, in the dream state as the Dream Master, and in the spiritual worlds as the Inner Master. Sri Harold Klemp became the MAHANTA, the Living ECK Master in 1981.

MAHANTA. *mah-HAHN-tah*   A title to describe the highest state of God Consciousness on earth, often embodied in the LIVING ECK MASTER. He is the Living Word. An expression of the Spirit of God that is always with you.

PLANES.   The levels of existence, such as the Physical, Astral, Causal, Mental, Etheric, and Soul Planes.

SATSANG.   *SAHT-sahng*   A class in which students of ECK study a monthly lesson from ECKANKAR.

SELF-REALIZATION.   SOUL recognition. The entering of Soul into the Soul Plane and there beholding Itself as pure Spirit. A state of seeing, knowing, and being.

THE SHARIYAT-KI-SUGMAD. *SHAH-ree-aht-kee-SOOG-mahd*   The sacred scriptures of ECKANKAR. The scriptures are comprised of twelve volumes in the spiritual worlds. The first two were transcribed from the inner PLANES by Paul Twitchell, modern-day founder of ECKANKAR.

SOUL.   The True Self. The inner, most sacred part of each person. Soul exists before birth and lives on after the death of the physical body. As a spark of God, Soul can see, know, and perceive all things. It is the creative center of Its own world.

SOUL TRAVEL.   The expansion of consciousness. The ability of SOUL to transcend the physical body and travel into the spiritual worlds of God. Soul Travel is taught only by the LIVING ECK MASTER. It helps people unfold spiritually and can provide proof of the existence of God and life after death.

SOUND AND LIGHT OF ECK.   The Holy Spirit. The two aspects through which God appears in the lower worlds. People can experience them by looking and listening within themselves and through SOUL TRAVEL.

SPIRITUAL EXERCISES OF ECK.   The daily practice of certain techniques to get us in touch with the Light and Sound of God.

SRI. *SREE*   A title of spiritual respect, similar to reverend or pastor, used for those who have attained the Kingdom of God. In ECKANKAR, it is reserved for the MAHANTA, the LIVING ECK MASTER.

SUGMAD. *SOOG-mahd*   A sacred name for God. Sugmad is neither masculine nor feminine; It is the source of all life.

WAH Z. *WAH zee*   The spiritual name of Sri Harold Klemp. It means the Secret Doctrine. It is his name in the spiritual worlds.

Notes

Part One—A Seeker in the Foothills

Chapter 1. Sparks in the Tinder

1. Harold Klemp, *The Living Word,* Book 2 (Minneapolis: ECKANKAR, 1996), 206

Chapter 2. The Mystery Man

1. Harold Klemp, *The Secret Teachings,* Mahanta Transcripts, Book 3 (Minneapolis: ECKANKAR, 1989), 157.
2. John 2:19 Revised Standard Version.
3. Betty J. Eadie, *Embraced by the Light* (Placerville: Gold Leaf Press, 1992), 40.
4. Paul Twitchell, *The Tiger's Fang,* 2d ed. (Minneapolis: ECKANKAR, 1988), 75.

Chapter 3. A Call to Adventure

1. Harold Klemp, *Soul Travelers of the Far Country* (Minneapolis: ECKANKAR, 1987), 17.

Chapter 4. The Caves of Ajanta

1. Harold Klemp, *Journey of Soul,* Mahanta Transcripts, Book 1 (Minneapolis: ECKANKAR, 1988), 221.

Chapter 5. Lost in Time

1. Klemp, *Soul Travelers,* 92.

Chapter 6. The Rosetta Stone of God

1. Paul Twitchell, *The ECK-Vidya, Ancient Science of Prophecy* (Minneapolis: ECKANKAR, 1972), 137.
2. Klemp, *Living Word,* Book 2, 1.
3. Klemp, *Journey of Soul,* 145.

Part Two—The Ascent of the Mountain

Chapter 7. The Wayshower

1. Harold Klemp, *The Dream Master,* Mahanta Transcripts, Book 8, 2d ed. (Minneapolis: ECKANKAR, 1993, 1997), 13.
2. *The Shariyat-Ki-Sugmad,* Book One, 2d ed. (Minneapolis: ECKANKAR, 1970, 1987), 130.
3. Harold Klemp, *The Eternal Dreamer,* Mahanta Transcripts, Book 7 (Minneapolis: ECKANKAR, 1992), 228–29.
4. Harold Klemp, *A Cosmic Sea of Words: The ECKANKAR Lexicon* (Minneapolis: ECKANKAR, 1998), 232.
5. Harold Klemp, *How to Find God,* Mahanta Transcripts, Book 2 (Minneapolis: ECKANKAR, 1988), 255.
6. Harold Klemp, *Cloak of Consciousness,* Mahanta Transcripts, Book 5 (Minneapolis: ECKANKAR, 1991), 78.
7. *The Shariyat-Ki-Sugmad,* Book Two, 2d ed. (Minneapolis: ECKANKAR, 1971, 1988), 15.

Chapter 8. The Dream Master

1. Harold Klemp, *The Drumbeat of Time,* Mahanta Transcripts, Book 10 (Minneapolis, ECKANKAR, 1995), 244.
2. Paul Twitchell, *Coins of Gold* (Las Vegas: Illuminated Way Press, 1972).
3. *The Shariyat-Ki-Sugmad,* Book One, 16.
4. Klemp, *Living Word,* Book Two, 65–66.
5. Harold Klemp, *The Art of Spiritual Dreaming* (Minneapolis: ECKANKAR, 1999); Harold Klemp, *The Spiritual Exercises of ECK,* 2d ed. (Minneapolis: ECKANKAR, 1993, 1997).
6. *The Shariyat-Ki-Sugmad,* Book Two, 1.

Chapter 9. The Guardian

1. *The Shariyat-Ki-Sugmad,* Book One, 119.
2. Klemp, *Cloak of Consciousness,* 258–59.
3. Harold Klemp, *Unlocking the Puzzle Box,* Mahanta Transcripts, Book 6 (Minneapolis: ECKANKAR, 1992), 235.
4. *The Shariyat-Ki-Sugmad,* Book Two, 44.
5. Klemp, *Unlocking the Puzzle Box,* 215.
6. Harold Klemp, *The Golden Heart,* Mahanta Transcripts, Book 4 (Minneapolis: ECKANKAR, 1990), 59–60.
7. Paul Twitchell, *The Spiritual Notebook,* 2d ed. (Minneapolis: ECKANKAR, 1971, 1990), 68.
8. *The Shariyat-Ki-Sugmad,* Book Two, 25.
9. Harold Klemp, *The Slow Burning Love of God,* Mahanta Transcripts, Book 13, 2d ed. (Minneapolis: ECKANKAR, 1996 1997), 120.
10. Klemp, *Living Word,* Book 2, 4.

Chapter 10. The Teacher

1. *The Shariyat-Ki-Sugmad,* Book Two, 105.
2. Klemp, *Eternal Dreamer,* 7.
3. *The Shariyat-Ki-Sugmad,* Book One, 2.
4. Twitchell, *Spiritual Notebook,* 141.
5. *The Shariyat-Ki-Sugmad,* Book Two, 204–5.
6. Harold Klemp, *We Come as Eagles,* Mahanta Transcripts, Book 9 (Minneapolis: ECKANKAR, 1994), 6.
7. Klemp, *Eternal Dreamer,* 128–29.
8. Harold Klemp, *How the Inner Master Works,* Mahanta Transcripts, Book 12 (Minneapolis, ECKANKAR, 1995), 17.
9. Klemp, *Slow Burning Love of God,* 239.
10. Klemp, *Cloak of Consciousness,* 130.
11. Harold Klemp, *The Secret of Love,* Mahanta Transcripts, Book 14 (Minneapolis: ECKANKAR, 1996), 86.
12. Klemp, *Drumbeat of Time,* 60.
13. Klemp, *How the Inner Master Works,* 201–3.
14. Klemp, *Slow Burning Love of God,* 145.
15. Klemp, *How the Inner Master Works,* 242.
16. Klemp, *Dream Master,* 33.
17. Klemp, *Drumbeat of Time,* 239.
18. Klemp, *Eternal Dreamer,* 114–15.
19. Ibid., 110.
20. Ibid., 123.
21. Ibid., 242–43.

Chapter 11. The Light Giver

1. *The Shariyat-Ki-Sugmad,* Book Two, 245–46.
2. Klemp, *Drumbeat of Time,* 43.
3. *The Shariyat-Ki-Sugmad,* Book One, 129.
4. *The Shariyat-Ki-Sugmad,* Book Two, 152–53.
5. Klemp, *Secret Teachings,* 112–13.
6. Klemp, *Journey of Soul,* 277.
7. Klemp, *Eternal Dreamer,* 133.
8. *The Shariyat-Ki-Sugmad,* Book Two, 229.
9. Klemp, *Golden Heart,* 73–75.
10. *The Shariyat-Ki-Sugmad,* Book One, 223–24.
11. Paul Twitchell, *Dialogues with the Master* (Minneapolis: ECKANKAR, 1970), 17.
12. Harold Klemp, *Wisdom of the Heart* (Minneapolis: ECKANKAR, 1992), 52.

Chapter 12. The Wind of Change

1. *The Shariyat-Ki-Sugmad,* Book One, 180.
2. John 3:8 Revised Standard Version.
3. Twitchell, *Tiger's Fang,* 127–28.

4. Harold Klemp, *Child in the Wilderness,* (Minneapolis: ECKANKAR, 1989), 277.
5. *The Shariyat-Ki-Sugmad,* Book One, 4–5.
6. Klemp, *Cloak of Consciousness,* 22.
7. Ibid., 115.
8. Klemp, *Journey of Soul,* 103.
9. Klemp, *Cloak of Consciousness,* 56.
10. Klemp, *How to Find God,* 211.
11. Harold Klemp, *What Is Spiritual Freedom?* Mahanta Transcripts, Book 11 (Minneapolis: ECKANKAR, 1995), 84.
12. Klemp, *Drumbeat of Time,* 77.

Chapter 13. The Healer

1. *The Shariyat-Ki-Sugmad,* Book Two, 227–28.
2. Ibid., 228.
3. Klemp, *Drumbeat of Time,* 180–81.
4. Klemp, *Cloak of Consciousness,* 21.
5. Klemp, *What Is Spiritual Freedom?* 35–36.
6. William Shakespeare, *The Merchant of Venice,* act IV, scene *i,* line 184.
7. Klemp, *Secret of Love,* 72–73.
8. Klemp, *Unlocking the Puzzle Box,* 190.
9. Ibid., 244.
10. Klemp, *We Come as Eagles,* 83–84.
11. Klemp, *Journey of Soul,* 292.
12. Ibid. 129.
13. Klemp, *Unlocking the Puzzle Box,* 26–27.
12. Klemp, *Wisdom of the Heart* 119–20.
15. Ibid., 159–60.

Chapter 14. The Redeemer

1. Twitchell, *Spiritual Notebook,* 175.
2. Klemp, *How the Inner Master Works,* 67.
3. Harold Klemp, *The Living Word* (Minneapolis: ECKANKAR, 1989), 80.
4. Klemp, *Living Word,* Book 2, 195–96.
5. Paul Twitchell, *ECKANKAR: Illuminated Way Letters 1966–1971* (San Diego: Illuminated Way Press, 1975), 255–57.
6. *The Shariyat-Ki-Sugmad,* Book One, 7.
7. Joel L. Whitton and Joe Fisher, *Life between Life* (New York: Warner Books, Inc., 1986), 39.
8. Ibid., 39.
9. Eadie, *Embraced by the Light,* 108–19.
10. *The Shariyat-Ki-Sugmad,* Book One, 34.
11. Klemp, *Living Word,* 81.
12. *The Shariyat-Ki-Sugmad,* Book Two, 4.

Chapter 15. The Godman

1. *The Shariyat-Ki-Sugmad*, Book Two, 185.
2. Klemp, *We Come as Eagles*, 26.
3. *The Shariyat-Ki-Sugmad*, Book One, 217.
4. Ibid., 195.
5. Ibid., 117.
6. Klemp, *Eternal Dreamer*, 7.
7. *The Shariyat-Ki-Sugmad*, Book Two, 8.
8. Klemp, *Golden Heart*, 37.
9. *The Shariyat-Ki-Sugmad*, Book Two, 18–19.
10. Ibid., 241–43.
11. Klemp, *Secret Teachings*, 50
12. Klemp, *Slow Burning Love of God*, 76.
13. *The Shariyat-Ki-Sugmad*, Book One, 94–95.
14. Ibid., 40.

Chapter 16. The Prophet

1. Twitchell, *ECK-Vidya*, 15.
2. Ibid., 15.
3. *The Shariyat-Ki-Sugmad*, Book One, 85.
4. Twitchell, *Spiritual Notebook*, 222.
5. Paul Twitchell, *The ECK-Ynari: The Secret Knowledge of Dreams*, 2d ed. (Minneapolis: ECKANKAR, 1980, 1985), 46.
6. *The Shariyat-Ki-Sugmad*, Book One, 186.
7. Twitchell, *The ECK-Vidya*, 119.
8. *The Shariyat-Ki-Sugmad*, Book Two, 34.
9. Harold Klemp, *A Modern Prophet Answers Your Key Questions about Life* (Minneapolis: ECKANKAR, 1998).
10. *The Shariyat-Ki-Sugmad*, Book One, 121.
11. Klemp, *Cloak of Consciousness*, 32.

Chapter 17. The Ancient One

1. *The Shariyat-Ki-Sugmad*, Book One, 92.
2. Ibid., 92–93.
3. Klemp, *Wisdom of the Heart*, 186.
4. Twitchell, *Spiritual Notebook*, 173–74.
5. Klemp, *Wisdom of the Heart*, 158.
6. Klemp, *Living Word*, 141.
7. Harold Klemp, *Wisdom of the Heart*, Book 2 (Minneapolis: ECKANKAR, 1999), 185–88.
8. *The Shariyat-Ki-Sugmad*, Book Two, 246.
9. Klemp, *Wisdom of the Heart*, 162.
10. Klemp, *Wisdom of the Heart*, Book 2, 180.
11. *The Shariyat-Ki-Sugmad*, Book Two, 162.

Chapter 18. The Living Word

1. Klemp, *Living Word*, 4.
2. *The Shariyat-Ki-Sugmad*, Book One, 38–39.
3. Ibid., 112.
4. *The Shariyat-Ki-Sugmad*, Book Two, 157.

292

FOR FURTHER READING AND STUDY

 **The Art of Spiritual Dreaming**

Harold Klemp

Dreams are a treasure. A gift from God. Harold Klemp shows how to find a dream's spiritual gold, and how to experience God's love. Get insights from the past and future, grow in confidence, and make decisions about career and finances. Do this from a unique perspective: by recognizing the spiritual nature of your dreams.

 A Modern Prophet Answers Your Key Questions about Life

Harold Klemp

A pioneer of today´s focus on "everyday spirituality" shows you how to experience and understand God´s love in your life—anytime, anyplace. His answers to hundreds of questions help guide you to your own source of wisdom, peace, and deep inner joy.

 Our Spiritual Wake-Up Calls

Mahanta Transcripts, Book 15

Harold Klemp

When God calls, are you listening? Discover how God communicates through dreams, the people you meet, or even a newspaper comic strip. Learn how you are in the grasp of divine love every moment of every day. The Mahanta Transcripts are highlights from Harold Klemp's worldwide speaking tours.

 35 Golden Keys to Who You Are & Why You're Here

Linda C. Anderson

Discover thirty-five golden keys to mastering your spiritual destiny through the ancient teachings of Eckankar, Religion of the Light and Sound of God. The dramatic, true stories in this book equal anything found in the spiritual literature of today. Learn ways to immediately bring more love, peace, and purpose to your life.

Available at your local bookstore. If unavailable, call (952) 380-2222. Or write: ECKANKAR, Dept. BK21A, P.O. Box 27300, Minneapolis, MN 55427 U.S.A.

THERE MAY BE AN
ECKANKAR STUDY GROUP NEAR YOU

Eckankar offers a variety of local and international activities for the spiritual seeker. With hundreds of study groups worldwide, Eckankar is near you! Many areas have Eckankar centers where you can browse through the books in a quiet, unpressured environment, talk with others who share an interest in this ancient teaching, and attend beginning discussion classes on how to gain the attributes of Soul: wisdom, power, love, and freedom.

Around the world, Eckankar study groups offer special one-day or weekend seminars on the basic teachings of Eckankar. For membership information, visit the Eckankar Web site (www.eckankar.org/membership.html). For the location of the Eckankar center or study group nearest you, click on "Other Eckankar Web sites" (www.eckankar.org/ekcenters.html) for a listing of those areas with Web sites. You're also welcome to check your phone book under **ECKANKAR**; call (952) 380-2222, Ext. BK21B; or write **ECKANKAR, Att: Information, BK21B, P.O. Box 27300, Minneapolis, MN 55427 U.S.A.**

☐ Please send me information on the nearest Eckankar center or study group in my area.

☐ Please send me more information about membership in Eckankar, which includes a twelve-month spiritual study.

Please type or print clearly

Name _____
first (given)   last (family)

Street_____ Apt. # _____

City _____ State/Prov. _____

ZIP/Postal Code _____ Country _____